THE KANSAS CITY PUBLIC LIBRARY
Ewing Kauffman
BOOK FUND
The purchase of this book was made possible
by the friends of Mr. Kauffman.

RACE, RAPE, and INJUSTICE

Documenting and Challenging Death Penalty Cases in the Civil Rights Era

RACE, RAPE, and INJUSTICE

Barrett J. Foerster

Edited and with a Foreword by Michael Meltsner

The University of Tennessee Press • Knoxville

First Edition.

The paper in this book meets the requirements of American National Standards Institute / National Information Standards Organization specification Z39.48–1992 (Permanence of Paper). It contains 30 percent post-consumer waste and is certified by the Forest Stewardship Council.

Library of Congress Cataloging-in-Publication Data

Race, rape, and injustice: documenting and challenging death penalty cases in the civil rights era / [edited by] Michael Meltsner.
p. cm.
Includes bibliographical references and index.
ISBN 978-1-57233-862-3 (hardback) — ISBN 1-57233-862-8 (hardcover)
1. Race discrimination—Law and legislation—United States—History.
2. African Americans—Civil rights—History.
3. Capital punishment—United States—History.
4. United States—Race relations.
5. African Americans—Civil rights—Southern States—History.
6. Rape—Southern States—History.
7. Civil rights movements—United States—History.
8. Foerster, Barrett J., 1942–2010.
9. Meltsner, Michael, 1937–

KF4757.R35 2012
345.73'0253208996073075—dc23 2012026774

To Tom Delbanco
M.M.

Contents

Foreword

After his first year in law school at UCLA, Barrett Foerster volunteered along with twenty-seven other law students for a summer internship collecting data on the sentencing practices of southern juries in rape cases. The year was 1965, the height of the civil rights movement, and the group of very green youth encountered hostility and resistance. Violence was often around the next corner. But these were not shock troops. They presented themselves as serious academic research assistants, not civil rights workers. Their role was to move quietly and deceptively, without attracting any more attention than need be as they begged, wheedled, and hounded court clerks, local lawyers both white and black, and even a few judges to gather the highly detailed data they needed to complete complicated research questionnaires.

They were sent to the South by the NAACP Legal Defense Fund, then engaged in trying to prove to the satisfaction of federal judges that blacks convicted of raping white women were common fodder for execution while defendants convicted of rape in other circumstances were usually sent to prison. This was a proposition that was not generally doubted by knowledgeable people, but which required objective, nonanecdotal proof if it was to lead to changes in the law. Unless jurors were to report that race had led them to dispatch the black men before them to the electric chair or gas chamber—an admission once conventional but no longer likely—the only way to proceed was through a massive statistical analysis of jury behavior in sentencing convicted rapists and measuring not only differential treatment of the races, but, crucially, investigating whether any nonracial factors—prior criminal record, use of extreme violence, and so on—could explain any differential.

Foerster, who had grown up in the South himself, decided that the story behind the students' efforts had never been fully told and that its impact on the decades-long struggle over the death penalty in the courts deserved to be better known. Despite a busy career as a practicing attorney in San Diego, and then, beginning in 2003, as a respected Superior Court judge in Imperial County, California, he interviewed colleagues from the 1965 project, collected their diaries, sent assistants to study the archived records of the cosponsoring student civil rights organization, and analyzed every court decision he could find that related to the use of the students' research and the ultimate passage of its findings into a kind of jurisprudential version of folk wisdom. Tragically, Judge Foerster died suddenly of a pulmonary embolism in November 2010, shortly after delivering a draft manuscript of this book to the University of Tennessee Press.

I was twenty-eight in 1965, a staff lawyer at the Legal Defense Fund. Responsibility and litigation experience came fast and furious at the Fund. After only four years as a practicing attorney, I felt like a hardened soldier in the civil rights struggle. I had argued a capital case before the Supreme Court so early in my career that I needed a special order from the court to appear before it. One of my roles as part of a talented, close-knit group of colleagues was to share supervision of the student researchers to the extent that their presence raised problems of access to court records or encountered practical difficulties as they moved through the South that summer. I'm sure our supposed availability comforted the students, but there was in fact little we could do. They were on their own, and to this day I am amazed that none were injured, faced trumped-up criminal charges, or were seriously distracted from the task at hand.

When the press asked me to consider readying *Race, Rape, and Injustice* for publication, I was eager to do so, but wary of the task. This is Barrett Foerster's story, and I wondered if I could fully honor his text and perspective while still making the modest changes I hoped he would have agreed to as part of the give-and-take of the serious editorial process required by the University of Tennessee Press. Fortunately, my views were not so different from Judge Foerster's on most, if not all, issues that I ever felt insecure in clarifying or slightly modifying his approach. Throughout, I have tried to ask the obvious questions: how would he have responded to this editorial comment or that, this or that rereading of a law review analysis, and so forth. If I have erred in my calculations, it probably comes from forgetting my experience with strong and wise editorial assistance going back to my first editor, Joe Fox of Random House, who not only bought *Cruel and Unusual: The Supreme*

Court and Capital Punishment (1973), from a then unpublished author but made sure I stripped the text of any hint of legal obfuscation.

As Foerster tells the story, the student experience in the South began with a general ignorance of the region but ultimately led to a finer-grained knowledge of its people, their customs, and common evasions when it came to race. The students worked hard, and despite the resistance they encountered, cleverly made public records public in fact; but even more important, their research was impeccable, and its reliability has never been challenged. The lawyers who used the fruits of the students' labors did so creatively and with a dedication and tenacity that ultimately produced a life-saving judicial outcome. But the hero of heroes in this story is an academic, Marvin Wolfgang, who despite being called the most influential criminologist in the English-speaking world was little known outside of his profession. Recruited to the project by Anthony Amsterdam, Wolfgang made it his own. He not only crafted the research approach and designed the critical data collection instrument, but he also presented the results in so powerful a manner that the courts were forced to concede their bona fides even while finding dubious legal reasons to defeat their implications. Wolfgang, a scholar whose work shaped modern criminology, shines in these pages, and having been able to spend time with him while he worked through his analysis of the massive data the students collected, I can only add, deservedly so. Marvin Wolfgang died in 1998 at the age of seventy-three, a great loss to science as well as to everyone who knew him.

Foerster argues that the yield of the law students' labor began a series of transactions: research analysis of the data, lawsuits based on that analysis, years in which because of the unsettled litigation no execution was permitted, an ebb and flow of Supreme Court cases producing some wins and some losses (but always educating the court about racism). Then, in 1972, there came a cleaning of the law books of virtually all death penalty statutes, and finally, four years later, there was court approval of a revised and thought-to-be more limited set of death laws, which, Judge Foerster concludes, amounted to a great improvement, at least insofar as racial discrimination is concerned, over the previous legal regime.

To fully accept this thesis requires one to realize that despite never linking its approach to statistical proof of racial death sentencing, the justices accepted that it was prevalent. The heart of the matter was the glaring disconnect between (1) an overwhelming factual record produced with great difficulty, but nevertheless backed by powerful indicia of reliability and analytic sophistication, *and* (2) a refusal of the Supreme Court to acknowledge that statistics mattered when evaluating the racial outcomes of criminal sentencing, even while justices, both "liberal" and "conservative," subtly signaled again and again that the statistics were probably right. Many reasons have been proposed for the court's unwillingness to own up to the code it was employing when it threw out death sentences for "arbitrariness," or for the court's refusal to apply statistical findings explicitly to death-case sentencing patterns, even as it relied on statistics in many other areas of the law. This is not the place to engage in an extended survey, but surely such reasons include an understandable if misguided reluctance to rely on the abstraction of numbers instead of concrete, case-specific proof of racial infection. Equally understandable, but surely cowardly to the edge of dereliction, the court was unwilling, regardless of the facts, to even implicitly claim that thousands of citizen jurors over the twenty years studied had voted on racial grounds and, even more poignantly, that the justice system had executed hundreds of men because of the color of their skin.

The other day I realized that I'd been involved with capital punishment issues for forty-nine years—first as a sleep-deprived frontline advocate, then as a sort of case manager, then as an analyst, consultant, teacher, observer, outraged letter-to-the-editor writer, and, most recently, simply as a campaign veteran lurking around the edges of the subject. These years brought remarkable changes: I never believed we would win *Furman v. Georgia,* or, that once won, the Supreme Court would back down in such a confusing and paradoxical fashion in the years that followed. And they brought equally remarkable stubborn constants—the political attraction of urging that the culpable be punished to the maximum, despite a range of contrary social facts and the many costs, not all of them financial, incurred by doing so.

The era of judicial death penalty regulation began somewhat inadvertently. The lawyers' main task was eliminating the formal props of racism: abolition wasn't on anyone's agenda in the beginning. The Legal Defense Fund came to believe in fits and starts that it had to push for total victory and that it was at least conceivable it might win. Often the lawyers felt they had been painted into a corner and had to go forward despite great fears of failure. Perhaps this random beginning in part accounts, through the nexus of a weak politics, for the moral stalemate we have today: where execution is statistically so small as to make it seem more a human sacrifice than a defensible, generally applied policy, but large enough, at least in certain regions of the country, to stifle its dismantling; where judge-and-jury, life-and-death distinctions are often unintelligible and incoherent; and where almost everyone not involved in a case of a particular heinous killing believes the entire condemning-and-killing system is tainted by choices based on race, caprice, bad lawyering, excessive costs, and a range of other systemic incompetencies. Such a system will eventually be discarded, but it may be in the long run. Of course, in the long run lives will be lost. With this dreary prospect ahead, it is fitting to celebrate in the pages that follow the ideals that moved Barrett Foerster and his peers to join and advance a cause of elemental justice.

Michael Meltsner
Cambridge, Massachusetts

Chapter 1

A Showdown Looms

The moon, partly hidden behind dense clouds, cast but a faint light onto the open fields racing by the windows of the green Buick. No street lamps pierced the Mississippi darkness. In fact, only a dim line of pebbles on the shoulder made the edges of the country road distinguishable.

The young driver of the car sported stubbly brown whiskers, and like his youthful companion, also in his early twenties, he was a first-year law student at a prestigious northern university. The pair had just completed a day of poring through old, dusty files in the cavernous basement of a county courthouse. They'd been sent on an undercover mission: gather data about white rape victims and their African American attackers for use in a legal assault on the death penalty in the South. The day's work had been tiring, and neither man was chatty. But what was soon to happen would drastically sharpen their senses and underscore the potential peril of their assignment.

As the Buick lumbered westward towards the Louisiana state line, a white Chevrolet truck sped by in the opposite direction. It braked to a squealing halt, and then spun about the isolated roadway. Its engine roared, its gears clashed, and its headlights wrenched the Buick from the night's shadows.

"Uh-oh! I bet they spotted our plates," one of the young students muttered, referring to the northern license plates they had meant to exchange for local ones. His companion, immobilized by fear, could only nod. His body was so tense he'd forgotten how to tremble. The fact hunters had become the prey.

The Buick cut through a corner, then skidded a half circle before leaping back onto the roadway and racing forward. But the truck had picked up the chase, and as it gained on the Buick, shouts of derision, mixed with rebel yells, came from the pursuers. The white truck drew closer, fell back, and then drew closer—*much* closer—again. Finally, the truck's front fender tore into the rear fender of the Buick, first once, then twice, and finally with a sickening thud that spun the Buick sideways and into a ditch.

The Buick's rear wheels spun wildly in the air to the accompaniment of sneers and laughter as the truck stopped briefly. Someone shouted derisively, "What's your business, Yankees?" After a momentary silence, the truck sped forward and disappeared into the black fog of night. The message was clear: "Outside agitators" weren't welcome in Mississippi.

The young law students, hearts racing, feared their tormentors' return. Certain parts of the South were still under Ku Klux Klan control and the Klan's brand of justice could be swift and brutal. Though left stranded at night in a roadside ditch somewhere in the southern countryside, the students dared not seek help. In the mid-1960s, their "foreign" license plates were enough to boil the blood of any southern segregationist. Racial and regional hatred was common. So the young men labored over the next few hours—by themselves—to build a ramp of earth and rock high enough to provide traction for the Buick's rear wheels and, thus, enable their escape.[1]

Stunned

When I first learned of our cohorts' misfortune, I was stunned by this assault on what until then had seemed our relative safety. We had been sent to the Deep South only to research discriminatory sentencing practices, not to become physical targets in the greater civil rights struggle. Phil Brown, a first-year classmate of mine at UCLA Law School, broke the news upon my return to our New Orleans hotel room. "No more nighttime adventures," he warned, referring to the risks that pervaded the southern countryside after dusk.

A month earlier, twenty-eight law students (of which I was one) had been selected for this project on the basis of academic performance and interest in civil-rights issues. Most of us had just completed our first year of law school and were in our early twenties. On June 21, 1965, we gathered in a classroom on the University of Pennsylvania campus in Philadelphia.[2] We'd been chosen by the Law Students Civil Rights Research Council (LSCRRC), an organization founded in 1963 that involved law students in summer research and legal assistance projects in support of the civil rights movement. We were a highly motivated group. The LSCRRC director, Steve Antler, had only started serious recruitment a few months earlier, but as far as I could tell, everyone selected had showed up at this mandatory first meeting. Our task was to work with the NAACP Legal Defense and Educational Fund, Inc. (commonly known as "the Fund" or the "Inc. Fund"), on one of its most important law reform initiatives. We were to learn the specifics by hearing from a legendary young law professor named Anthony Amsterdam and his colleague, Marvin Wolfgang, a sociology and criminology professor who also taught at Penn.

I arrived at the classroom disgruntled, tired and achy, having taken a "red-eye" flight from L.A. the night before. The soaring, muggy Philadelphia temperatures didn't help. Already mid-morning and my clothes stank from fresh perspiration. I flopped into a seat near the podium, hoping that my close proximity to the speakers would keep me awake. A few minutes passed, when suddenly the sounds of buzzing, youthful conversation stopped as a tall, athletic figure bounded onto the platform in front.

"Good morning," he said, crisply. "I'm Tony Amsterdam."

His piercing stare commanded our rapt attention as he glanced about the room seemingly measuring our meager capabilities. Only in his early thirties, Amsterdam already bore dark circles under his bloodshot eyes, a sign of too many all-nighters spent poring over court files and death penalty briefs. So here was the Great Professor I had heard so much about. The stories of his keen memory and persuasive powers were impressive. In oral argument he was renowned for citing cases by memory, some over 150 years old, and the breadth of his intellect was extraordinary. He spoke two foreign languages (French and Spanish) and was well versed in poker. While attending high school he audited lectures given at Bryn Mawr on art history. He graduated summa cum laude from Haverford College in 1957, and pursued a graduate degree in art history at Bryn Mawr while he was attending law school at the University of Pennsylvania, where he graduated first in his class. His achievements came not without adversity. He was stricken with bulbar polio in his youth and had to spend many days in an iron lung while he was quarantined.[3]

He leaned over the podium and turned in my direction. "You are about to embark on a mission that may change the course of this country's constitutional history," he thundered. Goosebumps riddled my back. Now I was fully awake, oblivious to the suffocating effects of the thick summer air. Slowly he unfolded the reasons for our calling and what he hoped would be accomplished. Our goal, he explained, was to determine statistically whether the death penalty in southern rape cases had been applied discriminatorily over the previous twenty years. If a disproportionate number of African Americans convicted of raping white women received the death penalty, regardless of the presence or absence of nonracial variables (such as whether violence was used, whether the victim was married, etc.), then capital punishment in the South could be barred because of its discriminatory application and the consequent violation of the Equal Protection Clause of the Fourteenth Amendment to the U.S. Constitution.[4] Additionally, because execution was the South's favored tool of vengeance to punish blacks convicted of interracial rape, the Eighth Amendment's ban on "cruel and unusual punishment" might also be breached.

Amsterdam then introduced Wolfgang, a world-renowned sociologist in his early forties. He was a soft-spoken man, humble and scholarly in demeanor, but he had already made his mark on the science of criminology, then still in its infancy. He had studied and worked closely with Thorsten Sellin, author of the then-leading study of the lack of deterrent effect of capital punishment. In 1958 he produced his "Patterns of Criminal Homicide" in which he evaluated 588 murders in Philadelphia and found many to have been precipitated by the victims. Wolfgang also pioneered an evaluation of crimes committed by sufferers of spousal abuse, which had never before been studied. In 1964 he coauthored a book, *The Measurement of Delinquency,* which stressed methods by which the severity of the crimes could be measured.[5] Wolfgang was also a master of statistical methodology. He would be, Amsterdam explained, the person to evaluate the data we would bring back from the southern court files.

When Wolfgang took to the platform, the contrast between the two men was immediate. Wolfgang was not as suave in his delivery, nor as tall. His rumpled sport coat and bookish mannerisms stood in stark contrast to Amsterdam's intensity and organized delivery. But when he distributed the "Capital Punishment Survey" booklets that would be our constant companions and calmly explained their use, he had our complete attention.

"I need to know everything about these cases," he stressed. "No exceptions. We'll have enough difficulty convincing judges to look at rape cases through the prism of statistics." He paused, and then smiled wryly at Amsterdam. "I hear those trained in the law hate math. Give them an excuse and they'll run from it. So, our statistics have to be based on accurate facts. That means you must be thorough! You'll have to examine court files, read trial transcripts, interview defense and prosecuting attorneys, study newspaper accounts of the trials, and possibly interview witnesses." He paused to allow the enormity of our task to sink in. "And in some states, state penitentiary or pardon-board files and appellate court records will be additional resources you can look at. All the information you gather from these sources will have to be entered."

I thumbed through the "Capital Punishment Survey" booklet and discovered to my horror twenty-eight pages of detailed questions with dotted lines waiting for answers. Information sought included the defendant's and the victim's age, family status, occupation, the defendant's prior criminal record, the victim's husband's occupation, the victim's reputation for chastity (how would I find that out?), and the prior relationship, if any, of the defendant and the victim, including their prior sexual relations. Page after page of such questions. Oh, my God. Did this sound like a lot of work! I needed to surface for air. I stared angrily at this mad professor, then reluctantly read on: ". . . the manner in which the defendant and the victim arrived at the scene of the offense, the number of offenders and victims, the degree of violence or threat employed, the degree of injury inflicted on the victim, whether the victim's home was broken into, whether other contemporaneous offenses were committed, the presence of members of victim's family and injuries or threats employed upon them, the nature of the intercourse . . ."[6] *The nature of the intercourse?* I winced in disbelief. Intercourse is intercourse, I thought, or at least that was what I had learned from my few years of youthful experience.

I plunged into the booklet again: ". . . whether the victim or defendant had been imbibing alcohol or drugs when the rape occurred, whether the defendant had been represented by retained or appointed counsel, whether the defendant pleaded guilty or was found guilty by a judge or jury, whether the accused raised the defenses of consent or insanity," and on and on.[7] Suddenly I wondered if I'd had enough and was ready to walk. It was summertime, for God's sake. I'd volunteered to do a little adventuring in the Deep South, of joining up with other civil rights activists, maybe even battling vicious southern police dogs. Definitely not doing this—sweatshop work.

Wolfgang then reminded us to be objective in the reporting of the data. "You are not to allow your personal assumptions about the probable results of the study to influence the manner in which you record the data."[8] He droned on, "Nor do I want you to write anything in the schedule not called for. Most of the questions are to be answered by checking the applicable boxes." His words reminded me of the tedious instructions given by proctors after standardized test booklets are handed out.

Then came the kicker. Because there was no way to resolve factual disputes, he wanted the facts to be reported, "in the light most favorable to the prosecution, and most unfavorable to the defendant, in every case." All conflicts in testimony were to be resolved in favor of how the complaining witness reported the incident.[9] So, a white female's denial that she ever gave her consent to intercourse would always trump a black male's claim to the contrary. Didn't seem right to me, but Wolfgang was insistent on making the statistics bulletproof.

When he was finally through, Wolfgang appeared ready for questions. If I had not been so delirious from lack of sleep, I would have surely kept my silence and allowed others to embarrass themselves. Instead, up popped my impetuous right arm signaling a question. Wolfgang motioned his head towards me.

"What if we're stonewalled?" I asked. "What if the court clerks refuse access to their records?"

My question was met with immediate snickering from a few surrounding students. "The records are public property!" somebody whispered. "They can't refuse!" My ears reddened.

A young man nearby overheard the retort and approached the lectern as Wolfgang withdrew to one side. "I'll answer that," he replied, followed by a pause. "A good question." Relief swept over me. Thank God someone didn't think I was such an idiot. My rescuer looked dapper, sporting a freshly ironed white shirt and crimson and blue tie (Penn's colors). He introduced himself and said he was one of the Fund's attorneys from New York.

"That might happen, "he warned. "Please realize that southerners feel they are under siege. To them you are northern invaders. This is their second Civil War. And many are angry at northern college kids for helping colored people stand up for themselves. They think you are traitors to the white race. Not only might the authorities close the public records, but you might also be targeted for harassment . . . or worse."

The ominous "or worse" cast a hush over the classroom. He went on, "I don't expect anyone here to get hurt. But you must not show what you're up to. Yours is an undercover operation. You are not to dress in jeans. If you do that, you'll be instantly marked as a civil-rights worker. You're to go dressed in white shirts, ties, and even sport coats. I know it's going to be hot down there. But you've got to look as respectable as you can. Not the traditional garb of 'troublemakers.' You are soon to enter what will seem like a foreign country. You are to tell no southern officials who sent you or what your business is. Have I made myself clear?"

No one responded. "Do you know what today is?" he continued. "Today is the first-year anniversary of the murders of those three civil rights college kids near Philadelphia, Mississippi . . . on June 21, 1964." He paused briefly, then asked more somberly, "You know what I'm talking about?" His question was met with subdued nods from around the room. The Schwerner-Goodman-Chaney murders. In early August 1964, the decomposed bodies of Michael Schwerner, twenty-four (from Cornell University), Andrew Goodman, twenty (from Queens College), and James Earl Chaney, twenty-one, were discovered by FBI agents under an earthen dam on a farm in Neshoba County, Mississippi. The three had been marked for murder by Edgar Ray Killen, a Baptist preacher, sawmill operator, and KKK member. Michael Schwerner was especially hated for his work over the preceding four months in operating a Congress of Racial Equality (CORE) field office in Meridian, Mississippi. On June 21 of that year, Deputy Sheriff Cecil Price, another KKK member, had arrested Schwerner, Goodman, and Chaney for allegedly speeding five miles over the posted limit. After holding the trio in the county jail for a time, Price released them, then pursued and rearrested them within an hour. He drove them to a deserted location, where he turned them over to two carloads of armed KKK members. The young men then were taken to an even more remote location where they were shot to death.[10]

The speaker continued, "For those of you being assigned to Louisiana, you must be especially careful not to show your hand. Last year we sent several law students into that state to do some preliminary investigating. We asked them to find out where the records for rape cases were kept."

After rummaging through a packet of papers he had been carrying, the speaker stopped at one document of seemingly particular significance.

"I want you to turn to this handout," he said, holding it, "which reads at the top 'Statewide Analysis–Louisiana.'" He paused while the students shuffled through their papers, finally catching up with him.

"You'll find on the first page of this handout the following warning: 'Because of this official attitude, it appears that a successful search for information at the state capitol in Baton Rouge must be made on the first try. Repeated attempts might arouse suspicion that would lead to *a closing of any possible source* [emphasis added]. And conceivably the State, if it got wind of the project, could alert all the Louisiana parish courthouses not to divulge information.'"[11]

I continued to read where he left off. The handout recommended that the records in Baton Rouge should only be sought after all information from the various surrounding parish courthouses had first been obtained. "Thus armed, one should be able to get the most mileage out of the visit to the Capitol."[12] For that reason, the students were to entice "the secretaries to unwittingly open up the files."[13]

> If pressed for an explanation [of our work] he should be prepared to state that he is engaged in some form of non-offensive project as e.g. a general study on capital punishment. Generally it is wise to be extremely polite and ask as few questions as possible. . . . If an important fact such as race . . . is missing . . . [indulge] in some general conversation and point blank [ask] just prior to departure.[14]

Spies, I thought. Are we now reduced to spying on our own countrymen? Or are they different from us? Are white southerners truly from another planet? I would soon find out. The speaker gave one more warning.

"I don't want anyone here drawing attention to yourself. And most obviously, please don't appear openly with any colored people or civil rights workers."[15]

These warnings came with good reason. A year earlier the LSCRRC had sent law student "interns" to work in southern law firms that represented civil rights activists. Some of these interns had been drawn into the crossfire between their firms' clients and angry local citizenry. Lorenzo Eric Chambliss, when he arrived in St. Augustine, Florida, in 1964, almost joined an interracial group of young demonstrators on a march. The march was short-lived after the demonstrators were met with bricks and rocks thrown their way. One young man returned in terrible shape. His mouth was bloodied and many of his teeth were missing.[16] Another intern, Jeremiah Gutman, was in Bogalusa, Louisiana, in 1965 as an observer of a voters' registration march led by, among others, CORE leader James Farmer. While walking along the roadside, he was told by a police officer to either be with the demonstrators or not. When he failed to respond immediately, he was grabbed and thrown among them.[17] Alan Lerner, while working as an intern in Jackson, Mississippi, was arrested.[18] We were told to avoid such confrontations with southerners. Otherwise we would become distracted from our rape survey mission, thereby lessening its accuracy.

"Scouts" First

As the day wore on and we heard from other speakers, I became increasingly impressed with the amount of preparation that had gone into this project. We were told that within the year preceding, law students and attorneys had been sent all across the South as "scouts" to report back the names of helpful secretaries and clerks and determine if the case records on rape convictions could be copied. These scouts also had researched the criminal laws and procedures of each southern state we were to visit.[19] And they made contact with a small but vital network of attorneys in the South who were not fearful of representing clients active in the civil rights movement. These attorneys later came to our aid when southern authorities resisted our investigating efforts.

In Florida, the "scouting" had gone a step further. There, a civil rights attorney from the Daytona Beach area, Tobias Simon, had marshaled several students from local law schools to travel by themselves through backwoods counties, retrieving information from court files that showed discriminatory sentencing patterns facing African American defendants in rape cases. Among those volunteers, Bennett Brummer and Richard Burns were handicapped with thick New York accents. Despite arousing suspicious glances from the court clerks, they remained naively impervious to the potential dangers they faced.[20] What they discovered was the almost exclusive use of the death penalty for the past twenty years on African Americans convicted of rape, whether the crimes were perpetrated on white or black women. The only white man executed for that same crime was an unrepentant homosexual. This data was later forwarded to the New York office of the Fund.[21]

DOJ Statistics

We were told of similar statistics available from the U.S. Department of Justice (DOJ) which merely showed that of African Americans convicted of rape, a far greater proportion were sentenced to death than of white offenders. The DOJ did not explain why these disparities existed.

In Texas from 1930 to 1962, 13 whites and 66 blacks were executed. In the remaining sixteen southern and border states, 30 whites and 333 blacks were executed for rape during the same period of time, a ratio of one to eleven. By contrast, the national average for capital murder was one black for every one white executed even though blacks made up just one-tenth of the country's population.[22]

But the courts had previously rejected such statistics as insufficient because discriminatory conduct by jurors could not be established explicitly.[23] Jurors would rarely, if ever, admit bias in sentencing an African American man to death, relying instead on the outrageous facts of each case for their justification. Additionally, because juror deliberations were, and still are, conducted in secret, proof of racially charged comments among jurors were difficult to come by. Our research efforts were not intended to breach the jury room's wall of inviolability as such but to test for the presence of the nonracial variables in each case. Then, through a complex series of statistical analyses, these variables would be compared with the sentences rendered to see whether the defendant's and the victim's respective races were what truly determined who lived and who died.

Civil Rights Activity

By the end of the day we were all exhausted. I retired for the night to temporary housing at a nearby dormitory. So much information and so many lingering questions. For instance, why had the Fund chosen to refocus its energies on abolishing capital punishment? And what had triggered the conduct of this survey? I am sure none of us then fully appreciated or understood the confluence of historical forces that had led to our soon-to-be assault on the southern criminal justice system. Three factors were at play, the most obvious being the burgeoning civil rights movement that challenged all forms of racial discrimination practiced primarily against African Americans. At the forefront of this struggle was the Fund, which was founded in 1940 to provide representation for blacks who could not afford to assert their legal rights and to challenge racial discrimination throughout the nation.[24]

Thurgood Marshall, who became a U.S. Supreme Court Justice in 1967, served as the Fund's director until December, 1961. Through Marshall's tireless efforts in the federal courts, legal segregation in public schools received a fatal blow in the seminal Supreme Court decision of *Brown v. Board of Education*.[25] The Fund's efforts in the early 1960s took a different turn under new director Jack Greenberg by also providing representation of civil rights activists who were charged with criminal offenses for participating in demonstrations primarily in the South. In 1960 interracial groups made up of African Americans and white college students participated in "sit-in" protests at southern restaurants, resulting in numerous arrests by local authorities.

In 1961 James Farmer of CORE led the Freedom Rides into the South. Busloads of civil rights activists challenged racial segregation in restaurants, restrooms, and other similar public facilities.[26] In 1963 the Student Non Violent Coordinating Committee (SNCC) conducted the "Freedom Vote Campaign," and in 1964 the "Mississippi Freedom Summer" brought white students from the North to help in registering African Americans to vote in southern states.[27] Each of these efforts prompted retaliatory arrest and prosecution by southern law enforcement authorities as well as civil lawsuits by angry white property owners.

Maintaining White Domination

These efforts to suppress the civil rights movement had an unintended consequence: they brought into focus the southern court system as a tool to maintain white control over all facets of southern life. Because of the apartheid-like ordering of the races that had persisted since the end of Reconstruction in the 1870s, southern judges and juries were almost entirely all-white and all-male. These triers of fact had long been known for their discriminatory sentencing practices. The southern justice system was built on keeping the races apart and maintaining white domination.

A black man found guilty of raping a white woman was dealt with harshly to serve as a deterrent to miscegenation, or interbreeding of the races. One case, which the students knew from law school classes, and which particularly inspired our participation, was that of the "Scottsboro Boys." During the 1930s nine black youths, ranging in age from twelve to twenty, were tried for the rape of two white women. All defendants were sentenced to death. One of the white women, Ruby Bates, later recanted her story, admitting that she and her companion had lied to avoid prosecution for conducting prostitution across state lines. Nevertheless, southern juries in Alabama ignored the evidence and repeatedly returned guilty verdicts after appellate courts had granted requests for retrials. After spending many years in prison, all the defendants were eventually released.[28]

Another example was the "Martinsville Seven" case. In 1949 Ruby Stroud Floyd accused seven African American males of raping her near Martinsville, Virginia. The victim was a thirty-two-year-old white married woman and a Jehovah's Witness. Within two days, all the defendants were arrested and signed confessions. Five of them were teenagers, the youngest being only seventeen. The oldest, a war veteran, was thirty-seven and married with children. The trials lasted only seven days, with all defendants convicted and sentenced to death by an all-white, all-male jury.[29] On February 2, 1951, three of the condemned "men" were electrocuted, and three days later, the remaining four were similarly put to death. The chair used in the killing of the seven became so hot that it needed time to cool before each subsequent execution. The youngest was quoted as saying moments before he died, "God knows I didn't touch that woman." The U.S. Supreme Court did nothing to intervene.[30]

Irrespective of the possible innocence of some of the youths, the punishment meted out underscored the relative value of human life as seen by the southern judicial system: One white female, wrongfully assaulted, deserved to be compensated by extinguishing seven black lives.

Execution as Cruel and Unusual

A second factor prompting the rape–capital punishment study was the growing view that execution, especially by electrocution, was a barbaric and unnecessary punishment. Death did not come instantaneously but in installments. Eyewitnesses reported seeing the condemned man cringe on receiving the first electrical current, then struggle to free himself from the straps as his limbs grew contorted. Some said they saw the inmate's eyeballs pop out and dangle on his face. He often excreted his waste and vomited blood and saliva. His body turned crimson, the flesh swelled, then burned and even caught on fire, causing a sweet smell that permeated the death chamber. The heat caused by the current in some instances became so extreme that the prisoner's blood reached the boiling level. The first shock wave of electricity was usually followed by a second jolt to finish him off.[31] Unfortunately, there had been many instances in which the condemned man did not die, only to be rushed back to the chair for another treatment.

One of the most notorious cases was that of Willie Francis, a sixteen-year-old African American accused of killing a white drugstore owner in Louisiana. Twelve Cajun jurymen sentenced him to die in the lap of "Gruesome Gertie," Louisiana's infamous portable electric chair, which sometimes performed erratically. Two horrific jolts of electric juice poured through Francis's body on May 3, 1946, as the chair skipped across the floor. The witnesses heard the condemned boy's screams, saw the convulsions of his face and the puffing of his lips. He finally cried, "Take this off. I can't breathe," referring to the hood placed over his head. Further efforts at killing him were immediately stopped, and the prisoner was able walk away from the chair.[32] But the State of Louisiana was not done with him yet. A second death warrant was issued, and not even the Supreme Court would block Louisiana's efforts.[33] A year after the first failed attempt, Francis died by electrocution on May 9, 1947.[34]

Goldberg's Dissent

The third and most recent factor at play was the rising chorus of discontent with imposing the death penalty in rape cases, symbolized by a surprising expression of discontent from Supreme Court Justice Arthur Goldberg in an opinion in cases the court declined to review known as *Rudolph v. Alabama*.[35] Joined in the dissent by Justices William Brennan and William O. Douglas, Goldberg pointed out that, as of 1963, thirty-three states had already abandoned capital punishment for rape. Only five countries, including the United States, still authorized that sanction. He raised three questions with his fellow brethren of the high court. First, does sentencing a man to death for rape violate "evolving standards of decency"? Second, is death an excessive punishment since no human life was taken? And third, can the aims of punishment (deterrence, isolation and rehabilitation) be achieved as effectively by punishing rape less severely, such as by imprisonment? If so, is death for rape unconstitutionally cruel and unusual?[36]

His questions signaled to the Fund's staff attorneys that at least some justices might be ready to declare the death penalty for rape in violation of the Constitution. And while Goldberg did not raise the issue of discriminatory death sentencing by southern courts and juries, the issue of racism was very much at play.[37] The case came out of Alabama. The victim was a white female and the defendant was a black male.[38] The Fund's leading anti–death penalty lawyers (Frank Heffron, Michael Meltsner, Leroy Clark, and others) could think of no better way to challenge this ultimate punishment than by using a two-pronged assault: first, that capital punishment for rape was excessive and therefore cruel and unusual in violation of the Eighth Amendment; second, that death sentencing was applied mostly to a select minority in the South. Therefore it violated the Fourteenth Amendment guaranteeing all persons equal protection (and treatment) under the laws.

This was where we came in. Success would remain elusive unless these claims were backed by our fact-finding efforts.

With all of these collective forces of history blowing at our backs, we were each drawn to this early mission in our lives to help finish off another vestige of the Civil War era left undone by the collapse of Reconstruction. We were to become white-collar guerrillas[39] working behind enemy lines, uncovering the incriminating evidence that would eventually topple the house of cards on which capital punishment in the South had been built.

Chapter 2

Into the Southern Cauldron

We were drawn from different reaches of the country. Three of us came from UCLA—Phil Brown, Tim Brayton, and myself. Henning Eikenberg, a German student who had graduated from the University of Heidelberg in 1964, came from New Haven, where he had just received a master's degree from Yale Law School. Charles "Chuck" Farnsworth and Karen Davis came from Stanford, Evan Frullman from Boston University, John "Chip" Gray from Harvard, Layton Olson from Boalt Hall (the law school at the University of California in Berkeley), and Douglas Hedin from the University of Pennsylvania, where he had studied under Anthony Amsterdam. These are some of names I was able to recognize first after peering back in time through the scope of yellowed newspaper articles, microfilmed briefs, and the recesses of my memory. But there were twenty-eight of us and some I never met: though we did the same work, we did it in different places.[1]

We were all similarly motivated. Just three months earlier, students from across the country had descended on Selma, Alabama, to join in the great march to promote voting rights for African Americans. It all started on Bloody Sunday, March 7, 1965, when six hundred civil rights workers left Selma on U.S. Route 60. Arriving at the Edmund Pettus Bridge over the Alabama River, they were billy-clubbed and gassed by uniformed southern lawmen and forced back to Selma. Later, Martin Luther King Jr. sought, and was granted, a federal court order protecting the marchers as they made another effort to cross the bridge and march to Montgomery. By March 21 the group had grown to thirty-two hundred. They walked by day and slept in the fields at night. Four days later they arrived at the state capital. By then their numbers topped twenty-five thousand, swelled by students from across the country. The Selma March became the beacon of civil rights activism for our generation.[2]

Now it was our turn. Most of us had comfortable, white, middle- to upper-middle-class backgrounds, and had been influenced by the ethical and politically liberal values of our families. Some of us went for adventure, to challenge the South's social order and survive its wrath. After all, newspapers and television reporting were then filled daily with lurid pictures of snarling police dogs, belching water cannons, exploding tear gas grenades, and other tools of war hurled at African Americans and northern white kids marching arm-in-arm toward martyrdom. Several members of our group were Jewish and were perhaps especially attuned to issues of social justice and minority rights.

Most of us went with our families' blessings. My grandfather had long been offended by the southern treatment of blacks and offered to pay my plane fare. Beyond that I was on my own with the exception of a per diem pittance each of us received from the Fund. But when John Gary called his mother to announce his arrival in Opelika, Alabama, she became frantic at the thought of his remains being later discovered in some Alabama cotton field. Her near hysteria "didn't help my state of mind," he later wrote.[3]

Defying the Mold

At first blush I did not appear to fit the role. I was born in Charleston, South Carolina, and had been raised in Virginia at a time when the races were still segregated and the Confederate flag sometimes adorned the stage of our school auditorium. I was taught to revere Robert E. Lee and refer to the Civil War as the "War of the Northern Aggression." Outdoor movie theaters were segregated with the whites' cars parked in the middle of the lot facing the screen. Blacks had to park on the sides. Regrettably, my parents were enmeshed in these southern cultural values of class and caste, which I hurriedly tossed aside during my first year at the University of Pennsylvania. Moreover, in my rebellious teen years, I had come under the influence of my grandfather, who long championed civil rights for blacks. A man of letters, he had authored many college textbooks on American literature used on campuses across the country. My admiration for him led me to loathe the racial prejudices of my environs.

Fueled by visions of racial justice, we broke into small groups and on May 22, 1965, headed south by car. We were divided into five "teams" of roughly five to six students each. One student in each team was named the "leader." He was charged with parceling out the investigatory tasks to the remaining team members who could either work singly or in groups while moving from county to county. All team members were to keep regularly in touch with their leader. If questions arose as to how the survey form should be completed, or how to interpret the data, we were not to hesitate in calling our team leader or attorneys at the New York office of the Fund for guidance. If no answer was forthcoming, then direct contact with Professors Amsterdam or Wolfgang was allowed. Each team would cover two to three states. A sixth team was available for special research assignments, to act as a liaison with local civil rights attorneys and provide courier services. Eleven states and more than 230 counties were targeted.[4]

The Lone Woman

Chuck Farnsworth, Karen Davis, John Gray, Henning Eikenberg, Douglas Hedin, and Evan Frullman were all sent to work in Georgia and Alabama. Karen seems to have been the only woman in the entire group of twenty-eight students. The Fund sponsors had anticipated that we would all be male. The printed instructions handed out at the Philadelphia meeting warned us to dress in "coats and ties" so as not to attract attention. Young ladies in the early 1960s were not expected to be at the front lines of the civil rights struggle, let alone pursue legal careers. Karen and her boyfriend, Chuck Farnsworth, both from Stanford, met in Philadelphia. Initially, the other male members of their team were surprised at the prospect of female accompaniment on what was expected to be an arduous, adventurous trip into the corners of the Deep South. The assumption of the times was that fighting bigots, dealing with police armed with tear gas, grenades, and dogs, or whatever other southern discomforts awaited—now that was manly stuff.

But Karen proved these expectations dead wrong. She adjusted as easily as the rest of the "guys" to the torrid humidity and slum-like accommodations the group faced in Atlanta. Always she wore a proper skirt and blouse, irrespective of physical hardships. But unlike some of the "guys," she would go about the day's business with aplomb, all the while ignoring the drone of overhead mosquitoes and the incessant beads of sweat that formed on her brow. She was a trooper, willing to burrow into the musty archives of newspaper publishing houses and courthouse files for hours, and only coming out for occasional glimpse of sunlight, or a bite to eat. Because Charles had been chosen by the Fund to be the leader of the six-person team, the other male members anointed him their "Chief." Karen, Charles's girlfriend, was duly dubbed "Chiefess." Almost immediately she gained her doubters' respect with her ever-radiant smile, sense of humor, easygoing nature, and most important, her willingness to withstand the sometimes-salty talk of her companions. Karen blended her toughness with her feminine ways, and she had to during this period preceding the feminist movement.[5]

The Trip South

The Alabama-Georgia team split up in two cars, one driven by Chuck Farnsworth and the other by Chip Gray. They left Philadelphia on June 22 and tried with mixed success to stay in sight of one another. Chip was bemused over Chuck's shifting speeds that were "inversely proportional to the intensity of the conversation."[6] When Chuck announced that he was the great-great-grandson of Jefferson Davis, the president of the Confederacy during the Civil War, Chip suggested a scandalous newspaper headline for the white people of Montgomery, Alabama, "which is so proud about being the capital of the Confederacy: 'Jeff Davis's grandson returns as a civil rights worker.'"[7]

The group followed one of the interstates that hugged the eastern seaboard, spending a couple of nights along the way in dingy motel rooms cooled by air conditioners that erratically turned off, then on again. Once the "real" Alabama was reached, the interstate gave way to two-lane roads that rambled through fields of corn, sweet potatoes, and squash punctuated here and there by "genuine mule-drawn plows" and shacks of tenant farmers.[8] The windows of many of these shacks were left open for ventilation. Flies swarmed about nearby outhouses saturated with the stench of feces, and roofs were pockmarked with holes chiseled from the pounding of the semi-tropical afternoon rains. Tim Brayton, who had been sent to South Carolina, expressed disbelief that such primitive conditions persisted into the twentieth century.

Henning Eikenberg, the German student, and most of his fellow travelers came from cooler climates and were almost crippled by the South's blazing sun and the accompanying humidity. Henning wrote in his diary, "Everything sticks to the body—disgusting!"[9] But he was in awe of the extent to which nature's forces predominated. The chirping of millions of crickets, the fields of cotton, the acres of timberland, the earth reddened by oxidized iron, and the frequent cloudbursts that unleashed torrents of rain all helped to intensify his senses to the extreme climate he had entered.[10]

Michael J. Henry was a student from Harvard Law School. His group was assigned to prowl the bowels of the antiquated courthouses scattered about the Arkansas countryside. He would later decide after graduation to shun the world of corporate law and its monetary rewards by spending his time instead at the Fund's offices in New York, working on the death penalty challenges that the Fund had launched.[11]

I was assigned to a team covering Louisiana and Mississippi in the heart of Old Dixie. I sat in the back seat of a rattletrap Chevy most of the way down while my two companions, who were from the same law school, chatted away in the front. All the fond memories of my youth resurfaced as we passed by the small towns between Little Rock and Shreveport—Malvern, Arkadelphia, Prescott, Texarkana, Gilliam, Dixie, and many smaller burgs in between. They spurred my remembrances of southeastern Virginia and the visits to my grandfather's three-story antebellum home in Chapel Hill, North Carolina. When we left Texarkana, we took a temporary detour to see more of the countryside, following a two-lane roadway through open fields and forests clustered with pines. There the land took on a quality of comfort.

Unlike my traveling partners, I relished the sight of shacks scattered about like leaves felled unevenly by the summer breezes, the tin roofs resting on crumbling pillars of cinder blocks, and half-sunken porches weighed down by white-enameled refrigerators and washers in disrepair. The front yards filled with squawking chicken and rusting trucks added to my sense that this place was authentic. It was real—not papered over with modern things. And always the little churches that popped up everywhere. In these parts of the South poverty knew no bounds between black and white, except on Sunday. There were black churches and white churches, each beckoning their congregations to leave the cotton fields and pecan groves and partake once each week in the Lord's bread and wine (or grape juice). The warmth of the geography made me feel like a prodigal son as the Old South tried desperately to twist its vines around my heart and lure me home to a cozier time when I was a boy. Only I wasn't a boy any longer, and I wasn't home. I was on a mission to change that which was part of me but which could not hold me.

Arriving at Our Destinations

As we approached Louisiana, the mournful sounds of "House of the Rising Sun" blared from the radio, as if to warn of our impending ruin. The Animals' version was still a hit from a year earlier. The air thickened, gradually smothering me with its heavy humidity and sweet aroma of honeysuckle. Finally we arrived at Shreveport and drove to the CORE office in the black section of town. It was early evening when we pulled in. The air was still moist and offered not a single breeze. Puddles of sweat dripped from our exhausted faces as we alighted from the car. Inside the office we were greeted with the buzz of chattering young people, some black, some white, hustling about with self-importance and oblivious to our presence. I saw our team leader huddling with the director of the office, planning for the next day's adventures.

I desperately needed to freshen up from the sun-drenched captivity I had suffered in the back seat of our Chevy and so, without telling anyone, I strolled down one of the unpaved streets, past a few well-lit drugstores situated strategically at intersections and where mostly young black men and a few of their girlfriends had gathered. Their eyes swept suspicious glances in my direction, staring at my every footstep. Soon I found myself in a residential part of town sliced in half by a well-lit highway teeming with cars, cruising aimlessly, a few packed with black teenagers. No longer was it just the young folk I noticed staring. Everyone was, whether from their porches, or while watering their front lawns, or in passing me by on the sidewalk. And their facial expressions were not friendly.

Finally, someone yelled, "Hey . . . white boy. 'Ere boy . . ." followed by cackling laughter. I knew it was time to leave. I had violated a southern code of conduct that the races do not mix, especially on their respective home turfs. For a white guy to enter a black neighborhood uninvited and alone was big trouble. I knew better but had been swept up by the naiveté of my colleagues. Just because we were on a civil rights mission did not shield us from the sins of our white forefathers. My legs could not carry me fast enough back to my companions and safety.

Opening Up the Records

The next day each of our team members received instructions from the team leader as to which courthouses we were assigned and what routes we would follow. Phil Brown was sent first to New Orleans and Baton

Rouge, Louisiana, to review the transcripts and other records in the Louisiana Supreme Court's files, and then to Jackson, Mississippi, to do the same at the Mississippi Supreme Court. I was sent to prowl about the Greco-Roman-styled courthouses of Red River, Jackson, Lincoln, Bossier, Ouachita, Richland, Catahoula, and Franklin parishes, to name a few. Almost simultaneously with our arrival in Louisiana, other law students were landing at their southern ports of entry and fanning out from there. The Alabama-Georgia group hit the appellate stacks of the Alabama Supreme Court in Montgomery. Tim Brayton visited South Carolina's antebellum courthouses scattered about its forty-some counties. Layton Olson checked out the appellate records in the Supreme Court building and the parole files of the state prison in Columbia. Chip Gray and Henning Eikenberg traveled about Alabama, stopping by the county courthouses in Selma and Livingston and the newspaper archives of the *Tuscaloosa News* and the *Selma Times Journal.*

On our respective journeys we learned much from southern attorneys about how their system of justice worked. I remember in Pascagoula, Mississippi, a long conversation I had with a young practitioner, a pug-faced man with a heavy build, mop-thick hair, and an unerasable smile beaming aggressive overconfidence. "There are two kinds of justice heah," he told me proudly, "white man's and black man's."[12] And there was a simple explanation for that. Two differing societies required their own brands of laws.

He claimed the southern courts were more lenient to "Negrahs," than to whites, "because we hold them to a lower standard." The district attorney of a Louisiana parish I later met explained this "lower standard" further. "Negrahs," he said, were by nature "highly excitable" and likely to take extreme actions over small injuries.[13] Also, they often charged each other with "make-believe" offenses. When taking these factors into account, most judges would give lenient sentences. I asked the D.A. why, based on my research, so many black defendants pleaded guilty to rape instead of going to a jury to fight the charges. He beamed widely. "'Cause he won't dare go to a jury. They'd fry 'em."[14]

The Case of the Available Wife

Chip Gray recounted his conversation with an attorney in Selma who spoke of a case in which the black defendant was charged with carnal knowledge of a minor. Even though the defendant had the worst local white lawyer representing him, he was acquitted. But Gray was told that if some "Harvard lawyer had interfered at all, the Negro would have been electrocuted."[15]

Another attorney told Gray of his representation of a young black male charged with raping a middle-aged white woman in her home while she was asleep. The facts suggested she might have been a willing partner in the alleged assaults. The prosecution contended that the young man and his black male companion overheard the white lady and her husband arguing one evening, prompting the "boys" outside to wonder if she might be available. They waited until after the argument subsided, then heard the husband leave for a separate bedroom, where he soon fell asleep. More time elapsed, and finally when all was quiet in the household, one of the young men brazenly jumped through the woman's open bedroom window and had a session with her. The other lingered patiently outside. When the first one was done, the other took his turn. He had sex with her once, left through the open window, and upon reinvigoration, came back for more. He left again, but his appetite still whetted, he came back for a third time. By now the husband was awakened by the commotion, saw the "boy" with his wife, and chased him away. The wife claimed she had taken a sleeping pill that night and was completely unaware of the young men and their actions. She had slept through it all. The hooligans were later caught and faced rape charges. To escape the "chair," and on their attorneys' advice, they pleaded to a lesser charge of burglary with intent to rape. Each received only fifteen years in prison, a merciful sentence by southern standards.[16]

The Court Clerks

The court clerks taught us much about southern justice as well. In one small parish I visited, I found the records of rape convictions incomplete. While the docket books had entries for the defendants' names, the charges, and the dates of the charges, they did not reveal the dates of conviction or the sentencing. And the files for those cases could not be located. When I asked the elderly clerk where they might be, he squinted his eyes and cast me a sinister smile.

"Son," he answered in an extended drawl, "'round he-ah, if they're Negrah, we Ku-Klan 'em."[17]

I shuddered at the photographic image stuck in my memory of a white mob gazing up at a shirtless young African American man with an extended neck and drooping head, hanging from an oak tree. This ugliness, though difficult to confront, spurred me to find the missing information that would make the statistics more reliable. I responded with some frustration, "You must have the files somewhere. They can't just disappear!"

"Well, son," he replied with a wry expression. "They might be in the attic. But y'all have to plow through the cobwebs to find 'em."

With that, he ushered me behind the clerk's counter, then down a hallway until we reached a flight of steps made of wide wooden planks spiraling upwards. The planks were furrowed from years of treading feet and creaked loudly as we climbed them. At the top was a small door left open. He flicked on a switch that lit three sixty-watt bulbs spaced evenly apart along the center ridge of the attic and motioned that I enter first. I hesitated and then ventured into this abyss of near darkness, planting my feet carefully on the rough attic flooring. I could barely make out through the feeble, dusty lighting the outlines of files piled precariously on top of one another.

The old clerk followed me in and found a desk with a small lamp I could work by. "You got three hours," he warned. "Then we close."

I nodded my understanding. After he left, a vague exhilaration overcame me as I began poring through the yellowed files, many enshrouded with spider webs, and examined the faded print under the lamp. I sensed ghostly voices speaking to me through the pages, demanding they be recognized for the misfortunes they had suffered. Slowly the minutes, then the hours washed away, and by the end of the afternoon I had discovered some of the missing information. The convictions of guilt were clearly stated as well as the means—a guilty plea, or a court or jury verdict. But the sentences imposed were not. Either the spaces were left blank, or the verdict forms or judgments had been misplaced, probably intentionally. And that is where the trail ended. I was disappointed in myself that I could do no more to bring recognition to those whispering voices I had to leave behind. I sent the Fund as much information as I could. Whatever became of those young men must be left to the ages.

The Alabama group had better luck at the Supreme Court building in Montgomery. The appellate files were more carefully documented than those I found at the trial court level because of the nature of appellate review. An appellate court depends almost entirely for its decision-making on the thoroughness of the trial court record it is provided. The less thorough the record, the less chance an appellant will gain a reversal if error was truly committed. That record usually includes transcripts of the testimony given by witnesses. It was from those transcripts that most of the facts were extrapolated in completing the

Capital Punishment Survey booklets. Gray described what he called a "typical frame-up" case:

> White girl violently raped by two Negroes. A month later she picks two people out of a police line-up. There was apparently a question as to whether the police had coached her [regarding] whom to pick. Both Negroes claimed they had been thoroughly beat[en] up; one had two broken bones in his hand broken by stomping.[18]

Over and over, these forced confession cases popped up in our investigations, particularly where African Americans were charged with rape, followed by quick and easy convictions. It was not until a year later in *Miranda v. Arizona*[19] that the U.S. Supreme Court attempted to end some of these police practices by requiring suspects to be advised of their constitutional rights and warned before their statements could be used in court.

"White on black" rape cases were particularly hard to find. Chip Gray mentioned one in his diary in which five white men were convicted. They had become "drunk and decided to kill the first Negro they came across. It happened to be a woman so they all raped her instead. They got a term of years which decidedly would not have been the case if the races had been reversed."[20]

Resistance from the Courts

In one of the handouts given to us at our Philadelphia meeting, we were warned of being "run out of town" should our civil rights affiliation become known.[21] While I never had to face that extreme difficulty, Chip Gray and Henning Eikenberg were not so fortunate. They encountered a particularly troublesome chief clerk at the Perry County courthouse who on their arrival strolled out of his office wearing a ten-gallon hat. He inquired of their business, and after listening to the young men's explanations, he curdled his fingers around a six-shooter pistol strapped into his holster, leaned over the desk and told them curtly, "I think you should go someplace else." They did. At the Montgomery Circuit Court, Gray also reported that "the clerk was a real bastard. He ranted and raved in a high temper, but finally did let me look at a book for a minute."[22] At the courthouse in Livingston, Gray observed, the clerk was a "real tough nut," adding, "I tried to use the utmost in humility, but he refused to let us see the records even after we said they were public. He said he would find us a case if we could give him the name but that wasn't going to do us much good."[23]

And at the Jefferson County Circuit Court, the clerk told Gray that the court's files were not open for public inspection to anyone coming from outside the state. Gray described the clerk as "white-haired, pinched looking with rimless glasses . . . [H]e would have been a sad case if he hadn't been so petty, mean and officious at the same time."[24] The clerk at first refused to allow any of the docket books to be viewed in the records room because he was "too suspicious." When he finally relented, he kept a wary eye on Gray and Eikenberg, following their every move.

A similar reception greeted them in Sumter County in the far western part of the state, and part of what was then called "Black Belt" country. These access issues became serious enough that calls had to be placed to New York and Philadelphia for some guidance. Professor Wolfgang huddled with his statistician, John Monroe, who had initially selected the counties to be examined. Their solution: replace Sumter with Greene County (another "Black Belt" part of the state). Perry was also presumably dropped.

Resistance to their investigatory efforts came not only from the court clerks but also from judges and lawyers. When Gray and Eikenberg stumbled upon Judge James O. Hare, he was reading a newspaper in his clerk's office at the courthouse in Selma. Gray described the judge as a genteel, "solemn faced little man" who at first put on his southern charms, showing them about the courthouse, recounting some history of the local bar and explaining why King Cotton had given way to the cattle industry. Then, unexpectedly, Hare changed course. In a growling baritone, he aimed some barbs at the U.S. Department of Justice for having orchestrated the civil rights march from Selma to Montgomery a few months earlier. When he learned from what schools Gray and Eikenberg had come, Hare expressed his displeasure with Vassar for refusing to admit his niece "because she was a southerner." As his demeanor grew increasingly chilly and distant, the young men took the hint, leaving with little information.

They fared no better with Judge Mallory, also of Selma. The judge began their meeting by unabashedly positioning a Smith and Wesson revolver on his desk before slowly withdrawing it to the middle drawer. Gray and Eikenberg became increasingly wary of the judge's display of manhood and decided it was best to leave. They also visited a prominent attorney in Selma, who asked them what they were up to. Gray let slip that they were working on a case for Oscar Adams, an African American attorney who had become infamous within the local white community for his pursuit of civil rights causes. The attorney needed no further inquiries and ended the interview abruptly. Not easily slighted, Gray retorted, "You're not showing much respect for the law!" and went for the door.[25]

One of the legal secretaries they met was as sweet and gracious as could be until she later discovered the true purpose of their visit. She hunted them down at a nearby courthouse and apologized for having shown them any assistance. She said she was so sorry she had "let down" her boss by having helped them on their civil rights mission. Chip Gray wrote: "She was one of the bitterest people we'd come across yet. She didn't accept our argument that 'even' a Negro was deserving of aid and information in preparing a case."[26]

Blue Collar Resistance

The response to our presence from outside the legal community was equally unsettling. On my trip across northern Louisiana, I recall visiting a diner packed full of mostly local farmers and working people. On entering, I was met with the blue haze of Lucky Strike smoke and the smells of sweat and burned cooking. I sat in a booth still dressed in a white shirt and red tie, barely noticing the drop in the din of chatter. Waitresses in white aprons scurried about pouring coffee.

One of them with red bangs hiding her eyes observed my attire and strolled over. After taking my order she asked, "You a civil rights worker?" The subsidence in conversation that immediately followed lasted longer than I care to remember. "'Cause they think you are," and she motioned to a table full of young toughs glaring in my direction. They were big-muscled fellows, three of them with cigarette packs protruding from under their rolled-up sleeves.

In the best southern drawl I could muster, I gave her repeated assurances of my Dixie roots, and that I came from Virginia and was working on a research project for one of my professors. My pretensions were met with disbelief.

Shaking her head, she warned, "We don' like outsiders. The Negrahs 'round here know their places. We like to keep it that way." I gulped down the rest of my meal and took the evening bus out of town.

Gray and Farnsworth had similar experiences while dining in Alabama. One waitress told Gray that her town was "touchy" from all the

"Negrahs" who had "integrated the place." She was especially indignant about the ones who came in to play the jukebox. "The nerve of 'em!"

Chuck Farnsworth recounted an instance at a small town café in Alabama. He had completed drafting a letter pertaining to a civil rights matter that he wanted published in one of Alabama's leading newspapers. He mistakenly placed the letter within eyeshot of their waitress who had wormed her way to his side. Later the waitress was observed whispering to a police officer seated a few tables away. After finishing their meals, Chuck and his group left the café and drove off in separate cars towards Mobile. Within minutes of their departure, Chuck's car became engulfed in flashing lights and siren sounds, forcing him to the side of the road. The police officer, he noticed, was the same one seen at the café. The officer sauntered over to the car and shone the beam of his flashlight on a lonely, empty beer can resting on the back seat. Panic set in, and Chuck reeled off whatever he could think of to avoid arrest. When he finally mentioned his destination, the officer nodded approvingly. "Good," he said. "Y'all need to get out of town."

Gray feared he and Henning were at times being followed. After visiting the courthouse in Linden, they were approached by someone who said he was an ABC (Alcoholic Beverage Commission) officer. He engaged them in friendly chitchat, and then asked if they were civil rights workers. In Tuscaloosa, during lunch at the courthouse cafeteria, a sinister-looking fellow approached their table and told them he had been watching their movements at the courthouse. He claimed he was an investigator for the Alabama legislature, asked what they were doing, and made a few racist remarks about African Americans to send a clear message about his sympathies.[27]

Other forms of hostility to our presence came in subtler forms. When Gray and Eikenberg asked to rent a room at a dollar a day from the Christian Student Center, the receptionist thought there would be no problem—that is, until he introduced his visitors as Harvard and Yale students. The receptionist's superintendent shook his head and replied that all rooms were taken. Southern officialdom had its own way of enforcing the old order in the presence of the FBI and other Justice officials. Sometimes, instead of allowing blacks and whites alike to frequent the same public toilets, the facilities were locked so that no one could use them.[28] Gray recalls staying at one hotel in Opelika, Alabama, which had been renamed a private "club," so that blacks could continue to be excluded. And Gray saw restaurants displaying new signs that announced, "We reserve the right to seat customers where we wish."[29] Since white management could no longer refuse to serve blacks (thanks to federal court orders desegregating places of interstate commerce), segregation of the races would be enforced from within.

But with all this resistance to outside authority came a paranoid mindset. Gray wrote of local clerks he came across who glanced at his suit and tie, then asked if he was a Department of Justice official. Eikenberg was told that the Communist Party had infiltrated most civil rights groups[30] and was responsible for sending so many young college students to the South that summer. And we were constantly lectured, as if that would convince us that the races must remain separated. Repeatedly, southerners, upon learning of our out-of-state origins, would speak of the "good and bad Negroes." The bad ones were "uppity." The good ones knew their own inferiority, appreciated the kindness of whites, rejected the civil rights movement, and knew their place in society—at the bottom. This attitude was reflected in the court transcripts we read. Blacks were greeted informally by their first names or nicknames. But whites (even the "lowliest white whore," wrote Eikenberg),[31] were addressed as "Mr." or "Miss," or given other titles.

The Chase

The greatest difficulty I encountered came from quarters where I least expected it. Generals speak often of the fog of war, of the confusion and chaos that reign over any battlefield. The civil rights clashes that waged across the South in the mid 1960s were not immune to this condition. The wildfires of racial anger and angst burned most furiously at night when their flames shot across human divides without distinguishing between friend and foe. I stumbled into one such wildfire after walking across the bridge leading to Natchez, Mississippi. I was well-armed, or so I thought, with my Virginia driver's license and South Carolina birth certificate stuffed in my wallet. I even sported my newly purchased broad-brimmed hat so popular with southern white men. But while my disguises might well have placed me beyond the clutches of the Klan, the white hat attracted unwanted attention from the very people I was there to help.

I walked alone that night guided by my tourist map. I had hoped I might catch a glimpse of a riverboat paddling down the Mississippi River, or maybe a historic southern mansion. I descended into Natchez from the bridge and then followed a sidewalk for a couple of blocks toward a darker part of town. Clouds drifted over the moon shutting out what little light remained. Suddenly, the roar of an accelerating car lunging towards me from a side street jarred me. The car pulled to my side, screeched to a sudden stop and two African American men jumped out while the other two remained behind. The quickness of their actions left me no time for rational thought or discourse. No time to explain who I was, the great mission I was on, or that I was helping in *their* civil rights cause. What trumped the moment were my primal instincts of fear and flight. I dashed across someone's front lawn to the back of their property, then scrambled over a low-lying fence and down a narrow dirt driveway leading past several houses, at speeds I had never run before. My sole focus was to return to the main thoroughfare I had strayed from, where I could find safety from better lighting and greater street traffic. But something lying in the driveway that I could not see blocked the forward thrust of one of my feet. In an instant I landed face down on hard gravel.

Gone was my white hat and tourist map, both lost to the darkness. I could hear voices from behind, then the roar of that same engine, and I knew the chase was still on. I leaped back to my feet, oblivious to the scrapes on my knees, face, and elbows, and I continued my flight toward the main thoroughfare, where I could see two streams of headlights moving in opposite directions.

When I arrived, I dashed along the side of the roadway looking for help. But no one paid any attention to my flailing arms and shouts of desperation. I noticed that a few homeowners on their porches glanced my way, then disappeared into their homes, and closed their front doors. They wanted no part of my troubles. So I looked for a hole in the two lanes of traffic traveling in opposite directions through which I could thrust myself. But my pursuers had not given up and pulled to within a few car lengths of me. Suddenly the rear right door swung open and two of the men leaned forward shouting taunts in my direction. I reversed course, running in the opposite direction from whence they were traveling. Now behind their car, I took a split moment to plan my escape. I knew if I stayed close to the traffic I would be too visible for them to pursue me on foot. And if I could successfully dodge my way back and forth across the two lanes, my pursuers would lose the chase because of my greater maneuverability.

The fibers of my body tensed as I swung into action. Soon I spied that hole in the traffic I had been waiting for and scurried through it like a rat, outdistancing the speeding cars barreling down upon me. When I reached the other side, my pursuers U-turned their vehicle and headed my way. Once more I dashed along the roadway opposite the direction they were traveling until I was behind them. I looked for another hole in the traffic and again slithered across the street. I must have repeated this process four or five times until finally my pursuers grew dispirited and disappeared into the night.

Chapter 3

Meeting the Klan

In 1965 it was the Ku Klux Klan and its many klaverns sprinkled across the southern countryside that posed the greatest threat to our mission and our safety. Had their members been made aware that the objective of our survey was to nullify the death penalty in the South, we would have become compelling targets for their wrath. To fully appreciate the peril we faced requires an understanding of Klan history and the evolution of white supremacist thinking in the South.

The Ku Klux Klan (KKK) enjoyed a long and sordid history in the American South. Founded in 1866,[1] its power sprang from a willing use of terror, including cross burnings, rape, and bombings.[2] Klansmen and other white supremacists understood the public spectacle of execution to be white society's most potent tool for keeping African American males in check.[3] In the nineteenth century, lynching that combined torture and hanging was commonplace. In 1868, the Klan murdered over 290 black men. In the next three years another 118 were burned alive, hanged, or killed by other sadistic means.[4] After Reconstruction ended in the South and federal troops pulled back to the North, Klan violence became public and condoned by local authorities as a way to maintain the racial caste system.[5] In 1892 there were 161 lynchings. By the 1880s and 1890s, African Americans accounted for 73 percent of all lynching victims.[6]

Lynching Replaced by the Death Penalty

Beginning in 1909, the NAACP campaigned to publicly expose the savagery of southern violence. Soon the national and international community voiced dismay at what was viewed as an uncivilized region in the United States. Southern businessmen grew concerned that outside investment would be redirected elsewhere. Also, many African Americans were leaving the South. Their departure meant that cheap labor was becoming harder to find, which put an added strain on a troubled regional economy. In the twentieth century the number of lynchings declined as southern community leaders proposed new laws and policies later adopted by their state governments to curb violence towards African Americans.[7]

As a result, white supremacists including Klansmen relied increasingly on the courts to impose terror by execution. The electric chair replaced the noose as the threat that would intimidate blacks and ensure their submission. White judges and juries would commonly impose capital punishment on black males, particularly if they were convicted of grave interracial transgressions. Terror imposed by lynching gave way to terror by capital punishment as the number of executions grew.[8] State legislatures authorized capital punishment for a panoply of crimes including robbery, burglary, and rape.[9] And the most serious transgression of all, whether real or imagined, was the rape of a white woman by a black male.[10] Miscegenation threatened the "purity" of the white race. The worst kind of miscegenation was that imposed by force (i.e., by rape).

The most compelling statistics supporting this perspective were published by the U.S. Census Bureau in 1932. There the federal government revealed that during the period from 1920 to 1929 there were 437 executions in southern and border states. Of those, 313 were African Americans. Though they only composed 25 percent of the population, about 72 percent of those executed were African American. Because of these disproportionate numbers, blacks were executed about twelve times more often than whites.[11] Later Census Bureau statistics reaffirmed this trend. Capital punishment had thus been transformed into a tool to maintain the caste system in the South and was only secondarily used as a means to dispense justice.

Resurgence of the Klan

In response to the "invasion" of the South by northern civil rights activists in the 1960s, the Klan enjoyed a resurgence. During that decade its membership grew to twenty thousand.[12] The Klan fanned the fears of southern whites with claims that their political and economic power was under siege by "outside agitators."[13] These agitators included a Communist-Jewish conspiracy to upset the South's social order and bring tumult to the region. The Klan was responsible for the 1961 attacks on the Freedom Riders who tried to integrate interstate buses, and during the sixties the KKK was responsible for numerous murders and bombings of African American churches.[14] White Citizens' Councils were also being formed as federal pressure to implement the Civil Rights Act of 1964 grew. However, the councils resorted mostly to economic reprisals against African Americans and not to acts of violence. Their members often met openly and often included prominent community leaders.[15]

When we descended into this cauldron during that sweltering summer of 1965, little did we appreciate the historical significance and potential consequences of our efforts, which were designed to nullify the death penalty by proving its discriminatory application. We were thus taking direct aim at a weapon of terror that had become one of the primary implements of white control. If we were successful, abolition of the death penalty would seriously undermine an important symbol of white intimidation of blacks, an intolerable circumstance to most Klansmen. In their most florid fantasy, if the black man no longer feared the electric chair, he would become defiant. Rampaging black men would impregnate white daughters and wives, and the white race would become polluted with mulatto offspring.[16] Such was the paranoid and perverted thinking of those times. Because our mission so threatened the southern social order, maintaining our cover was critical. Our safety and the success of our undertaking depended on it, particularly in the countryside where the Klan had emerged as a dominant political force.

Reminders of Racist Violence

There were plenty of reminders of the violence lurking beneath the southern veneer of hospitality. During Henning Eikenberg's visit to Selma, Alabama, he was eating lunch at a soul food restaurant known in the African American community as "Eddie's Place," or Walker's Café. But he quickly lost his appetite upon learning that a white Unitarian minister from Boston had recently been murdered there. On March 9, James Reeb and two companions had just finished their chicken dinners and were headed out the café's doors when four Klan members assaulted them. Reeb was struck on his left temple with a heavy stick. The blow crushed his skull and in two days he was dead. National outrage sparked a strong rebuke; reportedly President Johnson was so moved by Reeb's death that he instructed his aides to draft a voting rights bill.[17]

Eikenberg passed by Sheriff Jim Clark's offices.[18] Clark had become infamous for his manhandling of civil rights volunteers seeking to register blacks to vote. Although blacks formed a majority of Selma's population, only 350 were officially registered. Clark would direct his men to go up and down the registration lines, instigating fights, and then locking up anyone who resisted, including old women and children. He wore a "Never" button on his uniform and could easily be taunted into unleashing his temper.[19] The national press loved to catch his corpulent frame on camera as he strutted about with a billy club in hand.

And there were the daily reminders appearing in the press of other violent encounters between civil rights activists and white supremacists, the editorial pages castigating northern outsiders for their ties to communism, and the ever-sprouting John Birch Society signs calling for all white southerners to "Fight Socialism! Impeach Earl Warren!"[20] Confederate flags were everywhere. They adorned private and public buildings alike, reminding us we were unwelcome in this strange land.

Attending a Klan Rally

Despite the apparent dangers that tracked our every move, many of the students possessed a reckless streak. Tim Brayton heard about a Klan rally outside of Columbia, South Carolina, from an announcement on a local radio show and decided to attend. At about 6 p.m. he drove to the field where the Klansmen and their families were congregating. Several hundred people were in attendance. He followed the cardboard signs bearing the handwritten "KKK" initials, and arrows pointing along a dirt road. At a clearing, he was able to see a small five-foot cross and then a much larger one, about forty feet in height, looming over the crowd. The larger cross was wrapped in strips of old rags that had been soaked in oil and kerosene. Old GM trucks and cars were still rolling in. Those Klan folk already gathered were in a festive mood, their weekend enlivened by the festivities soon to occur.

Tim's impression of them was not charitable. They were a bedraggled-looking bunch, the men with their plaid shirts and hand-me-down boots caked with sun-dried mud and the women with their outdated hairstyles and faded floral dresses purchased from local discount stores. The male Klan members were dressed in white robes. The state officers wore red satin robes, and the Grand Dragon wore green. Colors adorned the sleeves of some of the men. None wore masks. By the early 1950s, South Carolina had enacted anti-mask legislation, along with Alabama, Georgia, and Florida. By then fifty southern cities had also approved ordinances banning the practice in order to better control Klan violence.[21] Brayton thought the spectacle was comical if not farcical—grown men wearing Halloween dresses and pointed hats with only their whiskered faces exposed.

In the background Tim could hear a loudspeaker blaring what sounded like marching music followed by a scratchy rendition of a familiar patriotic song. The music was followed by a recorded history lesson describing the emergence of the "Invisible Empire" during Reconstruction times after the Civil War. Long-deceased members were eulogized for their gallantry in saving the flower of southern white womanhood from rape at the hands of northern carpetbaggers and the "Negrahs."

A stage had been set up not far from the crosses. Different speakers approached the podium. They began with a prayer, then a series of racial harangues, and finally the speech by the Grand Dragon. He ended by commanding his fellow Klansmen to report to the cross. All those dressed in the Klan robes followed the Grand Dragon; they lit torches with the fires and embers spewing from the smaller cross and formed a circle around the larger one and walked towards it. On reaching the base, they circled it, then touched the ground with their torches and raised them in unison. In a final gesture the marchers laid their torches at the base of the cross, which burst into a firestorm.

The Klansmen continued to march around the base despite the smoke and sparks spewing forth. Finally they were told to halt and return to the speaker's stage. Watching the spectacle of this man-made inferno seemed to have a calming effect. As the flames died down, the onlookers one by one drifted away into the night, satisfied that God would fulfill their prayers for supremacy.

Meeting the "Imperial Klonsel"

Tim Brayton watched the ceremony from the outskirts of the field, daring not to mingle with the crowd and thereby draw attention, but Henning Eikenberg, the German law student, decided to enter the "lion's den" on July 25, 1965, by meeting with Matthew Murphy Jr., the "chief lawyer," or "Imperial Klonsel," for the Klan in Alabama.[22] Murphy was an imposing figure. He had the appearance of a bulldog, with large, drooping jowls perched on each side of his scowling, thin lips. He staggered with the burly frame of a professional wrestler. He had already attained national fame for defending several Klansmen charged with murdering Viola Liuzzo, a thirty-nine-year-old white housewife from Detroit.[23]

On the night of March 25, 1965, Liuzzo had been ferrying civil rights marchers back to Selma, Alabama, following their march on

Montgomery. Soon her car was overtaken by Klansmen speeding in excess of one hundred miles per hour in a Chevrolet Impala. One of her pursuers shot her in the face, killing her instantly.[24] The Klansmen were arrested and tried before an all-white, all-male jury. In his closing argument, Murphy launched into a one-hour tirade against blacks, Jews, Catholics, the NAACP, and President Johnson. His oration included quotations from biblical and Klan scripture. Two of the jurors were members of a local White Citizens Council and were moved by the rhetoric. They voted for acquittal. A deadlocked jury meant a conviction was avoided, despite the eyewitness testimony of Gary Thomas Rowe Jr., a Klan member and actually an F.B.I. informant.[25] On May 21, 1965, Murphy appeared on the cover of *Life* magazine, pugnaciously holding out two extended fingers in a victory gesture.[26]

Eikenberg wanted to question Murphy about several of the rape cases he had handled as defense counsel. But on learning of his visitor's country of origin—Germany—Murphy had other ideas. He beamed with delight at finding a presumptive racist soul mate and welcomed Henning to Alabama. Though Murphy was helpful in providing information that Eikenberg needed, their conversation soon turned to racism practiced outside the South. Murphy extolled the virtues of the former Nazi regime and mentioned that there were only three countries in the world where he would feel comfortable living: Germany, South Africa (still under all-white rule in 1965), and Australia (which then still practiced segregation of whites from the indigenous population). Henning, an avowed civil right sympathizer, was appalled at his supposed linkage to the Third Reich. But when Murphy finally learned for whom Henning worked, their conversation quickly cooled.[27]

The Klan in Louisiana and Mississippi

I had to be more discreet in my travels around Louisiana and Mississippi where the klaverns were plentiful and violent. In those two states three branches of the Ku Klux Klan operated without restraint and were responsible for countless bombings, murders, and arson attacks, including the burning of the Mount Zion Church in Longdale, Mississippi, and the Schwerner-Goodman-Chaney murders, both of which occurred in mid-1964; the drowning of two nineteen-year-olds, Henry Hezekiah Dee and Charles Eddie Moore, in southwest Mississippi, also in 1964;[28] the attacks on civil rights demonstrators in Bogalusa, Louisiana, in 1965; and the death of Frank Morris and the burning down of his shoe shop in Concordia, Louisiana, in 1964.[29]

The Original Knights of the Ku Klux Klan operated throughout Louisiana in the mid-1960s with the heaviest concentrations of members in Shreveport, Monroe, and Bogalusa. Klaverns were active in twenty-nine parishes, nineteen of which were in northeastern and central Louisiana. The Klan used fronts such as the Christian Constitutional Crusaders in Monroe and Winnsboro to hide banking transactions and other activities.[30]

The White Knights of the Ku Klux Klan were principally located in Adams and Franklin counties in Mississippi.[31] They were formed in 1963 in Natchez and were so secretive that they engaged in no public rallies. Imperial Wizard Sam Holloway Bowers Jr., a vending machine operator, headed the White Knights, which were responsible for the Schwerner-Goodman-Chaney murders and were subsequently infiltrated by the F.B.I.[32] Finally, the United Klans of America, established in McComb, Mississippi, in 1964, was headed by Imperial Wizard Robert Shelton. It was very active in Natchez under the front of Adams County Civic and Betterment Association. There were seventy-five klaverns in forty-two counties operating throughout the state of Mississippi in the mid-1960s.[33]

Meeting a Klansman

In my travels around rural Louisiana and Mississippi, signs of the Klan's presence became evident especially in communities such as Poplarville and other nearby rural towns. Poplarville appeared to be a quiet place, lined with trees along its main thoroughfares and populated with only a couple of thousand residents in southwestern Mississippi. It was noted for its Pearl River County courthouse, probably built in the late nineteenth century and majestically fronted with four massive white columns, but it had a violent and checkered history.

In 1959 twenty-three-year-old Mack Charles Parker, suspected of an interracial rape on thin evidence, had been dragged from his jail cell by a mob, taken by car to the Pearl River Bridge approximately twenty miles west of Poplarville, and shot twice in the chest from a range of about six inches. Parker died within seconds. The original plan had been to castrate Parker and hang him from the superstructure of the bridge; however, with Parker dead, the mob weighted his body down with logging chains and tossed him over the concrete railings of the bridge into the rain-swollen river.

I found a room for the night at a two-story Victorian home skirted by a wraparound porch. My grey-haired landlady, probably in her sixties, was too crotchety for my liking. As soon as I was shown to my room, she lectured me on a list of house rules that included times when I could not use the toilet and shower.

During my walk into town the next morning, I noticed posters tacked on trees and wooden fences advertising a Klan rally in nearby Crossroads, a rural community to the west. For those who could not come, the event was to be broadcast on a local radio station. I jotted down the station number and expected time of broadcast. Edward L. McDaniel was to address the crowd. McDaniel had been appointed Grand Dragon of the Mississippi branch of the United Klan of America (UKA) a year earlier. He was instrumental in launching new UKA klaverns in McComb and Natchez, Mississippi. He was also successful in encouraging many members of the White Knights to switch their allegiances to the UKA in Mississippi. UKA members were responsible for a rash of bombings in McComb, Mississippi, in 1964, not far from Crossroads.[34]

As I approached the center of town I spotted a barber pole with the usual rotating colors and decided on a quick haircut before starting my day's work at the courthouse. A close-cropped military style would be best for these parts. That would make me look more like a local boy than the shaggy Californian I had become. As I approached the barbershop I spotted two elderly, bespectacled white gentlemen seated on a bench outside, reading the *Times-Picayune,* which in the 1960s had a wide circulation. Their thin lips cracked not even a faint smile as they glared at me warily. I opened the screen door and was greeted by the pungent smell of cigar smoke and a balding, middle-aged barber eager for a customer.

"Y'er next," he said gesturing to an empty chair. After a few salutary exchanges and listening to my directions on how close the cut should be, he turned to a crony straddling one of the waiting chairs and resumed a conversation about local fishing that I had apparently interrupted. I knew a little about the subject from my days as a child on the Chesapeake, so I asked what kinds of fish were found here.

"Bass, catfish, and a lot more. We got almost forty lakes in Pearl River County," replied the barber. The crony seated in front of me flicked some loose ashes protruding from the end of his cigar and then joined the fray. I noticed his beady eyes had been studying my city clothes before the white apron that descended upon me hid them.

"Where y'all from?" he asked in a sneering tone.

"Virginia," I replied. The two then nodded their approval at the mention of a former Confederate state. The inquisition continued.

What kind o' fishin' yo' like?" he asked.

"Saltwater," I answered. The fellow promptly threw up a wad of spit and hurled it on the floor. He was probably no more than forty-something but looked much older, his face flushed red from too many beers. His head sat on his almost shoulder-width neck. His gut flowed over his belt, and the zipper to the front of his jeans was undone to allow more breathing room for his expanded abdomen. Despite his gesture of rebuke at my preference for saltwater fishing, I had at least inched my way into the conversation that preceded my arrival.

"So what's going on in Crossroads tonight?" I asked brazenly. My new friend returned to chewing on the wet end of his cigar, momentarily ignoring my question. After grinding his teeth back and forth for a while, he answered, "Klan meetin'." Then another pause, followed by, "Where yo' from?" I expected the question since my accent, though Virginian, wasn't a deep drawl. I gave my well-rehearsed talk about the harmless-sounding research project I was working on for my Virginia law professor.

"The Klan's bringin' changes in these parts," my friend said. "Good changes. People here don' march any more. That's not worked. The Klan's gone back to night ridin'"—referring to an earlier time when white-robed, masked Klansmen on horseback raced about the moonlit countryside, torching the homes of black families and lynching carpetbaggers and their sympathizers. "Now *we* use force!"

I stared at him thunderstruck. He said *we*! I was talking to one of them! I gingerly asked the next question. "Ever been on a night ride?"

He paused and looked down. "Been on a few. Ah like to keep that to myself. But we never went after nobody that didn't deserve it." I dared not ask him to explain the "it." "We don' want our daughters meetin' nice darkies, bringin' 'em home, and havin' little pickaninnies."

I listened in silence while watching the ceiling fan whirring overhead. A fly landed on my beaded forehead already dripping from the humid heat that had drifted north from the Gulf waters. There are no dry heat days in the South during the summer months. I had hoped the barber's clippers would hum louder to drown out the racist monologue, but then I realized I had encouraged him to talk. The conversation was going nowhere, so I tried changing the subject back to fishing. However, the barber, who had just picked up a long blade to shave my face with, thwarted my efforts. My sudden vulnerability would not permit any interruptions on my part.

"I think the Klan's gone underground," the barber said. "Too many Feds. They're everywhere. And too many Jews. These kids comin' down from New York." He shook his head and said in a sneering tone, "They're all Jews. They wanna destroy our Christ-shun faith and turn us into godless people. Well, the Klan's puttin' a stop to that!"

I felt disgusted and couldn't wait for him to stop shearing me. I dared not disclose my Yankee sentiments and waited patiently until my incarceration ended.

Later that night I listened on the radio to Grand Dragon McDaniel[35] harangue a crowd that purportedly numbered more than one thousand. He sermonized about white purity and proclaimed that this nation could not remain half-white and half-black. A country of mulatto citizens, he said, was inconceivable. He wailed repeatedly against the civil rights trash disrupting southern white society. Peace, he said, would not come until the "Negrahs" were all back in Africa. He echoed many of the same sentiments I heard in the barbershop earlier that day. After listening to so much white supremacist rhetoric, I wondered how integration could ever work in this part of the country.

Bogalusa Burning

My second brush with the Klan came a couple of days later on my visit to Bogalusa in southeastern Louisiana. Prior to my arrival I had received a clear warning from my team leader about daily clashes between Klan members and demonstrators. I was also well advised of the tense circumstances preceding my visit from the daily news reports I read during the first six months of 1965. The town was caught in a crossfire between the Bogalusa Voters League (BVL) and the Original Knights of the Ku Klux Klan. The BVL membership was mostly African American and sought equal employment opportunities in the paper mills of Bogalusa's principal employer, the Crown-Zellerbach Company. The BVL also pressed for rapid implementation of all the guarantees under the 1964 Civil Rights Act, including equal access to public facilities.[36]

The Klan was resolutely determined to break the BVL and intimidate its membership with its tactics of terror. It had no intention of giving up ownership of the town's political establishment. The mayor, Jesse Cutrer, had been summoned on more than one occasion by Klan leadership to resist the BVL and its allies.[37] Supporting the Klan was most of the town's police force and its police chief, Klaxton Knight.[38] The police had done little to protect CORE picketers and marchers from being punched, kicked, and beaten with sticks by angry white mobs spurred on by Klansmen. Many on the police force were either Klan members or sympathizers.[39]

The BVL's allies included CORE representatives, the African American community, and the Bogalusa Deacons for Defense. The Deacons only numbered a couple of dozen but exaggerated their membership to impress the Klan. They provided armed protection to CORE workers and stopped any vehicles driven by whites from entering African American sections of town at night. They patrolled the labor hall where the BVL frequently held meetings and posted guards outside the homes of threatened African American town leaders.[40]

There were daily demonstrations, first by BVL supporters and then by Klan members who soon lost all control of their hatred for anyone they felt was sympathizing with the African American community. Klansmen used their clubs to force African American patrons to leave restaurants.[41] Klan members threw bricks and rocks at BVL marchers. Two CORE representatives were chased to an African American café, where one of them was grabbed and beaten.[42]

The Deacons responded by providing armed escorts for CORE staff members. They stationed guards laden with guns outside the union hall whenever BVL meetings were held there and patrolled the black neighborhoods to insure unwanted visitors left those areas.[43] The Klan monitored the police radio stations to learn when and where the BVL would be picketing. The FBI was sent in to monitor and report what was transpiring. Special agents planned for a long stay and appropriated an entire motel for lodgings.[44]

The situation deteriorated. Newsmen were attacked and beaten by white mobs.[45] James Farmer was sent down to lead several marches. CORE members picketed white stores on Columbia Street to protest the lack of African Americans hired as store clerks. The Klan retaliated by posting sixty Klansmen outside the union hall during a meeting of BVL members and left a couple of coffins outside. On one coffin was the name of a CORE worker.[46] By the summer of 1965, Bogalusa had come to be known as "Klantown, USA."[47] and had attracted the attention of Governor John McKeithen of Louisiana and Vice President Hubert Humphrey. At one point the governor considered sending in the National Guard. Humphrey recommended against that action, fearing that Bogalusa might then be placed under martial law in perpetuity.[48]

No Room for the Night

My visit to Bogalusa followed the completion of research at the courthouse in Poplarville. I took a bus west along Highway 26 to cross into

Louisiana. I used the bus to get about, finding that I could better blend in with my fellow travelers and thereby lessen the chances of attracting any unwanted personal attention. Greater safety in numbers, or so I thought.

When I arrived, the sun was poised just above the horizon, its streaks of light still casting a golden glow over the lush green landscape. I grabbed my one suitcase, bounded down the steps, and glanced up the main thoroughfare towards the center of town. I was greeted only by the usual swarms of bugs that came out from their foliated hiding places at this time of day. Especially troubling were the mosquitoes, having finished laying their larvae in the nearby bayous and now gliding quietly about the Louisiana countryside in search of fresh blood. I felt a couple landing on the nape of my neck, but by the time I reached to crush them they had already left their venomous red marks.

The town was a dusty place with few architectural attributes. I had an eerie sense that there was something terribly wrong. There was a stillness, a lack of any human activity, as if all the town's residents had been evacuated from the clutches of an advancing hurricane. Not a moving car was in sight, and the grocery stores and diners had "closed" signs posted prominently to discourage prospective customers. Not even the gas stations were open for business. I lumbered up the street, swinging my suitcase with the pace of my walk, until I spied a large two-story motel not far from the bus stop. The motel was like an anthill, covered with officious-looking men bustling about in shirts and ties, some even in suits, with a few hats protecting their heads from the sun's descending rays. Most were probably in their thirties and forties, and all were white. At times a small group would cluster together on the second floor landing before ducking into rooms for a few moments and then reappearing. I glanced at the parking lot but could find not a single empty stall. I spotted an "Office" sign and peeked inside the front door window. There, three white-shirted men with pistol holsters wrapped around their torsos surrounded a beleaguered clerk. Fingers were pointing, heads were shaking, and voices were rising. I opened the door and was met by angry stares, as if I had interrupted a private family argument.

"I need a room for the night," I said hesitantly.

"We're full," the clerk answered dismissively. "And y'er not likely to find any place 'round here." I tried to smile at the thick South in his voice, and asked if there might be a guesthouse nearby. One of the armed gentlemen suggested a place at the far end of town.

I thanked him and hurried on my way. It was getting dark and I was not about to be left with only Bogalusa's hard sidewalks to sleep on. The thought of becoming easy prey to the town's warring factions sent my feet moving at a quick pace down the wide deserted street, alone, with no street lamps to light my way and no idea where I was headed.

Before long a hardware store appeared on my right, then a gas station on the left, a stationery store, and a baker's shop. All were vacant, the front doors snapped shut and "Closed" signs in the windows. As I passed a restaurant, I felt the crunch of glass beneath my feet and saw a smashed window without a shard left intact. Another shop was sealed from view with wooden boards nailed over its apertures. Then another motel appeared, much smaller than the first one I encountered. It had no more than six or seven rooms. A "No Vacancy" sign was planted on the front lawn, and again I saw more men in white shirts and ties scurrying about the parking lot packed with cars. So I walked on.

Perhaps another quarter mile up the street was a small boarding house, a comfortable-looking place with wood siding, built probably at the turn of the century. It too bore a "No Vacancy" sign. And so the search continued without the sight of a single pedestrian or moving car. I finally wandered into a neighborhood of small houses surrounded by picket fences and well-ordered rows of vegetables planted in front. The streets were well paved, an indication that I must be in a white neighborhood. In African American neighborhoods in the South, the roads were usually left unpaved, covered with dirt and some loose gravel. Little care was given to those neighborhoods by the white city fathers.

Meeting Charles

On the left of the roadway, I spied a "Guests Welcome" sign in the front window. The two-story home had a chimney and was enveloped by a deep roof. Small windows appeared on the ground level in seemingly random fashion. The place seemed inviting and for the moment at least was left undiscovered by Bogalusa's white-shirted intruders. As I approached the wide porch in front, a door quickly flew open and a hand ushering me inside greeted me. I entered and found a stout, mid-forties woman with a ruddy face hiding in the shadows. No lights were turned on in the house. The wrinkles on her forehead gave away her worried thoughts.

"Dangerous out there!" she exclaimed. "You mustn' be walkin' roun' at night!" Like a mother hen she continued scolding me for a moment more, then asked where I came from and what I was doing in Bogalusa of all places. I gave my usual explanation, after which she showed me into her parlor and introduced me to a visiting neighbor. He was seated in front of the fireplace and greeted me with a wide smile. "Welcome,

welcome," he sang, with an outstretched hand. "Name's Charles. Glad you're stayin' the night." I found southerners tended to avoid speaking anything the least bit controversial, particularly on first encounter. Now well imbued with northern culture, I went right to the point.

"What's going on around here?" I asked. "Nobody's walking around, I saw all these men wearing pistols, and this is the only place where I could find a vacancy!" I sat down beside him, sinking into a well-pillowed divan that consumed me with its softness. The friendly gentleman suddenly turned dour.

"FBI," he answered. "Taken over the whole town. Grabbed every room for rent." He went on, "And those northern agitators! They're out there paradin' the streets with the Negrahs and that Mr. Farmer. Why, we had three officers hit by rocks this afternoon. Saw it myself!"

Charles started to shake, incensed by all the commotion caused by these unwelcome visitors. He was respectable-looking enough, maybe twenty years older than I was. I later learned he received a college education from Louisiana State University and was studying to become a pharmacist. He sported a thin black moustache and was trimly built and neatly dressed in slacks and plaid shirt. But here too was another example of someone who, while better packaged than the Klansman I had met in Poplarville, was still unwilling to see the winds of change blowing across the South.

I asked him about the Klan. "Well, I'm not one of them," he answered. "But that's all we got left to protect our way of life. Nearly everyone here belongs. Take Martha's brother," and he pointed to the rotund lady who had greeted me at the front door. "He just joined when he found out his store been broken into after one of those marches."

"But how does he know it wasn't Klansmen that did it?" I asked. I had earlier seen photographs in a New Orleans newspaper of hooded Klansmen with big smiles walking Bogalusa's streets, unfazed by the presence of state troopers.[49]

Charles shook his head vehemently. "They're not the problem. Unless of course you're a sympathizer. Now a sympathizer's like a traitor. If they seat the coloreds at the counters, well . . ." and he shrugged his shoulders. "What can I say? They have what's comin' to 'em."

I asked him about Bogalusa's past. Our conversation diverted from present-day troubles, to a time when blacks and whites were invisible to one another, when white families structured their hierarchy according to a supposed aristocratic lineage. Charles pointed to the picture of a white-haired old gentleman perched on the wall with a bird dog at his feet. That was "Papa," Martha and Charles's great-great-great-grandfather who once owned much timberland in Washington Parish. Papa looked imperious, possessed of a formality distinguishable from those whites who had grown up in the country. Charles droned on about the lines of lineage that linked him and Martha together, all originating from this potent overseer of the Old South. Martha must have been in the kitchen when she overheard our conversation. She returned bustling in with a plate bearing some crackers and a spread of some sort. "Charles!" she exclaimed. "You're turning us all into bastards!" Charles responded with a polite guffaw, as if a full-throated laugh was too boisterous for the southern gentleman he claimed to be.

We moved on to more recent times when Mayor Sullivan ruled the town in the early part of the century. "Did the Klan keep him in place?" I interrupted, trying to steer Charles to a more current topic.

"He didn't need to.[50] He'd used his bloodhounds if a man broke the law. They'd track him down and tear him to pieces if they had to." Slowly Charles continued his trek through the twentieth century, finally arriving at the current decade when Crown-Zellerbach had decided on a course of plant "modernizing." To the locals, both black and white, that meant layoffs. Jobs long assumed secure vanished as faceless corporate types lodged in faraway places slashed payrolls. The United Paperworkers Union went on strike, but jobs were cut anyway.

Charles shook his head sadly. "Used to be we got along fine with the coloreds. My brother and I grew up with them. We played games in the forest with Mammy's boys. Mammy was our housekeeper but we treated her like family. Now our folks and theirs don't talk to one another. Or help each other. And it started when white jobs were taken away by the Negrahs who bid for the same work."

So that was root cause of Bogalusa's racial strife, I thought. A labor split that swept away the ruling white gentility. Whites of all shades, both country folk and townspeople, were turning to the Klan to save their jobs. The labor union proved useless, and it was a northern creation at that! But the Klan—now there was real muscle power. The sun had vanished by the time I heard the chimes ringing from the mantelpiece clock. Martha rescued me from Charles's ceaseless chatter by insisting I needed my rest and showed me to my room. Finally I could hear the screeching of the front door as it opened painfully and then closed behind Charles's departing steps.

The next morning brought new challenges as I tried to find my way back to the bus stop. I feared the risks I might face walking Bogalusa's sidewalks alone, so I called for a taxi. With the first one tried, I was greeted by an African American voice.

"Yo' wanna get us both killed?" he asked. "I can't do that."

Though taken aback at his abrupt refusal, I was more embarrassed by my own naiveté for having asked him. Undeterred, I scrolled down the Yellow Pages, making further calls and receiving similar responses until I finally found one brave soul willing to venture the short ride.

Chapter 4

The "Underground" Mobilizes

In 1965 almost anyone with authority in the Deep South, whether police officers, judges, attorneys, or politicians, was white and staunchly opposed to integration of the races. Some wore "Never" buttons on their lapels and blamed the Great Communist-Zionist Conspiracy for the invasion of longhaired, unkempt, "salt and pepper" college kids. Photographs appeared in small publications of young blacks and whites linked arm-in-arm at rowdy demonstrations, often urinating together in public streets, and suggestively clutching one another.[1] Southern whites who flocked in gathering numbers to the meeting halls of the Klan and the White Citizens Councils felt under threat from a culture they did not understand or respect.

From our perspective, whites were dominant and powerful. They held all the levers of power and presented a formidable, united front. The twenty-eight of us were coursing a terrain so treacherous that a single false step could have left us without access to the court files and derailed our mission—or worse. No wonder several Fund lawyers in New York expressed doubts we would succeed, let alone stay in touch with one another.

But those doubts failed to account for our own cunning, or the southern civil rights network that would we would come to rely upon. When he arrived in Montgomery, Chip Gray re-registered his vehicle and obtained Alabama license plates to disguise his Yankee origins. Chuck Farnsworth did the same, but only after being pulled over by a state trooper who, upon seeing the California plates, asked what he was up to. Chuck assured him he was just passing through, on his way to Mobile. The next day, Alabama plates were installed in place of the California tags.

While in Jackson County, Mississippi, I solicited the help of the president of a local bar association with my "University of Virginia research project." I had earlier plucked from a University of Virginia Law School faculty roster the names of two professors I could safely use as my overseers since they were both on vacation and could not be reached (I had checked into that beforehand). After convincing the bar president of my southern loyalties, he provided me with a passport of sorts, a typed letter addressed to "All Law Enforcement officers of Jackson County," explaining the legitimacy of my business and the courtesies I should be shown. This letter proved useful when I was stopped by a state trooper in Pascagoula and then let go. Much of the time I wore a tan Stetson hat to blend in with the locals. I even purchased a rebel flag. I had become a traitor to my cause—at least superficially.

But it was the loose network of civil rights attorneys who cooperated with the Fund that best shielded us from the massive resistance of southern officialdom. Thurgood Marshall first formed this network when he was director of the Fund. He and his attorneys sought out lawyers, mostly black and often NAACP members, but also some whites willing to face down the wrath of local communities and court systems. When Marshall left the Fund in 1961 for a federal judgeship, Jack Greenberg, the new director, redoubled the efforts to expand the network, which was needed more than ever as the civil rights movement gained steam. Greenberg, for example, sent Frank Heffron, a young attorney who joined the Fund in 1962, on several trips to visit the Fund's southern counterparts and offer them assistance. In 1963 Heffron and a student from Columbia Law School, David Copithorne, began the early research into discriminatory sentencing patterns with a visit to Birmingham, Alabama, to examine the courthouse files and fill out a survey questionnaire. Heffron maintained continuing contact with a group of attorneys who were willing to take on capital cases. The Fund in turn agreed to provide those attorneys with students from northern law schools (through the Law Students Civil Rights Research Council) who would work for modest stipends as law clerks performing legal research, serving legal documents, and writing briefs.[2]

Matthew Perry

This network proved critical to our own efforts in conducting the survey. One of the participants was a well-respected African American attorney, Matthew Perry, who practiced law in Columbia, South Carolina.

Perry was the most prominent civil rights lawyer in the state, but he was also well known for his representation of death row inmates. Perry also represented Harvey Gantt, who sought admission as the first black student to Clemson University in South Carolina. After several lower court defeats, Perry finally won Gantt's admission from the federal courts in 1963. Gantt was later elected mayor of Charlotte, North Carolina, and ran unsuccessfully for the U.S Senate. In 1973 Perry was appointed to the U.S. Court of Military Appeals by President Gerald Ford, and four years after that, President Jimmy Carter nominated him to a federal district court judgeship in South Carolina.[3]

Following Tim Brayton's arrival in Charleston, and before he began working on the rape project, he was sent to Perry by the Fund. Perry showed him around the state courthouse in Columbia, introduced him to the supervising clerks and a few friendly judges and attorneys they encountered in the hallways. The responses were consistent—big, warm smiles with reciprocal greetings of guarded respect. Tim was soon engulfed in transcripts, appellate records, and whatever else he needed brought to him by willing clerks. Perry spoke to Tim of his friendship with Thurgood Marshall and of his belief that his hard work would eventually secure equal justice for future generations of South Carolina African American litigants. Tim was totally impressed by Perry, describing him years later as a "mental giant" and a legal scholar who possessed calm and deliberate analytical skills.[4]

Oscar Adams

The Alabama group was also referred by the Fund to African American attorneys, Oscar Adams and Demetrius Newton. Both had graduated from black colleges. They had gone north to earn law degrees since they were barred from Alabama's segregated white law schools. Adams graduated from Howard University in Washington, D.C., in 1947. He was African American royalty: his father had been the publisher of the *Birmingham Reporter* and his great-grandfather a member of the Alabama legislature during the Reconstruction years.[5] Adams and Newton returned to their native state and formed an association of sorts in their private law practices. By the time Gray met them, both were well known in Montgomery for handling civil rights cases.[6] Adams would later be appointed to the Alabama Supreme Court in 1980 by Governor Fob Jones, and he would successfully stand for reelection in 1982 and 1988. Newton would become a municipal judge and state legislator.[7]

Adams quickly brought Gray and the other students up to speed on which clerks to go to for help, which cases to pay special attention to, and who could be safely interviewed without fear of too many suspicious inquiries. He invited the Alabama group to his home in an African American neighborhood of Montgomery known as "Dynamite Row." Adams explained that the title was attributed to the number of homes hit with dynamite sticks thrown by passing Klansmen and other white supremacists. The homes were large, mostly two-story, surrounded by sweeping lawns, and occupied by upper-income families.

Gray's group arrived at Adams's house on a hot muggy Sunday and was immediately ushered to the back, where Adams showed off his substantial swimming pool and bar. Inside the bar on one of the walls was an enlarged cartoon featuring a southern mansion fronted by white columns. Two African American men dressed in pink suits were lounging in wicker chairs on the front porch sipping their mint juleps. At the top of the drawing appeared the caption: "Now this is what Martin Luther King had in mind!" Gray cringed at the racist content, but Adams reassured him with a wide smile. He said he bought it from a white lady at a curio shop, who at first refused to let it go because he was black. Adams pleaded with her, repeatedly affirming that he found the caricatures hilarious. Finally she relented.[8]

David Hood Jr.

Another lawyer contacted by Chip Gray and Henning Eikenberg was David Hood Jr. of Bessemer, Alabama. They met Hood at his "elaborate" split-level home surrounded by nearby ramshackle houses, but only after driving past the "white" part of town to the "wrong" side of the railroad tracks separating the white from the black communities. Hood had been detained in court and arrived late. He was a big man, with a hearty, genial manner, and described as "another former football player gone to pot."[9] He had uncanny street smarts. Hood knew where all the speed traps were set for unwary "agitators," the suspicious court clerks, attorneys, and judges to avoid because of their segregationist sympathies, and where not to drive to at night. In the coming days, this information proved vital to Gray in surviving Bessemer's minefields.

Hood seemed particularly knowledgeable about some of the rape cases Gray had unearthed at the state courthouse. He gave him the names of witnesses and family members of the victims to contact and recounted a case he prosecuted against a white man who was convicted by an all-white jury of raping two young black girls. Hood explained that he was appointed a special prosecutor because the white district attorney dared not touch the case for fear of not being reelected. One of the female victims was only six years old. The conviction was quite an accomplishment, considering the times.

Hood was even prouder of his representation of Bessemer's African American schoolchildren in a class action lawsuit the Fund filed in 1964 against the Jefferson County Board of Education. A federal court found that the school board maintained a racially segregated school system and ordered the board to submit a desegregation plan.[10] Hood and other counsel from the Fund attempted to negotiate a plan acceptable to both the board and black parents, but their efforts proved unavailing. No plan was put in place until 1967, when the court of appeals ordered black children to attend the formerly all-white schools in Jefferson County, Alabama.[11] The court also ordered the integration of faculties, facilities, and school activities. During the course of this litigation, Hood's efforts had not come without risk. Several times his home had been firebombed, and he had received numerous telephone threats.[12]

Hood's interests extended well beyond his law practice: like many black lawyers, he was increasingly active in Democratic politics, culminating in his selection as a delegate to the Democratic National Convention in 1972.[13] As Gray, Eikenberg, and Hood spoke into the late-afternoon hours, their conversation was periodically broken by the comings and goings of civil rights activists asking for advice, as well as by two northern women from the federal Department of Justice's Community Relations Service. Hood apologized for the interruptions, explaining his belief that wealthier African Americans, such as himself, must take leadership roles in the "freedom movement."

C. B. King

C. B. King of Albany was the most prominent African American attorney in South Georgia. King had helped Frank Heffron identify the best sources of information for us to investigate to complete the rape survey in the state.[14] He was known for what he called the "brickbat theory" of practicing law.[15] He would never compromise his client's interests. He would go to court at the slightest provocation, making litigation so nasty that white judges and attorneys alike would do almost anything to appease him. The Fund generously staffed King's office with volunteer students and low-paid young lawyers from the North who relished the opportunity of associating with a man so reviled by the southern white bar. Many of them came from top-rated schools; some later became judges, law professors, and one, a member of Congress.[16] King loved training them and holding forth about the local racial culture.

Once King was asked if he had a chip on his shoulder. He replied, "I have the law on my shoulder."[17] The antipathy towards him was so widespread that whenever he went to court he took precautions to protect himself. He parked his car next to the police station to discourage potential vandals. The seat of his car had been hit on at least one occasion with acid.[18] One intern recalled a preliminary hearing during which the family members of a rape victim were waiting outside the courtroom in the hallway, pacing impatiently and brandishing their shotguns. Some of the spectators inside were sharpening their knives. King represented the accused rapist. The interns wondered how they would ever leave the courtroom alive. At an opportune moment, King grabbed his interns, marched them uninvited past the bench, into the judge's chambers, down a back staircase, and into the street, where the getaway car had been parked.[19]

King had no fear of responding in kind to whatever indignity he was shown. If a judge called him by his first name, King addressed the judge in the same manner.[20] He possessed a mastery of the English language, using words opposing attorneys sometimes did not comprehend. He had a photographic memory and was known to cite cases and statutes in detail. His clients included civil rights activists Ralph Abernathy, Andrew Young, Martin Luther King Jr., and many others.[21]

In 1962 Bill Hansen, a white SNCC field worker, had been arrested and beaten unconscious by a white deputy sheriff. King went to see Sheriff Cull Campbell to find out about Hansen's condition. Campbell replied, "Nigger, haven't I told you to wait outside?" The sheriff then pulled out a walking stick and slammed it furiously on King's head. With blood gushing down his face and clothes, King staggered across the street, and a *New York Times* photographer took a photo. The photograph was flashed across the world by the wire services, appeared in numerous newspapers and magazines, and stirred the international community's outrage at this latest display of southern white brutality.[22]

Sidney McMath and John Sizemore

There were not many white attorneys in the South who dared to assist our efforts. But there were a few. Most notable was Sidney McMath, a former governor of Arkansas who advocated racial moderation. When public service no longer beckoned him, he returned to private practice and established a labor law firm.[23] Prior to the summer of 1965, his associate, John Sizemore, provided the Fund with contacts at the state penitentiary in Grady and the names of state officials who would allow access to records needed for the rape survey as long as our purposes were not disclosed. He offered to let the students use his name as their employer.[24] Any mention of the Fund would arouse suspicions.

Clifford Durr

Clifford Durr was another white lawyer referred to the Alabama group. By 1965 he was one year into retirement but had embarked on a new phase of his career by opening his home to visiting graduate students, journalists, activists, attorneys, and others engaged in the civil rights struggle in Alabama.[25] Douglas Hedin had just completed his first year of law school at the University of Pennsylvania and was invited to Durr's house along with Chip Gray, Charles Farnsworth, Karen Davis, Evan Frullman, and Henning Eikenberg. Needing a place to stay, the students agreed to rent the second floor of the white clapboard, two-story home situated in an older, quiet neighborhood not far from downtown Montgomery. The apartment was sparsely furnished with only rollaway beds. When Doug Hedin entered one room, he was astonished at the sight of "rows of leather bound volumes of the opinions of Supreme Court Justice Hugo L. Black." He learned from the Durrs that Josephine Black, who was Hugo's first wife, was the sister of Virginia Durr, Clifford's wife. Hugo would give members of his family and selected friends the bound volumes of his opinions at the end of each Supreme Court term.[26]

On weekends, the Durrs invited the students to their one-story cabin in Wetumpka called "Pea Level," located in the foothills of the Appalachians, twenty miles outside of Montgomery.[27] The cabin had a large screened-in front porch and creaking floors, and was surrounded by nearby forests. Gray would later learn from Virginia Durr that their neighbors in Wetumpka were mostly Klan members.

Hedin and the other law students were fascinated with Clifford Durr's accounts of his experiences working in the Roosevelt and Truman administrations. Clifford spoke often in a low, growling tone of voice, probably because so many of his subjects were people he disdained. The students spent many a weekend afternoon walking with Durr through the woods and along the banks of the creek running through the property, listening to the old man's tales of the Great Depression, the Red Scare era in Washington, D.C., and his representation of African Americans in Alabama during the period before the civil rights movement of the 1960s.

Hedin learned from Clifford and from subsequent readings much about the life histories of both of the Durrs. Clifford first went to work with the Reconstruction Finance Corporation, a New Deal agency, in 1933 after receiving a recommendation from Black, then a U.S. senator from Alabama. Later he was appointed to the Federal Communications Commission, where he became an advocate for public broadcasting. In the latter part of the 1940s, he bitterly opposed the investigation of FCC employees accused of disloyalty. In 1948 he refused reappointment to his FCC position and focused his law practice on representing government employees accused of "Un-American" activities.[28]

In the early 1950s he returned to Alabama and soon encountered controversy when Senator James Eastland of Mississippi subpoenaed Durr's wife to testify at hearings concerning the Southern Conference Education Fund, an alleged Communist front organization operating in Mississippi that was promoting the cause of civil liberties for African Americans. Eastland had targeted Virginia Durr for her outspoken opposition to the poll tax. The tax had long been employed in southern states to discourage African Americans from voting. Clifford was allowed to cross-examine the principal government witness who gave scurrilous testimony about Clifford's wife. Clifford responded by throwing a punch at the witness. The punch was caught on camera and the picture displayed in newspapers across the country.[29]

By the mid-1950s, Clifford Durr's law practice had been left in shambles by the Eastland hearings. With his white business clients gone, Clifford turned to civil rights litigation, representing African Americans who certainly could not afford to pay his usual rates. In 1955 he posted bail for a young African American woman who had been arrested for sitting in the white section of a public bus. The woman, Rosa Parks, was a friend of the Durrs who had worked for them as their seamstress.[30] However, Clifford was insistent that he was not a civil rights lawyer. Too narrow a term, he claimed. He was a "civil liberties" attorney. But Durr would later express his dismay at not having been more assertive in the civil rights movement of the sixties. And he told Chip Gray that he had little respect for northern lawyers who wore their sympathies proudly but assigned their legal work to white segregationist law firms who could curry more favor with the local judges.[31]

Clifford also spoke of his family and life prior to the Great Depression, when he was like any other southerner, steeped in the fashionable prejudices of the times. He had been born into a patrician family in Alabama.

Both of his grandfathers had fought in the Confederate army in the Civil War. His father founded the Durr Drug Company, which established the family on firm financial footing. Clifford received a Rhodes scholarship to Oxford and graduated in 1922 with a law degree. But his way of life changed dramatically with the Wall Street Crash of 1929 and the emergence of the New Deal years.[32]

The students' stay with the Durrs was made more enjoyable by Virginia's fine cooking. They especially appreciated how her baked hams made a splendid dinner. They tried to minimize their "mooching" with small contributions of hot dogs and bread. More significantly, they rewarded their hosts with manual labor that included hauling cement tiles and sand for a new patio being built on the back of the house, scything weeds, and digging up trees. On one occasion Gray asked Clifford if there were any gloves he could wear to protect against the blisters forming on his hands. Clifford replied that he could only offer "hand grown" ones. Virginia had a more sympathetic ear and handed Gray a few Band-Aids. The second-floor apartment lacked air-conditioning, and the students found the heat punishing. But the only difficulty in their stay with the Durrs came when Karen Davis arrived with two African American friends who were members of SNCC.[33] When Farnsworth told Virginia Durr of the new guests, she became visibly distressed. She spoke tremulously about the time several Montgomery police officers bullied her with threats of arrest for boarding an African American lady friend for the night. Gray and Farnsworth engaged in a private, heated debate over what to do and eventually decided the "SNCCers" had to go.[34]

Daytime visits from black civil rights activists were welcomed as long as they did not stay overnight. Gray recalled the Durrs introducing him to Edgar D. Nixon, who was principally responsible for the Montgomery bus boycott of the 1950s, which had been organized to protest the bus company's segregationist policies. Nixon, together with Martin Luther King and the Reverend Ralph Abernathy, eventually forced the company to come to terms. The boycott lasted 381 days, longer than anyone expected. Gray recalled Nixon speaking proudly of his achievements and somewhat resentfully of King gaining most of the publicity and credit.

Tom Lawson

There were also a handful of white jurists sympathetic to the plight of the African American community, although they had to be especially careful in espousing their views due to the elective nature of their offices. Chuck Farnsworth and Karen Davis discovered one of them accidentally. They were huddled over a reading table in the basement of the Alabama Supreme Court building in Montgomery, poring through bound transcripts of cases that had been presented to the court. They were preoccupied with the curled, faded pages facing their bleary eyes when Chuck thought he recognized the faint sounds of creeping footsteps and rustling clothing coming from behind. He tried not to notice until his better senses awakened him to the presence of a specter whose shadow was enveloping them. Chuck remained quietly seated, pretending to be unperturbed. Suddenly a booming baritone voice pierced the basement's previous solitude.

"Whatcha doin' here?"

Chuck and Karen flinched in unison, quickly rising to their feet to face a large man hovering above them by several inches. The man was around sixty years old, dressed in a white dress shirt, tie, and impeccably tailored pinstriped dress pants. Their hearts pounded, fearful of the grilling to come.

"We're graduate students," Chuck stammered as he collected his thoughts. "We're working on material for a paper."

"Now don't B.S. me, young man. Y'er here working for the NAACP aren't you?"

"Well . . . yes," Chuck replied, thoroughly embarrassed he had been caught in a lie. He decided to bare all and explained why they had been sent to check the court records and what the rape study was to investigate. He resigned himself to whatever dire consequences would follow. Much to his surprise and relief, the older gentleman smiled broadly, baring a set of teeth well preserved from years of accumulated gold fillings. "Well, no matter. I'm Tom Lawson, one of the justices here." Lawson explained that he was the most moderate one on the bench, at least on racial issues, which probably was why he was frequently challenged around election time. Before departing, he told Chuck and Karen to call on him if they ran into trouble. "I know how hard y'er workin' and I'll help you where I can."

Karen and Chuck were left speechless and deeply in awe of the man. A state supreme court justice . . . willing to help a couple of young law students in their research project . . . and willing to buck the segregationist policies of Alabama's courts, of its legislature, and of then Governor George Wallace. They needed Lawson's intervention sooner than they expected. The following day Chuck and Karen visited the Office of the Clerk for Montgomery County to look at the court files. The chief clerk was a small, baldheaded, bespectacled, older man, probably in his early sixties. He studied the young couple at length, undoubtedly questioning their motives, and then shook his head. "Can't do it," he said coolly.

"We can't look at public records?" responded Chuck with exasperation.

"Nope. They're not for you." The clerk turned his back and walked away, leaving Chuck and Karen in disbelief at his rudeness and disregard for the law. The Supreme Court building was close at hand so they immediately paid Justice Lawson a visit. As soon as they announced where they had been, Lawson interrupted.

"Willie giving you a hard time?' he asked. Karen and Chuck nodded indignantly.

"That figures. Now, you go home, and come back tomorrow." He nodded reassuringly. "Willie'll have better manners."

They did as they were told. The next day Willie was already waiting for them.

"Well, come on in," he said, looking much chagrined. "Guess I have to show you the files." He took them behind the front counter and into the stacks, muttering to himself about the impudence of young people.[35]

Justice Lawson did even more. He opened the doors of the Supreme Court building to the law student researchers on Saturdays when it was closed to the public. He gave Chuck Farnsworth a key to the justice's consultation room with its full set of Alabama Reports that the students utilized.[36] Lawson stood for the more tolerant racial attitudes that were then emerging in the South.

That had not always been so. In 1935 he represented the State of Alabama in his capacity as an assistant attorney general in its rape prosecution of one of the "Scottsboro Boys." The U.S. Supreme Court reversed the conviction, finding that the African American defendant, Clarence Norris, had been deprived of due process by virtue of the "systematic exclusion of negroes from juries." The high court rejected the notion that "the black race . . . were utterly disqualified by want of intelligence, experience, or moral integrity to sit on juries."[37]

Thirty years later, Clifford Durr described Lawson as the most liberal of Alabama's justices.[38] Lawson's actions in giving an assist to the rape survey provided ample evidence of his willingness to recognize the need for change in Alabama's racial practices. In the years after the Scottsboro case, he enjoyed a distinguished career in Alabama. He was elected attorney general in 1938, and in the same year, elected to the Board of Trustees of the University of Alabama. In 1942 he became an associate justice of the Alabama Supreme Court, not retiring until 1972.[39]

The Old and the New

In that faraway summer of 1965, we were sent south to discover if there was a link between the race of a man convicted of rape and the severity of his punishment. Along the way we saw an Old South still vibrant, and not a gray caricature of itself relegated to the corner of some staid textbook. We saw African American tenant farmers behind mule-driven plows tilling the soil as their ancestors had done after disembarking from slave ships. We saw blacks and whites eating at separate restaurants, entering separate restrooms, and drinking from separate drinking fountains. African Americans drove across roads in their communities that were barely paved and crooked. They lived in shanties. Chuck Farnsworth was put up for the night at the farmhouse of an African American couple. There was no running water and only a small electric generator to give light at night. But while the accommodations were primitive, they were clean.[40]

We also saw a white culture struggling uncomfortably between opposing behaviors: rudeness bordering on violence towards blacks and graciousness showered on whites. At his girlfriend's insistence, Farnsworth delivered a bouquet of flowers to a helpful white female clerk at the Montgomery courthouse. The lady was so enthralled with the "nicest Yankees" she ever met that she almost performed cartwheels, effusing gratitude after gratitude upon her astonished young customers. On his visit to the courthouse in Selma, an older, white female clerk who was also accommodating to his inquiries helped Chip Gray. But her voice, pleasing in its musical qualities, turned shrill, loud, and vulgar upon the approach of a young African American woman to the front counter.[41]

Gray especially noted the separate social lives of blacks and whites. He and Henning Eikenberg were invited to a Sunday service at an African American church. They sat in the back row. There was no air-conditioning and no overhead electric-driven fans. Instead, they were handed fans with advertising promoting prominent black businessman "H. G. Gaston," and left to their own means to cool the sweat gathering on their faces.[42]

Henning was deeply impressed by the "intensely bright colors" of the clothes worn by the women seated in the pews and the dialogue that the "old-school" pastor held with his congregation. The pastor's preaching did not encourage the usual nodding off. Instead he pounced on his flock with fiery oratory that allowed no room for sleep.

The Pastor: *"The Lord is our light isn't he?"*

The Congregation: "Right he is! The Lord is all right!"

The Pastor, with arms gesturing emotionally: *"I don't know about you, but the Lord has told me he will save me and the Lord keeps to his promises, doesn't he?"*

The Congregation: "That's right, pastor!"

The Pastor: *"And all of you will read the Bible, won't you?"*

The Congregation: "Yes we will!"

The Pastor: *"But those of you who aren't Christian, don't tell me you will! You shut your mouths if you aren't Christian!"*

Then his tone softened as he spoke of the good the Lord had given him and of being blessed with forty-six years of marriage. Once he was done, the choir began a slow and sentimental song punctuated by occasional bursts from the trumpet player seated on stage beside the minister. Gradually the music increased into a crescendo of energetic rhythms and harmonies that sounded like rock-and-roll. During the services there was not a single mention of the civil rights struggle. The lay issues of the day and religion were kept apart. The pastor held to his role as a messenger of faith and made no effort to enter Caesar's world. Only after the services were completed did the tone of the congregation turn social and political. Requests were made for help with voter registration drives and donations were solicited for different causes.[43]

In contrast to this simpler affair was the elaborate dinner party Gray attended at the invitation of the father of a local girl he had met near Birmingham. The father was a well-to-do white lawyer who had been considered for a judicial appointment to the U.S. Court of Appeals for the Fifth Circuit. The home was lavishly decorated and dinner was served buffet-style. There were no black faces in the crowd. The men wore tuxedos and the women were dressed in long gowns. Chip made the rounds, but shallow conversations were about all he could solicit from the many inebriated guests. Henning Eikenberg had better luck upstairs with the younger brother of John's girlfriend, a bright young man still in grade school. The two engaged in a lively discussion about Greek authors.[44]

As the summer wore on, it became apparent to all of us that the Old South's segregationist policies were beginning to dissolve under the onslaught of civil rights legislation, the infusion of the watchful FBI agents planted about local governmental buildings, and the changing mores of southern students attending northern colleges. A new South was emerging alongside the old, with each struggling for its place. Chip Gray recalled meeting a young, white Montgomery woman who had just graduated from Concord Academy in Massachusetts. He gave her a ride to her parents' home in Birmingham. Along the way she marveled at the loving look of the green Alabama landscape and disparaged segregationist views on race. She smoked a pipe, which seemed at odds with the traditional culture in which she had grown up. But she felt uncomfortable with the "SNCCish" views held by her northern student counterparts. John described her as "caught between the North and the South."[45]

The old and new faces of the South appeared elsewhere in our journeys. During their stay in Selma, Gray's group observed on their visits to the Selma courthouse a continuous line of African Americans, mostly women, waiting to register to vote. But in Marion, they saw African Americans taking a voting, or "literacy," test in one of the courtrooms. These tests were used to delay or disqualify African Americans from voting.[46] Not until later that summer was the Voting Rights Act of 1965[47] enacted. The act prohibited states from imposing any "voting qualification or prerequisite to voting, or standard, practice, or procedure . . . to deny or abridge the right of any citizen of the United States to vote on account of race or color."

The New Politicians

These new federal rules brought about sweeping changes in Alabama's political landscape, and with it, a new breed of politician. Henning Eikenberg observed one of them speak before the congregation of the largest African American church in Montgomery. On July 25, 1965, Alabama's attorney general, Richmond Flowers, delivered a thundering oration in which he called for equal voting rights for Alabama's black population. He characterized Alabama's segregationist policies as little more than a "gesture of defiance that must be put behind us."[48] He took aim at Governor George Wallace and urged Alabama to stop looking to the past and return to the Union. The congregation responded to Flowers's bold talk and courage with raucous applause. Eikenberg was inspired as well. Here was a white man who had the "guts" to speak in front of "such a large Negro crowd"[49] while at the same time taking on the white supremacists. Flowers's willingness to personally prosecute the Klan defendants for the murder of Viola Liuzzo in their second trial earned him numerous death threats. Henning viewed Flowers as Alabama's "silver lining" despite his having "gambled away his political career."[50]

Even in sports, change was underway. Gray recalls watching a baseball game in Montgomery with Douglas Hedin. They saw most of the game from a high clay bank while downing a couple of beers and then went inside the park to watch the last two innings for free. Both the crowd and the teams were integrated. According to Clifford Durr, the city had lost its minor league team, the Rebels, for five or six years due to a state law banning interracial sports competition. With the passage of the 1964 Civil Rights Act, the integrated Rebels were back. However, that night belonged to Asheville thanks to its better pitching staff.[51]

Student Interactions

The changed thinking about racial separation was most evident within the groups of white and black students who worked that summer side by side as equals. CORE, the Mississippi Freedom Democratic Party (MFDP), the NAACP, and SNCC each had contingents of young black and white college and graduate students.[52] They had volunteered for the summer and some had taken a year off to participate in voter registration drives, sit-ins at public facilities, and lunch counter boycotts. Our own group of researchers exchanged telephone numbers and addresses with other students we came across. From those contacts we learned what was happening in the "hot spots" around the South and places to avoid, but also where we could stay at little cost.

We also interacted socially. Henning Eikenberg wrote of his experiences one hot July evening at a "Negro bar" located somewhere in the African American section of Montgomery. Supposedly segregated, it soon became filled with students, both black and white, who bubbled their youthful enthusiasm in conversations so loud that the background sounds of Motown artists were soon drowned out. Henning danced with a black student from Kansas City and admired her grace.[53]

But some of us were so incensed by the harsh, impoverished, and segregated world we encountered that we briefly ignored the warnings given to us in Philadelphia earlier that summer to stay clear of civil rights activities that could divert us from our research mission. Henning and others assisted in handing out two hundred copies of the *Southern Courier* to several African American churches in Montgomery. Several Harvard and Yale students had started the weekly newspaper. As an "underground" paper, its purpose was to disclose what was happening in the civil rights movement, dispensing news that the traditional, southern "white" press refused to print or only presented from the segregationist perspective.[54] On the other side of the ledger, we learned much about the southern whites' attitudes on morality, which were refreshingly high-minded and strict. Fidelity to one's family was paramount.[55]

Exchanging Ideas

We also exchanged ideas, particularly those of us from different racial backgrounds. I recall a bull session I had with one African American college student. We met at a CORE office not far from Baton Rouge. He was perhaps a year or two younger than I was and had been attending a nearby community college. He decided to take a year off to work on a voter registration drive in Louisiana. He offered to drive me to his mother's home for dinner. He said he lived alone with her. She worked as a domestic at a nearby retirement home. He was the youngest of four siblings, all of whom had left to raise their own families.

His mother must have been forewarned of our arrival—though it was still early. She had already set the large dining table with plates filled with macaroni and cheese, rolls, tomatoes, squash, and some beans. I complimented her on the fresh taste of the vegetables. She was gracious and hospitable. Everywhere I looked there were knickknacks strewn about, mostly pretty things—vases, little ornaments, family pictures—which gave the house a warm, cluttered look. Our dinner conversation focused mostly on the happenings of her church life—the new pastor and the money raised for a scholarship fund. After the dishes were cleared, she went upstairs to allow us to talk between ourselves. Her son and I then spent a good part of what was left of the evening in a nonstop debate over a wide range of civil rights issues. I argued that integration would never come to the South and that the black power movement, just then in its infancy, would lead the way to greater civil rights. "With black pride comes acceptance of blacks!" I exclaimed. I don't think my companion knew what to make of my radical rhetoric. He insisted on the more traditional approach of integration into the white communities. I compared the South's use of lynching and electrocuting African Americans to the Holocaust in Nazi-occupied Europe. While the southern methods did not physically exterminate large numbers of a race, their use effectively terrorized and silenced generation after generation of African Americans. My friend took issue with me, claiming that blacks only pretended to be suppressed. By evening's end the humanizing effect of our discourse had washed away our respective skin colors.

Henning's Reflections

Many members of the group had similar experiences. They gave us pause to consider whether the differences we perceived between cultures, religions, and races of man were real or imagined. And we wondered why these supposed differences aroused such hatred. In his diary, Henning Eikenberg poured forth the shame he felt for his own country allowing the Nazis to seize control of the German state and the collective mind of its people. He found little difference between the horrible prejudices directed against the Jews and those that white Americans held toward blacks. He wrote: "Negroes and color are exchangeable variables [and] in different cultures [become] replace[d] with other social . . . groups."[56]

What bothered him most about his own countrymen was their apathy and failure to react to the crimes of the Nazis. And he found that same apathy evident in America. The reluctance of many white Americans to push for an end to segregation while knowing it was wrong put them in a league similar to that of the German people, whose indifference forever stained their country's honor. Claiming that "some of my best friends are Negroes," he wrote, provides no cover for ignoring the pleas of those who are disenfranchised.[57] The only difference Henning could find between the treatment of blacks in the South and the Jews in Germany was in the degree of barbarity.

But Henning discovered that northern liberals could be equally prejudiced when they viewed the South solely through the lens of racial discrimination. The South was not just about race. It was a complex region bearing the faces of a diverse people. "The South is not a gang of bandits," he wrote, ". . . or a [group] of lawless states. . . . [I]t cannot be compared with the Third Reich."[58] He met conservative southerners who, though entrenched in their racist values, showered him with their hospitalities. He attended their church services and learned how deeply committed they were to one another. He came to respect the religiosity of the University of Mississippi law professor with whom he stayed, particularly after observing his host teach Sunday school. He also developed a respect for the American ethos, much of which he saw in his companion, John Gray. He described Gray as "very athletic . . . intelligent, practical, confident, and . . . convinced [of] the advantages of American democracy."[59] Henning heard much about American football from Gray, a former Harvard player, and was even prodded into some practice sessions in a field near the Durr's Montgomery home.

As the summer waned, we had much to think about. Slowly each one of us returned to our safe, all-white communities feeling self-righteous about our contributions. But there was a surprise waiting for us all at home, one that we never contemplated would erupt so far away from where we had just come. A racial inferno was boiling deep beneath the crust of the nation's consciousness. Tim Brayton returned to his native

Los Angeles late on the afternoon of August 11, 1965. From his plane hovering over LAX, he saw that inferno erupt into billowing smoke and flames shooting from rooftops. The first fires from the Watts riots spewed into a racial rage of a magnitude never before seen. More would follow. Tim could not help but wonder where the rest of us had gone wrong.[60]

Chapter 5

Wolfgang Fuels the Assault

Jack Greenberg, the Legal Defense Fund's director in New York City, had assigned Frank Heffron to oversee the law students' research efforts in the South. Heffron had been an editor of the *Columbia Law Review,* and his first job was as a Fund staff attorney. A "straight arrow" New Englander,[1] he'd been blunt in his pessimistic assessment of this project. He feared the uncertainty of the outcome and stressed the need for "specialists" who could better mine the required data.[2] First-year law students, untrained in the social sciences, might not be up to muster. Or they might be dissuaded from their search by threats, bullying, or worse. And there was always the fear that the vaults of the southern courthouses harboring the treasured data would be sealed once word leaked of the students' mission.

But as the weeks rolled by, the survey booklets relentlessly trickled in. Heffron examined them with intense concentration and soon had to admit that the amateur sleuths he'd sent south had succeeded in beguiling the entire southern legal establishment—judges, attorneys, court clerks, and peace officers alike. The students' deceptively candid, open, and youthfully sincere demeanor had gained them access to virtually every shred of data needed from every county and state to which they had been assigned.[3] The soft underbelly of the South's rigid, apartheid-like system of justice now lay exposed in over three thousand ponderous booklets, waiting to be sliced and microscopically examined.

A Delivery

Marvin Wolfgang was not so sure. The criminologist from the University of Pennsylvania knew that student researchers, often enthusiastic at the start, could find their interest soon waning as more tempting distractions (usually from the opposite sex) came along. The blazing Philadelphia sun that boiled its inhabitants that September of 1965 in the Gulf Stream's humid, suffocating embrace, further tempered whatever optimism Wolfgang harbored. But Wolfgang's guarded outlook would not last long. A knock on his office door jarred him to his feet. In walked a uniformed mail carrier bearing several packages bulging with mysterious contents. The postman slung the packages with a resounding thud onto Wolfgang's desk. One of them, damaged by its ride from New York, ripped open and spewed a torrent of booklets.

These were the surveys he had been waiting for, arduously assembled from over 250 counties across eleven southern and border states. The completed surveys contained what he needed to assess whether southern juries and judges had been discriminatory in their application of the death penalty.[4]

More packages were waiting in the mail carrier's truck outside.[5] Once they were all unloaded and signed for, Wolfgang immediately solicited his brightest graduate students for help in sorting out the data.[6] He had no problem finding willing volunteers. The students were a devoted bunch, due in large part to the countless hours he had spent guiding their theses, paying their way to conferences, and trying to find them teaching jobs.[7] But, though he had plenty of help, he did not have much time. His friend and faculty colleague Tony Amsterdam of Penn's law school insisted on a quick and accurate assessment of what lay in the schedules. The lives of scores of black defendants were at stake as their execution dates neared. Amsterdam was sure many had been sentenced because of their race, but he had to prove it. And soon.

Within a matter of days, his students assembled in one of the Wharton School's classrooms. Wolfgang paced back and forth across the full length of the lecturer's platform. He launched into a comprehensive explanation of how he wanted the data assembled and fed onto the computer punch cards. These were the days when computers were still a novelty, and the university's technology was primitive. Wolfgang prioritized much of the work by state or county according to how soon a defendant faced execution.[8] Frank Heffron and Norman Amaker, another Fund attorney, were assigned to keep Wolfgang abreast of pending execution dates.[9]

Buying Time

Meanwhile, the Fund's lawyers did their best to buy time. They requested continuances to permit Wolfgang time to complete his analysis of the data. But they were not always successful. In the case of Louis Moorer Jr., a black defendant convicted of rape in South Carolina, District Court Judge Robert Hemphill denied Frank Heffron's request for a sixty-day extension of a hearing to allow completion of a statistical analysis of 355 rape-conviction schedules. Hemphill was somehow offended by the idea behind Heffron's motion, and he lost his composure, hurling his fury at Heffron for trying to prove discrimination through statistics. When Heffron offered the schedules into evidence, Hemphill refused to admit them and then directed that the schedules be seized and sealed. It took an order from the U.S. Court of Appeals for the Fourth Circuit to have them returned to Heffron many months later.[10] With only a few days before Moorer's scheduled execution date, Moorer's other attorney, Matthew Perry, managed to gain a stay, or postponement, from Chief Judge Clement Haynsworth.[11]

In Alabama, delays were secured by bluff and bluster. Norman Amaker threatened the judges and prosecutors that if his requests for continuances were disallowed, he would have every court clerk in the state subpoenaed to deliver every court file and record of every rape conviction examined by the law students. The judges, fearing a statewide disruption in the orderly business of the courts, relented and postponed the trial dates so as to allow Wolfgang time to complete his analysis of the capital punishment schedules.[12]

Wolfgang's Background

Then in his early forties, Wolfgang had already published two books[13] and numerous articles. He was a founding director of the Sellin Center for Studies in Criminology and Criminal Law, served as a full-time professor in the Department of Sociology at the University of Pennsylvania, and was on his way to becoming a world-renowned criminologist. He received both his master's (1950) and doctoral degrees (1955) from Penn.[14] By the end of his life in 1998, he had written or contributed to more than thirty books, and written 150 articles that paved the way for criminology to become an independent discipline in its own right.[15] Beginning in late 1965, he and his graduate students worked steadily to beat the execution clock ticking away in southern prisons. And while busy on his statistical analyses of southern rape convictions, he was collaborating with Franco Ferracuti, the Italian forensic psychologist and physician, on an influential book, *The Subculture of Violence,* which was published the following year.[16]

Wolfgang's passion for education and intellect was fostered by his Pennsylvania Dutch grandparents who had raised him from an early age following the death of his mother, Pauline Sweigard.[17] He was the first person in his family to enter college.[18] His interest in criminology may have stemmed from his abhorrence of the battlefield mayhem he saw during World War II.[19] Drafted into the army after only a year at college, he was sent to North Africa and, later, Italy. During the Battle of Monte Cassino, he suffered from severe heatstroke and was sent home.[20] He strongly opposed capital punishment, considering it a barbaric form of retribution with no deterrent effect.[21] And he once wrote: "I am as strong a gun-control advocate as can be found among criminologists in this country. . . . I would eliminate all guns from the civilian population and maybe from the police. I hate guns—ugly, nasty instruments designed to kill people."[22]

But he insisted on the primacy of scientific methods in evaluating data and ensuring that the conclusions he reached were empirically supported with all necessary evidence and were free from any influence of personal bias. For that reason, he would not let his sympathies for those waiting on Death Row influence the findings he was preparing for the Fund. He wrote that he would publish his research findings according to whatever the data revealed, even if that meant risking damage to the abolitionist cause.[23] For that reason also, he decided the law students should concentrate on convictions rather than on an earlier stage in the processing of suspects or defendants, partly because "good empirical data prior to conviction were not readily available. Feelings, sentiments, intuition and anecdotes are not the kernel of scientific research. . . . Hence, no effort was made whether there was discrimination in the processing of suspects and defendants prior to the determination of guilt."[24]

He was adamant that "failure to abide by the known rules of scientific inquiry can only damage the evidence as well as the presenter. . . . The social scientist should not try to convert his design, his data, or his conclusions to conform to the litigation process."[25]

Nor did Wolfgang hesitate to attribute the disproportionately high rates of crimes committed by black males to what he termed a "subculture of violence." Relying on his 1958 study of 588 criminal homicides in Philadelphia, he faulted that subculture for an idolization of violence, which if deviated from, would be punished by ostracism and similar sanctions. His views proved to be controversial.[26] In acknowledging that the black subculture shares major values with the general society of which it is a part, he could have shifted the blame to the larger southern white society's reverence for force as a means to enhance one's honor and reputation.[27] He might even have found the origins of black violence in the whip lashes inflicted on the naked backs of black slaves in the antebellum South. He did none of that, *not* because these were not plausible theories, but because they could not yet be supported empirically. He was determined to maintain the impartial sanctity of this new science of criminology he had done so much to spawn.

The Numbers Speak

A different season. Another cold Friday evening in Philadelphia. The monotonously grey clouds sprawled across the sky, their bulging bellies seemingly ready to release another snowfall. Wolfgang exited his car with haste. He was oblivious to the freezing January winds that were whipping off the choppy waters of the Schuylkill, bringing with them flecks of snow that sent shooting pains across his near-frozen face. His eyes stung, but the professor ignored the pain. He was on a one-track mission, consumed with the numbers he knew were waiting for him. *The numbers!* That was his love, to apply science to the vagaries of human thought. He had been amazed at how admirably his graduate student assistants, all from Penn's Center of Criminological Research, had performed. The factual data from the capital punishment survey booklets for seven critical states had been transferred from the punch cards and run through the computer program he had devised.[28] Now what remained was to let those numbers sing and his analysis would fall into place.

Wolfgang's effort, to ascertain through statistical analysis the role racial prejudice played in sentencing, had never before been undertaken. Though he was the author of what was then the leading study of the deterrent effect of capital punishment, his great mentor, Thorsten Sellin, had not been that ambitious. Sellin was a Penn penologist of international renown and the supervisor for Wolfgang's PhD thesis. The two men, thirty years apart in age, had developed a close bond, almost equivalent to a father-son relationship,[29] and Wolfgang had Sellin's full support in deciding to collaborate with Amsterdam on the litigation-related research.

Wolfgang Prepares

"Start from the beginning," Wolfgang told himself as his steps quickened. He passed by the Ben Franklin statute, already coated with splashes of snow. "The two null hypotheses," he muttered. "*Everything* springs from them." These he had rehearsed in his mind many times before: first, that among all defendants convicted of rape, there were no significant differences between the proportions of black defendants with white victims and all other classes of rape defendants sentenced to death; and second, among all defendants convicted of rape there was no significant association between the race of the defendant and the type of sentence imposed.[30] Or to put it in laymen's terms, Wolfgang would assume that the southern white judges and juries had been completely colorblind over the past twenty years in deciding who would live or die for committing the crime of rape. Instead, nonracial variables (such as the degree of violence used, whether the victim became impregnated, and whether the victim's home was broken into) would be presumed the determinant factors. These assumptions would then be tested against the evidence gathered by the law students from the previous summer.

His pace quickened as he silently calculated the preliminary numbers drawn from the schedules for Arkansas. He knew Amsterdam was pushing for an early turnaround on this state because of Billy Maxwell, a young black man convicted of rape, only months away from the electric chair.[31] Wolfgang and his statistician colleague, John Monroe, had devised a "theoretical or expected frequency" of death sentences to be imposed on black and mostly white defendants, namely that the ratio of death sentences to convictions was the same between the two groups, even though blacks suffered a greater number of convictions.[32] Those frequencies would then be compared to the actual data collected. To the extent that there was a discrepancy between the expected and actual frequencies of death sentences, that difference would either be attributed to the "real phenomena tested" (such as race, use of violence, etc.) or chance.[33]

Wolfgang had already determined that for all seven states studied, black defendants whose victims were white were sentenced to death approximately eighteen times more frequently than defendants in any other racial combination (such as black on black, white on white, and white on black).[34] Because the difference was so great, chance was ruled out as an explanation.[35]

But his task did not end there. Perhaps nonracial variables played a role in the greater frequency of death sentences. Perhaps the black defendants carried out the rapes with such horrific force that a punishment greater than mere imprisonment was deserved. He had lectured his graduate students extensively on the chi square statistical test that was intended to determine if a distribution of observed frequencies differs from the expected frequencies of an event, such as a death verdict, by summing the squares of the discrepancies over all categories of cases.[36] But that was theory. The numbers gathered from the seven southern and border states were *real*—real crimes, real convictions, and real executions together with all the accompanying human pathos that could affect the sentencing outcomes. He could not leave his students alone on such a pioneering venture. This phase of the analysis he would have to do himself to insure his future testimony could withstand the relentless courtroom crossfire of examination and cross-examination.

The Analysis

Wolfgang arrived at the Wharton School on this lonely night, breezing through the glass entrance doors and into the classroom where he stored his computerized calculations in a locked cabinet. There was not a human sound coming from anywhere in the building. He opened the cabinet and pulled out the sheets of numbers arranged by state, race, and category of nonracial variables. Painstakingly he plotted their course, first by examining each nonracial variable relative to the type of sentence imposed. If no significant relationship existed between the nonracial variable and the type of sentence, he knew that further analysis would not be needed because the variable apparently had little impact on the jury's sentencing verdict.[37]

However, if there was a significant association between the nonracial variable and sentence, that variable was cross-tabulated with the race of the defendant. He next applied the chi omega statistical analysis to each variable. And there were thirty-four variables in all.[38] The hours ticked by as he pondered what to do with the data showing "a significant association between the presence or absence of contemporaneous offenses and racial combinations of defendant and victim."[39]

From the far recesses of Penn's campus, the tower bell chimes resonated through the thin winter air. Wolfgang sat up with a groan and contemplated what course he would next follow. Radiating about a set of tables he had pulled together were stacks of papers he had not yet waded through. His bloodshot eyes wandered about the classroom, staring vacuously at nothing in particular. Then came a flash of inspiration that jolted him back to the numbers. He would later write, "Although it might appear that the presence or absence of contemporaneous offenses is a contributory factor, more refined procedure shows that it does not play a significant part in explaining the association between black defendants and the imposition of the death penalty."[40]

What he meant was that if a robbery or some other "contemporaneous offense" was committed at the same time as a rape, the frequency of death sentences was the same—greater for a black man convicted of raping a white woman than for any other racial combination. He came to this conclusion after splitting the cases into two subgroups: one that included all cases in which the defendant had committed a contemporaneous offense, and one in which no contemporaneous offenses were committed. After applying the chi omega statistical test, he found in both groups a "significant association between racial combinations of defendant and victim and imposition of the death penalty."[41] He concluded, "Over two dozen possibly aggravating nonracial variables that might have accounted for the higher proportion of blacks than whites sentenced to death upon conviction of rape have been analyzed. Not one of these nonracial factors has withstood the tests of statistical significance."[42]

After reciting some of these other factors, such as a prior criminal record, the use of force on the victim, the commission a robbery or burglary with the rape, the use of a weapon, and the impregnation of the victim, he concluded that in each of the states he analyzed, all of these nonracial variables "'wash out,' that is, they have no bearing on the imposition of the death penalty in disproportionate numbers on blacks. The only variable of statistical significance that remains is race."[43]

A Picture Emerges

Many days and nights followed as Wolfgang and his graduate students continued assembling and analyzing the data state by state according to the litigation needs of the Fund attorneys and their clients. Toward the end of 1966 a clearer picture was emerging. More than three thousand men had been convicted of rape in 230 counties over the twenty-year period investigated by the law students in the eleven southern and border states investigated.[44] In the seven states selected for early examination there were a total of 1,238 rape convictions, of which 317 were of black defendants with white victims. The remaining 921 convictions were of other racial combinations (black on black, white on white, or white on black). Of the blacks convicted of raping white women, 36 percent were sentenced to death. Of the defendants in other racial combinations, only 2 percent received death verdicts. Black defendants whose victims were white were eighteen times more likely to be sentenced to death than the defendants in other racial combinations, regardless of the presence or absence of any nonracial variables. The probability of this happening by chance was less than one in one thousand.[45]

In Arkansas, the results were not as extreme but still compelling. Forty-seven percent of black defendants convicted of raping white women were sentenced to death. By contrast, only 14 percent of white and black offenders convicted of raping a member of their own race were given the death penalty.[46] The truth of race-based death sentencing in the South was now laid bare. The southern white jury's wall of inviolability was broken. What remained to be seen was whether it could be scaled in the courtroom battles that lay ahead.

Toughening Up Wolfgang

To prepare for those battles, Amsterdam, Greenberg, and the other Fund attorneys believed that Wolfgang needed to learn what it was like to be a witness. Wolfgang had never before been employed as a forensic expert, and was naive as to the ways of the courtroom. So Norman Amaker and Michael Meltsner, two of the Fund's more seasoned litigators, were sent to Philadelphia to "teach" Wolfgang what to expect from devious and combative attorneys. Ironically, as to some aspects of his testimony, it was Wolfgang who taught them. When Amaker tried to convince Wolfgang to use the word "discrimination" as early as possible in his testimony, Wolfgang resisted:

> As I laboriously indicated to all of the attorneys, despite the elaborate nature of the information we had concerning the victim, the offender, the character of the offense and the judicial proceedings, we had no direct evidence of discrimination. . . . I was uncomfortable using the term "discrimination" until all of the evidence was documented.[47]

Wolfgang also had to find a way to explain to a judge the meaning of such terms as "differential" and "disproportionate" from a social scientist's perspective and how these terms differ from conclusions like "discriminatory."[48] But the two lawyers forced him to take them through the elementary steps of the chi square statistical test employed in his calculations in laymen's terms, with all of its attendant, convoluted formulae. Amaker and Meltsner also provided Wolfgang with "long lists of questions" before critiquing his answers. The attorneys were most concerned with making Wolfgang's testimony understandable to a judge not schooled in scientific lingo,[49] and they readied him for likely areas of cross-examination such as the "scientific limitations" of his research.[50] What most impressed Amaker and Meltsner was Wolfgang's convincing appearance. He showed himself as he was—a scientist—searching for the truth and cautious about any opinions he might come to. He did not fit the mold of a case-hardened forensic expert ready to spout whatever his questioner wanted as long as the opinions were amply paid for.[51]

During 1966 the Legal Defense Fund jockeyed between state and federal courts, trying to stave off executions while using Wolfgang's findings and the data gathered in 1965 to launch a series of assaults on southern death penalty sentencing. Altogether by 1970, the Fund had raised the issue of discriminatory death sentencing in thirty-five cases.[52] Fund attorneys hoped that at least one of their cases would make its way to the United States Supreme Court.

Three Paths

Three paths might be taken to the high court. One involved filing a petition for writ of certiorari that would grant a defendant a review if he lost a death penalty appeal in a state supreme court. The writ's purpose was to seek federal judicial intervention to rectify the infringement of a defendant's constitutional or other federal rights. The lower state court would be required to transfer the entire record provided a minimum of four U.S. Supreme Court justices agreed to hear the matter. Insufficient evidence for conviction would rarely be a proper basis for a writ.[53]

A second path would open up if the first failed. The defendant could file a petition for writ of habeas corpus in the lower federal district court seeking the release of the defendant wrongfully convicted and detained, again usually because of some federal constitutional or statutory right being deprived. If the defendant lost at the district court level, he could proceed up the federal appellate ladder, again resting his final plea with the U.S. Supreme Court. (Today the habeas corpus writ is not as readily available. The petitioner has to meet an "extraordinarily high threshold" of proof and the constitutional error must have had a "substantial and injurious" influence on the jury's verdict to warrant relief.[54] But back in the 1960s, these restrictions were not present.[55])

The third path to the high court was to raise the defendant's federal claims in the lower state courts and, if rejected, appeal to the state appellate courts. Once state remedies were exhausted, then a final appeal to the U.S. Supreme Court would be available.[56]

The Sims Case

One of the first cases Wolfgang worked on involved Isaac Sims Jr. In 1963 Sims, an illiterate, indigent black man from Georgia, said to be "ignorant to the point of incompetency,"[57] was apprehended by two state patrolmen and charged with raping Nola Jean Roberts, a twenty-nine-year-old white woman. Sims had purportedly driven closely behind Roberts's vehicle, forced her off the road into a ditch, and taken her from her car into the nearby woods, where he raped her. He left the scene on foot because he could not start his own car.

Four hours later he was apprehended and taken to the office of a physician, Dr. Jackson, who had previously examined the victim. Dr. Jackson stripped off Sims's clothing, knocked him down, then kicked Sims above his right eye, and pulled him around the floor by his privates. Sims was kept in continuous police custody for over eight hours and not fed or given access to family or friends. He had only a third-grade education, and his mental capacity was "decidedly limited."[58] Finally, Sims was taken to an interview room at the jail, where he promptly signed a written confession. The "confession" came into evidence before an all-white jury, which found him guilty and sentenced him to death by electrocution.[59] Sims's appointed attorney chose to withdraw from the case and leave Sims to his fate without filing a motion for a new trial. The Georgia Supreme Court first reversed the conviction because Sims had been deprived of his right to counsel but, after a second trial, then affirmed the conviction.[60] It found that execution was a fitting punishment for rape, the most heinous of crimes a (white) woman could suffer:

> She is the mother of the human race, the bedrock of civilization; her purity and virtue are the most priceless attributes of human kind. . . . [S]he has resisted even unto death the bestial assaults of brutes. . . . Even a dog is too humane to do such an outrageous injury to the female. . . . [W]e permit the sovereign State . . .

> to guard and protect the mothers of mankind . . . and
> the zenith of God's creation.[61]

In 1966 the Legal Defense Fund took over Sims's representation and filed a petition for writ of certiorari with the U.S. Supreme Court challenging his coerced confession and Georgia's discriminatory death-sentencing practices.[62] In August the law student researchers, including me, received letters from Michael Henry of the Legal Defense Fund advising us that "the product of your labors is nearing fruition."[63] He added that the issue of discriminatory sentencing for rape "has finally been accepted for preliminary argument by the U.S. Supreme Court this Fall in *Sims v. Georgia*." But because Professor Wolfgang had only completed the survey analysis for Arkansas, Alabama, and Louisiana, other "easier issues" would first be addressed. Henry warned us that our sworn testimony in court or by deposition might become necessary. Enclosed with Henry's letter were two recent news articles from the *New York Times* describing the Sims case, the rape survey we had conducted in 1965, and the announcement that the Supreme Court had agreed to hear the appeal challenging "the entire southern system of capital punishment for rape as a façade for legalized 'racial repression.'"[64]

On January 23, 1967, the court, acting on the Fund's petition, reversed Sims's conviction and returned the case to the Georgia trial court to set a hearing on the voluntariness of Sims's confession. The sentencing issue was not addressed.[65] The Georgia trial court went through the motions of compliance and found the confession to be voluntary. Once again, the Georgia Supreme Court affirmed the conviction.[66]

With Sims's confession now seemingly secure from further attack, A. L. Dutton, the warden of the Georgia State Prison at Reidsville, was about to end Sims's years of legal maneuvering as well as his life. Georgia's electric chair had been used on several hundred inmates since its installation in 1924[67] and could easily handle another. The chair's high back, long armrests, and glistening coat of white paint looked regal to those who dared gaze upon it.

But the Legal Defense Fund attorneys had other plans for Sims. They instructed Wolfgang to ready his analysis of the statistical data for Georgia. "Long and elaborate depositions" then followed for Wolfgang in five southern states, including Georgia.[68] The Fund, on behalf of Sims, also filed a motion to perpetuate the deposition testimony of three of the law students who had served as field researchers in Georgia in 1965. The motion was eventually approved by the Fifth Circuit Court of

Appeals.[69] But before the evidence of racial sentencing could be finalized, the Supreme Court took another look at Sims's case. On December 18, 1967, it reversed the Georgia convictions and death sentence, finding that Sims's confession was coerced and that blacks had been unconstitutionally excluded from Sims's jury panel.

A second case Wolfgang participated in was that of Wheeler Billingsley Jr., Robert Butler, and James Liddell, who were convicted of taking turns raping a white woman from Alabama in 1964. All three were sentenced to death. Wolfgang, John Monroe, Frank Heffron, and eight of the law students[70] submitted to written interrogatories explaining how the survey in Alabama was conducted and what conclusions were reached. Seventeen counties representing 53 percent of Alabama's population were covered, and 212 schedules were completed.[71] Wolfgang found that

> among the 130 cases known to have involved a Negro defendant, the death sentence was imposed in 21, whereas, among 62 cases known to have involved white defendants, the death sentence was imposed in only one case. . . . None of [those] 22 cases contained Negro victims. . . . [A]mong the 70 cases involving Negro victims, not a single defendant was sentenced to death; whereas, among the 90 cases involving white victims, 22, or 25 per cent of the defendants were sentenced to death.[72]

Further, black defendants convicted of raping white females were "disproportionately frequently sentenced to death as compared to all other defendants." After applying the null hypotheses and chi square statistical tests, Wolfgang concluded that this disproportionate sentencing "could have occurred less than one time in a thousand by chance."[73]

Following the convictions of Billingsley, Liddell, and Butler, Norman Amaker stepped in to help with a motion for a new trial. Amaker had been described as a "great bear of a man"[74] who possessed a "brilliant mind" but he was best known for his tenacity.[75] He offered the 212 capital punishment survey schedules into evidence together with Wolfgang's and Monroe's deposition answers.[76] The motion being denied, the Fund took the case up the state appellate route and finally to the Supreme Court.[77] Meanwhile the defendants' dates with the electric chair were put on hold.

The Swain Case

Wolfgang also offered his expert opinions in the case of Robert Swain, a black man who was convicted of raping a white, married, seventeen-year-old female at her home in Talladega County, Alabama.[78] The same jury returned a death verdict. The Fund on behalf of Swain intervened to file a petition for writ of *coram nobis* seeking to vacate the judgment of conviction. This writ is used in court to secure relief against a criminal judgment (usually a conviction) because of some fact that the trial judge did not know about due to no fault of the defendant. However, that fact must be of such importance that if known, the judgment would not have been rendered.[79] The trial judge in Swain's case denied the petition, and an appeal was taken to the Alabama Supreme Court.

Amaker appeared for the defendant at the appellate level. He presented nine reasons to vacate the conviction, including the discriminatory death sentencing of black males convicted of raping white women. The Alabama Supreme Court acknowledged receipt of the depositions of Wolfgang and Monroe that contained the same evidence as was introduced in the Billingsley, Liddell, and Butler cases discussed previously. But the court rejected that evidence because there was no showing that the individual members of the jury acted with discriminatory intent, that not every possible variable was taken into account, and that the data on rape convictions the law students retrieved in 1965 came not only from Talladega County where the defendant was tried but also from sixteen other counties.[80] The Alabama Supreme Court affirmed the trial court's denial of the *coram nobis* petition, whereupon a petition for writ of certiorari was filed with the U.S. Supreme Court. When the court agreed to review Swain's case, it ordered a postponement of his execution.

The Surprise

Wolfgang's statistical evidence was also used in Billy Maxwell's case, which first came to my attention in late 1966. An Associated Press article appeared in the *Los Angeles Times* announcing, "Negro Rape Executions Challenged." The article described at length the rape survey conducted by the twenty-eight law students and the statistics they marshaled at a cost of $35,000, which "are now being pressed on the Supreme Court in what could become a landmark case."

Then came the surprise. Instead of Isaac Sims against the State of Georgia, as Mike Henry from the Fund had predicted, a new name and state appeared: the case was called *William Maxwell v. O. E. Bishop* (superintendent of the Arkansas State Penitentiary). The article covered some of the issues our survey group had been told about but contained only a bare outline of the facts of the case.

I decided to dig deeper at my law school's library. I spent a couple of days in the stacks reading cases and uncovered the Maxwell case's sorry past. It all began in 1961 when a black man wearing a nylon stocking over his head broke into a thirty-five-year-old white woman's house where she cared for her invalid father. She managed to call the police before the man grabbed her and dragged her two blocks away, where he raped her. Questioned in the hospital soon after the attack, she could not identify William Maxwell as her assailant but did so later at his trial. Maxwell was twenty-one years old at the time of the offense and was sentenced to death.

Christopher Mercer was Maxwell's black attorney, who at trial in 1962 introduced evidence of twenty men convicted of rape who were executed between the years 1930 and 1960. All but one was black. The Arkansas Supreme Court quickly dispensed with the claim of discriminatory application of the death penalty by finding the evidence flimsy and incomplete.[81] It held that no evidence was offered suggesting that the ratio of violent crimes by blacks and whites was different from the ratio of executions. Most significantly, it objected to striking down the death penalty statute due to the resulting "chaos" that would befall the courts. The court never defined what "chaos" it feared.

With the help of George Howard Jr. (another black attorney and, years later, an Arkansas federal judge) and Frank Heffron in New York, Maxwell filed a petition for a writ of habeas corpus with the federal district court. The constitutional questions were broadened, but again the primary issue was the discriminatory application of the death penalty. Judge Gordon E. Young accepted the petitioner's premise that in the counties of Garland, Jefferson, and Pulaski, black men convicted of raping white women were sentenced to death whereas white and black men who raped black women were either not charged or given a lesser sentence. Nevertheless, he held that the choice of punishment was in the sound province of the jury. Further, the statistics failed to answer whether consent was presented as a defense. Judge Young termed the statistical evidence "naive."[82] A year after Young's decision, the Eighth Circuit Court of Appeals denied Maxwell's appeal,[83] and the U.S. Supreme Court denied Maxwell's petition for review.[84] The execution date was set for September 2, 1966.

Two New Arguments

By mid-1966 Wolfgang had completed his analysis of the statistics in Arkansas and six other states and had submitted to several depositions. Because of this new evidence, a second habeas corpus petition was filed in the federal District Court. Arkansas's lieutenant governor, acting in Governor Orval Faubus's absence, agreed to stay the execution of four other death row inmates pending resolution of Maxwell's petition.[85] With Maxwell's life in the balance, the Fund attorneys led by Amsterdam decided to advance two new bases for constitutional attacks on Maxwell's conviction and death verdict in addition to contentions that Arkansas practiced race-based death sentencing and that blacks were systematically excluded from his jury.

The first of the new bases was that Maxwell's jury not give any standards to evaluate whether the defendant's life should be spared. Without standards, the "covert discriminator" gains "absolute license to practice his biases in the matter of taking human life."[86] Also, those few selected to die are subjected to "freakish, whimsical [and] erratic" treatment different from that of "similar men guilty of similar offenses." And without standards, a death verdict is more likely for those who cannot provide a full defense because of lack of funds or because they are "'friendless, uneducated, and with mentalities bordering on being defective.'"[87]

The second new claim was that Maxwell had been denied a bifurcated trial. In the 1960s the same jury in death penalty cases commonly decided guilt and punishment at the same time ("a unitary trial"). The defendant was therefore placed in a terrible predicament. He could waive his constitutional right against self-incrimination so that he could testify about mitigating circumstances (such as intoxication) that would lessen his culpability for the crime. In so doing he would most likely be convicted by his admission that he acted wrongly. Or he could not testify to lessen his chances of a conviction, and in so doing he would give up the opportunity to tell the jury why he should not be punished by death (called the common law "right of allocution"). With separate trials on the issues of guilt and punishment, he could choose not to testify during the guilt phase of the trial, yet still be able to testify during the punishment phase should a guilty verdict be reached.[88] Both his right to remain silent and right of allocution would thereby be preserved. Maxwell's unitary trial abridged both those rights.[89]

Maxwell had been on death row for most of the years since his conviction in 1962. His habeas corpus petition, set for hearing on August 22,

1966, was his last hope before he was to be executed on September 2. Amaker joined Amsterdam to represent Maxwell. But the center of attention was the professor from Philadelphia, Marvin Wolfgang, and those bundles of booklets filled out by the law students a summer earlier.

Chapter 6

Maxwell Climbs the Appellate Ladder

Anthony Amsterdam knew Wolfgang as a teaching colleague at the University of Pennsylvania. He was aware, of course, of Wolfgang's fame as a criminologist with a global reputation, and he admired his intellect. So, soon after Amsterdam was approached by Fund lawyers to join them in launching the attack of the death penalty, he recommended that Wolfgang be part of the team.[1] Establishing racial discrimination using statistics had never been done to the satisfaction of a court. It would take an expert witness of Wolfgang's caliber and proof of sound methodology to convince even an enlightened judge of the Fund's claims. Courts were inherently slow to accept any new concepts, especially those coming from disciplines outside the law.

Amsterdam soon met with Wolfgang to secure his participation. Though Wolfgang may have been indispensable for his sociological expertise, Jack Greenberg believed that in the end Amsterdam's superior legal mind would be able to assemble the arguments that would give them any hope of victory.[2] The death penalty was an established institution in the United States, was mentioned in the Constitution, and was deeply embedded in the American psyche. Greenberg was well aware of the battles the Fund faced and needed the best general he could find.

Amsterdam's Acumen

Anthony Amsterdam was first introduced to Greenberg at a meeting in New York to discuss the representation of Charles Clarence Hamilton, a black man from Alabama. Hamilton had been sentenced to death for breaking and entering a residence "with intent to ravish." No harm had befallen the victim. Greenberg was so impressed with Amsterdam that he asked him to speak at an upcoming conference at Dillard University in New Orleans.[3]

"Tony," as Amsterdam was known to his friends and associates, was endowed with an amazingly keen memory. One oft-repeated story came from his days as an assistant U.S. attorney. Appearing before a three-judge panel of the U.S. Court of Appeals in Washington, D.C., Amsterdam during argument cited a Supreme Court case by volume and page number. One of the judges called for the volume, and not finding the case at the page number Amsterdam had provided, he called the young attorney to task. Amsterdam replied politely that the citation was correct but that the judge's book must have been mistakenly bound. Upon closer examination the judge found Amsterdam to be correct. The volume had been incorrectly engraved on the outside as volume 211, but the pages inside showed the volume number to be 210.[4] The judges who witnessed this encounter were amazed; the story traveled through the courthouse like wildfire.

Amsterdam grew up in West Philadelphia, the son of a business executive who, prior to his return from World War II, had served as a military lawyer in Luxembourg.[5] In his youth, Amsterdam played pick-up basketball with Wilt Chamberlain.[6] He graduated from Haverford College with extraordinary grades. While at the University of Pennsylvania Law School he was editor-in-chief of the law review and graduated first in his class. He was then selected by Justice Felix Frankfurter to work as his law clerk. In 1961 he became a government prosecutor. A year later he returned to Philadelphia to teach at Penn's law school.[7] Greenberg knew that with Amsterdam on the Fund's side, a successful assault on the death penalty in the South needn't necessarily remain a fantasy. Tony had the skill and tenacity to make it happen.

But there was more to Amsterdam than just his brilliance. He was incredibly industrious, working late, often past midnight.[8] For him, sleep was an incidental luxury lasting only four to five hours.[9] Michael Meltsner, soon to be the Fund's First Assistant Counsel, described his experiences with Amsterdam during the heyday of the southern civil rights movement in the early 1960s. He recounted how Tony would often be called to represent civil rights demonstrators who had been arrested for their acts of civil disobedience. He was continually traveling between southern cities, grabbing whatever grub he could along the way to fuel his tireless energies.[10]

On one occasion he was called to Jackson, Mississippi, to help prepare some pleadings that sought to move to federal court a number of state cases filed against civil rights workers. When he arrived, he found virtually nothing to work with except a manual typewriter and an inoperable mimeograph machine. Without a secretary, he and another Fund lawyer, Melvyn Zarr, hammered away at the removal documents in the stifling heat, then repaired the mimeograph machine and cranked out the copies he needed. He was a one-person law firm, a "legal computer," as Meltsner described him.[11] He was continually called upon for advice by lawyers from around the country, asked to sit on various boards, speak at conferences, and assist on appeals. Once Amsterdam became allied with the Fund in 1963, its impressive record of courtroom successes grew even longer.[12]

Forebodings

Everyone hoped that Billy Maxwell's case would be the proper vehicle to prove how race had infected sentencing for rape. But Amsterdam and Amaker had their forebodings. They both knew that even under the best of circumstances it would be a hard sell to convince a judge—any judge—to accept statistical testimony as a method of proving race discrimination in sentencing.[13] Even harder would be to get a judge to accept such testimony from a professor schooled in a relatively new science such as criminology. Some southern judges might react as Hemphill had in South Carolina by angrily denouncing the research and insisting they had nothing to do with purely legal questions of constitutionality.[14]

But the Fund attorneys thought they were lucky in the assignation of a federal judge to hear Maxwell's case.[15] Jesse Smith Henley was an intelligent, temperate man appointed by President Eisenhower twice to the federal bench, first in 1958 in a recess appointment, and again in 1959, when the Senate confirmed him. Henley later risked local criticism because of his orders to desegregate housing at the University of Arkansas, public parks, and swimming pools. He was a Republican of the moderate mold who will best be remembered for the reforms he enforced in the late 1960s and early 1970s on the Arkansas State Prison System.[16]

Maxwell's attorneys were impressed with Henley's questions about the information contained in the survey booklets. He appeared to have taken the time to read the materials, and he listened intently to Wolfgang's opinions.[17] Wolfgang testified that the law student investigation in Arkansas uncovered fifty-five rape convictions from 1945 to

1965 involving thirty-four black and twenty-one white males. He separated the convictions into three categories: black on white (blacks males convicted of raping white women), white on white, and black on black. There was not a single rape of a black woman by a white man ending in conviction in the sample. Of the thirty-four blacks convicted of rape, ten had been sentenced to death and seventeen to life imprisonment, whereas only four white offenders were given death verdicts. The remaining seventeen whites were given life. Of the nineteen blacks convicted of raping nine white women, nearly 50 percent were sentenced to death. In all other racial combinations (white on white and black on black), only about 14 percent were given the death penalty.[18]

Cross-Examination

Wolfgang expected to be cross-examined about the scientific limitations of his research. Instead, Assistant Attorney General Fletcher Jackson Jr. asked Wolfgang if he had ever been in Arkansas before. He answered that this was his first visit. Then how could he fully understand the "social conditions" in Arkansas? And were any of the rape convictions in the survey drawn from Garland County? Wolfgang replied they were not. Well, why not, demanded Jackson. Wasn't this a flaw in the statistical analysis not to focus on the county from which Maxwell's jury pool was selected?[19] Wolfgang thought this criticism was "absurd," replying: "If we had drawn our sample counties purposely to pick counties in which *Maxwell* had occurred, we would have destroyed the statistical randomness of the selection of counties and would have also distorted the character of the scientific inquiry."[20]

John Monroe, the Philadelphia statistician, explained: "[A] sample is the procedure of drawing a part of a whole, and if this sample is drawn properly according to the law of chance, or with known probability, by examining a small part of the whole, and using the appropriate statistical methods, one can make valid inferences about the whole population from examining a small part."[21]

But there was an even bigger flaw to Fletcher's contention that the data should have been limited to Garland County. The Fund correctly argued that "it was not Garland County that convicted Maxwell and sentenced him to death *but the State*. . . . [T]he purpose of Mr. Monroe's testimony was to show the counties selected were *representative of the State* [emphasis added]."[22]

Nevertheless, Judge Henley agreed with Jackson, pointing out that the statistics did not show that Maxwell's jury in particular "was motivated by racial discrimination when it failed to assess a punishment of life imprisonment."[23] Henley's 1966 decision denying the habeas petition left Maxwell with only seven days before he was to be electrocuted. To support his decision, Henley added other propositions to his ruling: (1) that the fifty-five samples of rape convictions were too small, (2) that they were drawn in part from large urban areas in the southern and eastern parts of the state where the black populations were concentrated, (3) and that not every conceivable variable was included in Wolfgang's analysis (such as consent).[24] Henley also rejected Maxwell's other constitutional arguments.

Judge Henley's decision was not entirely adverse. He wrote that Wolfgang was a "well-qualified" criminologist, that John Monroe was likewise "qualified,"[25] and that:

1. The schedules filled out by the law students covered nineteen counties in Arkansas for the twenty-year period from 1945 to 1965. Those nineteen counties held 47 percent of the state's population.[26]
2. The State of Arkansas agreed at the hearing in the District Court that the basic facts contained in the schedules, such as the "age of the victim, the race and so on of the individual defendants or the alleged victims" would be admitted into evidence, as would Marvin Wolfgang's written report.[27]
3. Compared to other rape defendants, African Americans convicted of raping white victims were disproportionately sentenced to death. "A Negro man convicted of raping a white woman has about a 50 percent chance of receiving the death penalty regardless of the facts and circumstances surrounding his crime, whereas a man convicted of raping someone of his own race has only a 14 percent chance."[28]
4. The disproportionate sentencing could not have been due to the laws of chance.[29]
5. The statistical data produced was more extensive and sophisticated than had previously been produced.[30]
6. The sample of cases were drawn in a manner which was statistically acceptable.[31]

James M. Nabrit III, the Fund's second in command, along with Amaker and Amsterdam, rushed to the Fund's offices in New York City, where they worked through the ensuing weekend, barely completing in time the paperwork needed to file an application on Monday to stay Maxwell's execution. Amaker then traveled to St. Louis to file the legal documents with the Eighth Circuit Court of Appeals. Judge C. M. Mathes rejected Maxwell's application and even refused issuance of the "certificate of probable cause" required for an appeal.[32] Maxwell was on a fast track to meet his maker.

The only remaining hope was a stay from a Supreme Court justice. Amaker, Amsterdam, and Nabrit met in Washington, D.C., where they filed Maxwell's application . . . and waited. Tension gripped the hotel room where the three attorneys were lodged. Finally, they received word that Justice Byron White had granted the stay but only to give the remaining justices time to consider whether the Eighth Circuit should hear Maxwell's appeal.[33] Despair gave way to euphoria. Maxwell's September 2 execution was now on hold until after the summer recess. Four months later, the high court unanimously reversed Judge Mathes's ruling denying Maxwell a certificate for probable case. Maxwell could now file his appeal with the Eighth Circuit.[34]

The Public Mood

In 1966 a Gallup poll reported that a 47-percent plurality of Americans opposed the death penalty,[35] but after reaching its lowest point of approval in the twentieth century, capital punishment's popularity changed course. By early 1972, 51 percent of Americans favored it.[36] The seeds of this turnaround began in 1967 while Maxwell's appeal was waiting to reach the appellate docket. In that year, thousands took to the streets of San Francisco and New York City in mid-April to denounce the Vietnam War.[37] In July 1967, race riots erupted in Newark, Detroit, and other northern cities.[38] Other disturbing trends were developing. The inner cities were becoming dangerous places in which to live. Crime rates soared by as much as 350 percent since 1964.[39] Shopkeepers could not retain their workers and found their insurance rates rising to unacceptable levels. They blamed governmental indifference.[40] Law and order became the calling card for conservative politicians seeking election, who urged more severe punishments for convicted criminals. In 1966 Ronald Reagan won the governorship of California, riding a rising tide of fear and disgust over the student riots at Berkeley and the Watts riots in Los Angeles. He "preached cracking down on demonstrators and rioters," while his opponent, Governor Pat Brown, was portrayed as ineffectual.[41]

This change in public mood affected not only public but also judicial perceptions of capital punishment. The two were inextricably linked because of a Supreme Court opinion written in 1958 by then Chief Justice Earl Warren. In *Trop v. Dulles,* the court held that because the Eighth Amendment's ban on "cruel and unusual punishment" is not precisely defined, it "must draw its meaning from the evolving standards of decency that mark the progress of a maturing society."[42] Later decisions linked the "evolving standards of decency" test to the continued constitutional validity of the death penalty.[43] As capital punishment began gaining in popularity in the late 1960s, its chances of passing the "evolving standards of decency" test also improved. The death penalty's enhanced legitimacy in the public mindset also lessened the Fund's chances of a constitutional attack on the southern rape statutes.

Broadened Scope

Time was running out. Thus, instead of narrowing the scope of the assault, a conscious decision was made to broaden it. No longer would the focus be confined to blacks convicted of raping white women in southern and border states. The Fund decided to take on death cases of all color and stripe, whether the defendant was white or black and irrespective of the crime.[44] This decision received a sharp boost when the Ford Foundation announced a $1 million grant to the National Office of the Rights of the Indigent. The Fund's director, Jack Greenberg, decided to funnel some of the money towards assisting Death Row inmates, who were almost always indigent, to stave off their executions.[45]

Also, because of the unfavorable reactions of southern federal and state judges to the 1965 rape study, other avenues of constitutional attack were explored in addition to challenging the failure to require bifurcated jury trials ("split verdicts") or to provide the juries with standards by which they could decide whether a defendant lives or dies.[46] Another point of attack was the exclusion of prospective jurors who expressed general reservations about the death penalty. In *Witherspoon v. Illinois,*[47] despite leaving some loopholes, the Supreme Court banned this widespread practice, finding that not allowing such persons to serve produced a jury "uncommonly willing to condemn a man to die."[48] Race-based jury selection procedures in southern courts were also targeted.

In *Whitus v. Georgia*[49] the court held that prospective jurors could not be drawn from racially segregated tax digests.

But constitutional arguments about legal procedures could only go so far. Fund attorneys still had to meet the claim by prosecutors that capital punishment was still widely accepted by the American people. But if the Fund could gain delays in the executions of significant numbers of the condemned, then, as Michael Meltsner put it, the "more hollow would ring claims that the American people could not do without them,"[50] and the more likely the *Trop v. Dulles* test could be met. The hope was that as the numbers of Death Row inmates grew, the less likely political officials and jurists would want to be responsible for a "bloodbath" in the nation's execution chambers.[51]

And so a "moratorium" strategy unfolded. The Legal Defense Fund's willingness to take on all death cases led defense attorneys from around the country to seek help. As the calls came in, Greenberg hired a new lawyer, Jack Himmelstein, to oversee all the death cases the Fund was taking on. He was then twenty-six years old and a Harvard law graduate."[52] Himmelstein worked continuously with Amsterdam over the next five years, enrolling scholars, prison wardens, and psychologists as experts in the fight against capital punishment.[53] He assembled and distributed nationally a "Last Aid Kit" consisting of easily adapted draft pleadings and other documents for use by defense counsel whose clients faced imminent execution.[54]

The plan seemed to work as lawyers from around the country sought stay upon stay, grinding the death business to a snail's pace.[55] In January 1967, the Fund's strategy bore fruit when the Supreme Court directed the Eighth Circuit to issue the certificate of probable cause in Maxwell's case. This meant that the justices thought enough of the Fund's contentions to allow him to appeal. Later the court "held all death cases . . . [on its docket] in abeyance while it considered" Maxwell's fate.[56] Never before in this country's legal history had the continued viability of the death penalty seemed so much in doubt. State and federal judges alike issued stays of execution, unsure of what to expect from the federal courts. The last man to die was a mentally unbalanced Luis Jose Monge in Colorado's gas chamber on June 2, 1967. He had killed his pregnant wife and three of his ten children.[57] By 1971 the nation's death row population had swollen to 650.[58]

When Amsterdam appeared before the Eighth Circuit in the fall of 1967 to argue the appeal, Judge Harry Blackmun scribbled his evaluation on a scrap of paper: "A—; tall, twenty-eight, suave."[59] Nevertheless, Blackmun remained unresponsive, as was Henley, to Marvin Wolfgang's statistics for most of the same reasons expressed by Judge Henley.[60] But Blackmun ended his opinion with a glaring admission: "We do not say that there is no ground for suspicion that the death penalty for rape may have been discriminatorily applied over the decades in that large area of states whose statutes provide for it. There are recognizable indicators of this."[61]

And what were these "recognizable indicators"? It had to be the schedules completed by the law students and the testimony of Wolfgang and Monroe that the research supported. Perhaps for Blackmun the statistics were too provocative—a reaction that would haunt judicial response to statistical proof of racial sentencing for decades. After all, giving them credence would "cast serious doubt on every other rape conviction in the state courts of Arkansas."[62] Even worse was the doubt cast on many executions that had already taken place—that hundreds of black males may have been electrocuted because of their skin color while those of lighter pigmentation continued to live. These questions he never answered. Doing so could have risked undermining the very legitimacy of Arkansas's legal institutions and those of other states as well.

New Student Vistas

By 1968 most of the twenty-eight law students who had traveled south in 1965 had graduated. Some of them remained within the relatively safe confines of academia, honing their legal skills. Henning Eikenberg worked on his doctoral thesis at Yale for another year, and then returned to Germany, where his thesis was accepted at Saarland University in 1970. John ("Chip") Gray pursued a master of laws degree in a civil rights program from New York University Law School and also served as a staff attorney for New York City Legal Services. Phil Brown decided not to become an attorney and enrolled in an urban planning program (called "Advocacy Planning") at Hunter College in New York. His mother's eyes swelled with tears on learning of what she believed to be Phil's career mistake. To appease her, he agreed to take the California bar exam and passed on the first try. The planning program turned out to be less than what Phil had hoped for. By December 1967 he had left Hunter College and returned to Los Angeles. A few years later, he formed a partnership with his brother-in-law, which has lasted to this day.

For many of us, our experience in the South and the travails of the times—the assassinations of Robert Kennedy and Martin Luther King Jr., the Tet Offensive, the body bags brought home from Vietnam, continuing campus protests of the war, the My Lai massacre, the violence attending the 1968 Democratic National Convention—left their mark. For example, Layton Olson took a job with the Vista Project. Almost immediately following King's death, his neighborhood on Chicago's South Side erupted in riot, with murderous street demonstrators, fires sprouting from the smashed windows of nearby buildings, and overturned vehicles. I received my orders for Vietnam, leaving behind a young wife who was seven months pregnant.

But the many preoccupations of that year, both personal and national, did not distract the Fund's attorneys from their efforts to save Maxwell's life and expose the southern death machinery as another pawn of racism. Blackmun's written opinion was published on July 11, 1968. Once again Maxwell faced the electric chair. Once again the Fund's attorneys working under Amsterdam asked the Supreme Court to intervene,[63] but their hopes remained tempered. Petitions for writs of certiorari were, and still are, rarely granted. In some years, nearly 99 percent of the cases filed are disposed of without oral argument.[64] Review is only granted for compelling reasons such as resolving conflicts among lower courts or to resolve serious legal questions of federal legislative and constitutional import.[65] To be seriously considered for review at all cases must make the "Discuss List" at the justices' weekly conferences. Eighty-five percent of the cases filed do not even make the list, and those that don't are almost always denied without any discussion or vote taken.[66] While capital cases are treated seriously during this process, the presence of a death sentence is hardly a ticket to Supreme Court review. Only a small minority of such cases are given full consideration by the court.

The Surprise

Richard Nixon was elected president, and ultimately his selections would change the composition of the court. Fund attorneys and the Arkansas attorney general's counsel waited for word from Washington. Finally, on December 16, 1968, the court broke its silence by announcing that Maxwell's case did indeed have sufficient merit to be fully briefed and then argued orally before the justices. But what issues would the court consider? The three the Fund had served up to the Eighth Circuit appellate court were (1) whether the death penalty in Arkansas was being applied discriminatorily in violation of the Equal Protections Clause of the Fourteenth Amendment; (2) whether Arkansas's practice of permitting the trial jury absolute discretion, uncontrolled by standards or directions of any kind, to impose the death penalty violated the due process clause of the Fourteenth Amendment; and (3) whether Arkansas's single-verdict procedure, which requires the jury to determine guilt and punishment simultaneously, violated the Fifth and Fourteenth Amendments.[67]

The court announced it would limit its review to the second and third issues,[68] implying that the court had no interest in Wolfgang's statistics or whether death sentencing was being racially applied. But the justices were to hear about the rape survey anyway. By agreeing to consider the "standards" issue, the court effectively permitted the Fund to argue the reasons that standards were needed—including, of course, helping jurors steer clear of racial considerations when deliberating on a death verdict. Rules governing life-death jury choices would focus the jurors on a set of guidelines pertaining to the circumstances of the crime, the defendant's culpability, and other racially nondiscriminatory factors.

Maxwell's brief would argue that arbitrary and random death sentencing pervaded the courts across the country: "[U]ncontrolled and undirected jury discretion in capital sentencing" was "at the root of arbitrary and discriminatory imposition of the death penalty."[69] Death sentencing without standards gives "the covert discriminator . . . absolute license to practice his biases in the matter of taking human life."[70] Even when discussing death verdicts as being freakishly, whimsically, and erratically applied, an effort was made to tie in the race issue: "The very extremity of this arbitrariness may effectively conceal the workings of racial discrimination and of every other invidious prejudice forbidden by the Constitution."[71]

Delivering the Evidence

To support its position, the Fund laid out in detail the statistical evidence introduced in the district court below showing that in Arkansas, as in other southern states where juries were allowed unfettered discretion, death verdicts were strongly influenced by "racial and caste discrimination." The brief contained an extensive discussion of Wolfgang's "empirical study of sentencing patterns in rape cases . . . undertaken in 1965."[72] Attached to the brief was a twenty-three-page appendix describing the results of the law student's survey and Wolfgang's conclusion that "Negro defendants who rape white victims have been disproportionately sentenced to death."[73]

Wolfgang's conclusion was buttressed by a much shorter, three-page discussion of the breakdown by race of executions in the United States maintained by the Department of Justice's Bureau of Prisons. These "National Prisoner Statistics" covered the period from 1930 to 1962 and showed that of the 446 persons executed for rape, 399 were African Americans, 45 were white, and 2 were Indians.[74] "All were executed in southern or border states or in the District of Columbia." The Fund acknowledged that these "suspicious figures" might be explained by a higher black crime rate. Because the bureau's statistics were subject to challenge, Professor Wolfgang had been engaged by the Fund to conduct "a more systematic and rigorous examination of the evidence of racial differentials in capital sentencing."[75]

The Views of the Justices

Fund attorneys were, of course, apprehensive over how their provocative arguments would sit with the court. Notions of fairness guided Chief Justice Earl Warren, a principled man. He supported many of the new criminal procedure reforms such as extending the Sixth Amendment right to counsel to the states in the landmark decision of *Gideon v. Wainwright*.[76] His opinion in *Miranda v. Arizona* required that a person suspected of crime be informed of rights such as his or her right to counsel and to remain silent. But despite his civil libertarian views, no one knew what he thought of the death penalty. He had worked for eighteen years as a state prosecutor.[77]

Lyndon Johnson had appointed Justice Abe Fortas to the Supreme Court in 1965. By 1968 Fortas had established himself as a progressive on juvenile justice issues. He supported the expansion of due process rights to juveniles in an important case, *Kent v. United States*,[78] but his views on criminal procedural rights were largely untested. In *Malloy v. Hogan*[79] Justice William Brennan made clear that for him state criminal justice systems should embrace the fundamental values contained in the Bill of Rights through the Due Process Clause of the Fourteenth Amendment. William O. Douglas agreed. While Douglas had been sympathetic to law enforcement interests during the 1940s when he still held presidential aspirations,[80] he was thought to be a vote for the Fund position. And there was Thurgood Marshall, who would surely be sensitive to the racial dimensions of Maxwell's case.

There were four other justices who could not be counted on, though the Fund's attorneys hoped for a vote from at least one of them. Justice John Harlan was known as the "great dissenter" to the Warren Court, but he had a healthy respect for the Due Process Clause.[81] Potter Stewart had dissented in *Miranda v. Arizona,*[82] believing as did Justices Harlan and White, that the Warren Court was reading into the Constitution more than what was there. White had dissented in the Witherspoon case where he wrote that the court should "restrain its dislike for the death penalty."[83] leaving the propriety of the matter to the people's elected representatives. Justice Hugo Black, who also dissented in Witherspoon, repudiated any efforts to chip away at the death penalty.[84]

The oral argument took place on March 4, 1969. Tony Amsterdam squarely addressed the place of race in sentencing. He castigated the state legislatures for ducking the issue of when a convicted rapist should live or die. Because jury verdicts were rarely reversed, juries could act shamefully and without reproach. Amsterdam gave as one example the survey performed by the law students in Arkansas. The lower courts had conceded the strong evidence suggesting the death penalty had been applied discriminatorily. Without standards, he argued, such practices would continue.[85]

Questions from the Bench

From the questions the justices asked, it was difficult to predict which way the case would turn out—whether it would embrace a sea change in the way capital jury trials were handled, or leave matters as they were. Justice White asked whether a judge doing the sentencing had any more standards to be guided by than a jury.[86] The inquiry suggested that if a judge was equipped to sentence in a capital case without guidelines, so was a jury. Justice Harlan asked about the constitutionality of mandatory sentencing.[87] His question hinted at a possible resolution, to require automatic death sentences for certain heinous crimes so as to relieve the jury (or judge) of having to choose between life imprisonment or death.

Justice Fortas asked if standards could even be formulated.[88] The State of Arkansas had already addressed that concern, pointing out that the circumstances of each capital offense were so individual that drafting broad guidelines to fit the facts of every case simply could not be done. As to the bifurcated trial issue, Chief Justice Warren asked whether there was a limit to the questions directed at a defendant about his past life.[89] Warren's notions of fairness seemed to be at play.[90]

Justice Stewart's questions were the most troubling. He asked about the availability of the trial transcript and whether it could be determined from that if a *Witherspoon* violation had occurred.[91] The Supreme Court in *Witherspoon v. Illinois*[92] had held that jurors expressing only general reservations about the death penalty could not be discharged for cause. What Stewart seemed to be looking for was a way to avoid the larger issues and send the case back to the trial court for retrial because of error in the improper exclusion of prospective jurors.

The questioning left Amsterdam and the Fund attorneys feeling confident that the "standards" and "bifurcated trial" arguments remained intact. No justice had voiced his opposition to them,[93] but Stewart's questions about a possible *Witherspoon* violation concerned them. If the case was bounced back to the trial court on that issue alone, then the constitutional attacks on the death penalty would no longer be before the court, making it more difficult to secure stays of execution.[94]

Chapter 7

Momentum Builds, Then Stalls

Justice William O. Douglas sat quietly, watching this public display of bantering and cajoling. A fury enveloped him, and he knew in such times that it was best not to speak. Otherwise, his anger would surface much like lava struggling through the earth's crust, finally unleashing its uncontrolled fury every which way. He was a frustrated man. Twice he had been considered by President Franklin Roosevelt as his vice-presidential running mate, the last time in 1944. Only the intervention of certain leaders of the Democratic National Committee, Douglas believed, allowed Truman to emerge. Otherwise Douglas would have been president.[1]

There he sat, a quarter of a century later, still on the Supreme Court, where, some thought, he still suffered from frustrated ambition. His opinions had grown short and pithy over time. He had been accused of sloppy work.[2] Perhaps he didn't care any more, as he was nearing the end of his life and had already left his mark on constitutional law. But this case, this *Maxwell* matter—now here was something he was going to take a closer look at. Because he didn't like how it smelled. All those numbers, those ridiculous numbers of blacks who had been electrocuted. He hated such abuses. And he could identify with Maxwell, a black man disadvantaged at birth and now cast aside, because at heart Douglas always thought of himself as an outsider, someone not welcomed by those at the pinnacle of power. He had grown up that way. He worked his way through Whitman College as a janitor and waiter, and in the summer he picked cherries. "I worked among the very, very poor," he once said, "the migrant laborers, the Chicanos and the I.W.W.'s who

I saw being shot at by the police. I saw cruelty and hardness, and my impulse was to be a force in other developments in the law."[3]

He had become the longest-serving Supreme Court justice, appointed in 1939 by Roosevelt. He had engaged in a protracted feud with Justice Felix Frankfurter, who had fretted over a possible Douglas presidency[4] and did not respect his work on the court. To Frankfurter, Douglas was not a team player. He was "impetuous," "unstatesmanlike," results-oriented, and unwilling to abide by legal intricacies. Douglas thought little of Frankfurter's detailed, elaborate opinions.[5]

His sympathies for the disadvantaged were legendary. No other justice was as resolute in dispensing with judicial restraint to advance the cause of equal justice, irrespective of what path of life a person came from.[6] Because the Fourteenth Amendment's Equal Protection Clause applied only to states, not private persons, the other justices had struggled over how to rein in the discriminatory practices of private southern restaurateurs. Not Douglas. He wrote: "[O]ne who operates an enterprise under a license from the government . . . enjoys a privilege that derives from the people. . . . The business is not a matter of mere private concern. Those who license enterprises for public use should not have . . . the power to license it for the use of only one race."[7]

He abhorred discrimination in any form. In 1951 he renounced a state's imposition of a poll tax on the right to vote. The exercise of democracy, he reasoned, should not be dependent on how much was in a person's wallet. Years later he would write again, "Wealth, like race, creed or color, is not germane to one's ability to participate in the electoral process."[8] His total rejection of racial discrimination propelled him to renounce it even by private clubs.[9]

He had a strong reaction to the data produced by the law students and related evidence of discriminatory death sentencing by southern white juries. Douglas studied the Fund's brief, the evidence contained in the schedules, and Wolfgang's conclusions. No more, he vowed. Patiently he waited for the lawyers to finish their *Maxwell* arguments. There was no question what he was going to do. He would give his colleagues a piece of his mind at conference.

Discussion Begins

With the *Maxwell* hearing finally concluded, the justices retired to discuss the case. On March 6, 1969,[10] they met in the conference room adjacent to the courtroom with no one else present, as was the custom. While there exists no verbatim account of what was said, the debate must have been heated.[11] Justice William Brennan later reported that the court was having a difficult time resolving a range of views: "[I]t was not clear there were five votes for any single rationale."[12] What was clear was the final tally. Eight justices were in favor of reversing Maxwell's conviction, though for differing constitutional reasons. Hugo Black was the sole dissenter. Probably because of Douglas's passionate views, Chief Justice Warren assigned him the task of preparing the majority opinion.

Of course, the vote was tentatively nonbinding. The justices were free to change their minds at any time before each signed off on a final written opinion. The next day Justice John Harlan wrote to Warren suggesting that a second conference be scheduled because he (Harlan) was "not at rest" with his decision "to reverse this case on the . . . 'split trial' issue."[13] Warren agreed. Later that month the justices met again, and this time the reasons behind earlier votes became clearer. Douglas explained his views in the draft of a majority opinion he prepared. He cited the Arkansas court's failure to give Maxwell's jury any standards before they condemned him to the electric chair: "Where there are no guidelines . . . one jury may decide that *one defendant is not 'fit to live' . . . because he is a black who raped a white woman,* while another defendant is 'fit to live' because he is a white who raped a black [emphasis added]."[14]

There it was—an indication that our 1965 survey work and Wolfgang's statistical conclusions might move the court. No other evidence had been presented to the court that would have triggered that reference. The execution statistics of the Federal Bureau of Prisons provided to the Supreme Court only reflected the higher number of blacks sentenced to death for rape, not the interracial aspects of their transgressions." Marvin Wolfgang's statistics had finally found their mark.[15] Douglas may have been receptive to them because he believed in "fresh air blowing from other disciplines" to "ventilate the law."[16] Three other justices agreed with him and backed the imposition of standards to guide juries before setting penalties in capital cases. In his private notes, Brennan identified two of the three: himself and Warren.[17]

The impact of the Wolfgang study on Brennan is not difficult to discern. He believed that jurisprudence had much to learn from other disciplines and that a lawyer is "unwise . . . who rejects what can be learned from history and sociology and psychology."[18] He quoted Arthur T. Vanderbilt that "the law cannot be isolated from the other social sciences or understood without them."[19] Brennan wrote:

> [T]he legal scholar's role is . . . a creative one. He is more likely to have the leisure and range of thought necessary to reach across the arbitrary divisions between disciplines in the academic world and sense values that the law may properly serve and techniques it may profitably use . . . judicial decision must be nourished by all the insights that scholarship can furnish and legal scholarship must in turn be nourished by all the disciplines that comprehend the totality of human experience.[20]

Establishing constitutional violations through the use of sociological and statistical methodology was just the sort of "reaching across the arbitrary divisions between disciplines" that Brennan relished. And so when the Fund's brief in Maxwell's case arrived, Brennan could be expected to have given significant weight to Wolfgang's conclusions.

As for Chief Justice Warren, he too likely would have responded well to the statistical arguments of the Fund. Warren had limited regard for the legal rules in place, as they tended to complicate his search for social justice. "You sit up there," he said, "and you see the whole gamut of human nature. Even if the case being argued involves only a little fellow and $50, it involves justice. That's what is important."[21] Here the "little fellow" was the African American defendant convicted of rape who was more likely to face the electric chair than his white counterpart. For Warren, unfair and unequal punishment demanded judicial intervention.

The fourth justice in agreement on the need to reverse the lower courts in Maxwell's case was almost certainly Thurgood Marshall. Marshall also had a healthy respect for "reaching across the arbitrary divisions between disciplines" and using sociological and statistical tools to nourish judicial decision-making. He had done so when he was one of the lead counsels in *Brown v. Board of Education,* using sociological studies in oral argument to show the demeaning effect school segregation had on African American children.[22]

Marshall was particularly in tune with the drawbacks to standardless death sentencing. Putting aside his own ethnicity, as the former director of the Fund (from 1939 to 1961[23] when he resigned to accept a judicial appointment),[24] he well knew the issues of racial death sentencing, having represented many capital case defendants himself, including participating in the "the Martinsville Seven" defense. Marshall was frustrated with his colleagues on the court for their narrow views about the effects of racism on American society.[25] He believed they knew nothing about the lives lived by people of color.[26] He also believed that the minorities, the poor, and the undereducated were most often destined for the death chambers.[27] Brennan reported that Marshall favored reversal of Maxwell's conviction because his trial was not bifurcated between the "guilt" phase and the "punishment" phase. But Marshall never voiced any opposition to the standards argument. He would, however, later show his support for it when he joined the dissenting opinion of Justice Brennan in *McGautha v. California*.[28]

Seeking a Fifth Vote

With nine justices on the high court, Douglas needed a fifth vote to form a majority. But try as he could, he found the task to be Herculean. Fortas was resolutely opposed to giving juries any guidelines. He wrote Douglas: "The basic fact is that it is impossible . . . to state standards which justify capital punishment. The Model Code provisions are entirely unacceptable to me."[29]

Fortas was referring to the Model Code promulgated by the American Law Institute, whose eminent director, Herbert Weschler, had drafted a set of sentencing standards to govern the life-death decision. But Fortas was still willing to vote for reversal of Maxwell's conviction provided the basis be that the defendant was not given a bifurcated trial, leading Brennan to suggest that more emphasis be given to that issue in the draft opinion Douglas was preparing.[30] Harlan was undecided but leaned toward Fortas's view that a "unitary trial" on the issue of guilt and punishment deprived a defendant of due process. And Hugo Black, the lone dissenter, had voted to affirm the judgment, believing that the death penalty should never have been made a constitutional issue.[31]

Douglas finally decided to see whether a majority could be formed around the "bifurcation" issue as the sole basis for reversal.[32] But as soon as he found that majority, Warren announced his retirement due to age. At Harlan's urging, the remaining justices decided to put Maxwell's case on hold to allow Warren's replacement, whoever that might be, to weigh in.[33] New winds were blowing in from the White House with Nixon's assumption of the presidency. The majority that Douglas had painstakingly formed had now dissolved. Nixon, of course, would have liked to replace all of the justices who were part of the "Warren Court." That group included Warren, Brennan, Marshall, Douglas, and Fortas.[34] The remaining justices—Potter Stewart, Hugo Black, Byron White, and John Harlan—were viewed as "conservative" to "moderate" and were at least acceptable.

Enter Burger

After Warren retired, Nixon appointed Warren Burger as the new chief justice.[35] In 1955 Burger had been appointed to the United States Court of Appeals for the District of Columbia. He was known in legal circles for articles and lectures suggesting a less permissive attitude toward those accused of crime, particularly an easing of the legal barriers for admissibility of evidence against accused defendants in criminal cases. He once stated that "No nation on earth goes to such lengths or takes such pains to provide safeguards as we do, once an accused person is called before the bar of justice and until his case is completed,"[36] and he praised the approach of Scandinavian countries because "they go swiftly, efficiently and directly to the question of whether the accused is guilty,"[37] requiring the accused to testify if necessary.

Then the purge began. The conservatives within the administration viewed Douglas as their principal nemesis and also wanted him gone.[38] He had written over thirty books by 1970, including *Points of Rebellion,* in which he defended the antiwar movement. He likened "today's Establishment," to "King George III," and called for a revolution if the king's tactics were followed. By 1970 Congressman Gerald Ford of Michigan had started impeachment efforts against Douglas in the House of Representatives. Ford disapproved of Douglas's penchant for finding new wives and his endorsement of every youthful fad.[39] The impeachment attempt was eventually abandoned, thanks to the efforts of Douglas's allies on the House Judiciary Committee.[40]

After failing to remove Douglas, conservatives next targeted Brennan. He was attacked for hiring "radical" law clerks, including Michael Tigar, "a leading radical activist" from Boalt Hall at Berkeley. J. Edgar Hoover's assistant at the FBI, Clyde Tolson, visited Justice Fortas, warning him that Hoover was aware Tigar had gone to a youth festival in Helsinki, Finland, where representatives from the Soviet Union were also in attendance. When word of Tolson's visit leaked, Brennan reluctantly informed Tigar he could not clerk at the court.[41]

Brennan also came under scrutiny from federal investigators soon after Nixon was sworn into office. Brennan had provided funds for a limited partnership and was joined by several of his friends who were lower court judges. They included David Bazelon of the U.S. Court of Appeals for the District of Columbia and J. Skelly Wright, a district court judge. Brennan was criticized because sharing in such an investment might compromise his impartiality should the decisions of his fellow judges come up for review at the Supreme Court. Brennan quickly withdrew his venture capital and in so doing, he secured his survival on the bench.

Fortas's Removal

Abe Fortas was not as fortunate. President Lyndon Johnson had appointed him in 1967. He was close to Johnson, to whom he had often given legal advice. Fortas, an unabashed liberal, was sympathetic to the Great Society reforms the White House was promoting. As the defense attorney for Owen Lattimore during the Red Scare years of the late 1940s and 1950s, he was frequently at odds with Senator Joseph McCarthy when appearing with his client before Senate committee hearings. But Fortas was forced to resign from the Supreme Court in 1970 to avoid impeachment when the press disclosed he had signed a contract with one of Louis Wolfson's foundations that obligated the foundation to pay Fortas $20,000 a year for life. At the time Wolfson was under investigation for securities violations. Fortas's enemies claimed the payments were intended to help Wolfson avoid prosecution, although no proof of this was ever presented.[42]

After two nominees failed to receive support in the Senate, Nixon finally chose Harry Blackmun[43] of the U.S. Court of Appeals for the Eighth Circuit to replace Fortas. In what Fund lawyers must have taken as a great irony, Nixon had picked to replace Fortas the one appeals court judge in the nation who had written an adverse opinion in Maxwell's case. Blackmun was thought to be a thorough and meticulous, if somewhat bookish, judge. He was modest in demeanor and appeared at times to lack self-confidence. His early opinions revealed his support for law enforcement and adherence to the positions taken by government. Still, it was hard to predict what sort of justice he would be, and during his confirmation process the press emphasized what was thought to be the best predictor: he was a longtime friend of the chief justice.

Re-argument

Blackmun could not, of course, participate in the appeal from a judgment he wrote in the court below, so there were only eight justices to hear the re-argument of Maxwell's case set for May 4, 1970. This time the questions were more hostile. Burger asked one that implied Amsterdam had not come up with a compelling constitutional justification for the procedural challenges being proposed. And he asked why the statistics on racial discrimination shouldn't be better presented to the state legislatures for consideration as opposed to the courts. Justice Black asked if jurors do not have sufficient life experiences to allow them to pass judgment on whether a defendant is to live or die. Justice White asked whether a judge could order a new trial under Arkansas law if he disagreed with the sentence. The question suggested that there might be other ways already in place to remedy an ill-advised death verdict and that a drastic change in criminal procedures, as advocated by the Fund's counsel, was not necessary.[44]

The Court retired to deliberate for a second time on this case, leaving the Fund's counsel more pessimistic than ever because of the new composition of the bench and the queries posed during re-argument. On June 1, 1970, the court announced its decision. It ventured no comment on the statistics that pointed to discriminatory application of capital punishment in the South. Instead, the court seemed intent on ridding itself of the controversy those statistics had generated by sending the case back to the trial judge to see if a *Witherspoon*[45] violation could be uncovered—that is, whether a prospective juror had been disqualified for expressing only general reservations about the death penalty.[46]

Deferred Issues

Once again resolution of the "standards" and "bifurcated trial" issues was being deferred. So far, the court had seemed terribly reluctant to tackle anything to do with racial animus within the southern court system, preferring instead to nibble at the edges by tinkering with jury selection procedures. For instance, in *Alexander v. Louisiana*[47] the court held that the Equal Protection Clause of the Fourteenth Amendment prohibited the state from systematically excluding potential grand jurors of the same race as that of the defendant. In *Sims v. Georgia*[48] prospective jurors had been selected from a county tax digest, which separately listed taxpayers by race. The court concluded that the jury commissioner had too great an opportunity to make racially induced selections of potential jurors. In the *Maxwell* case, however, the race issue was exceedingly risky for the court to wrestle with. Questioning the ability of jurors of one race to be fair to a defendant of another could place the entire American jury system on trial. For the majority of the justices, it was safer to avoid the issue once more.

But the court did move ahead to reconsider the standards and bifurcation issues in two new cases, *McGautha v. California* and *Crampton v. Ohio,* to be heard "at an early date in the 1970 term."[49] Those cases were consolidated and became known collectively as *McGautha v. California.*

As the Fund did not represent the defendants in the two cases, its views were presented via *amicus curiae* brief. But by presenting itself as a "friend of the court," the Fund sought to bring its unique perspective on the issues once more and to influence the outcome of the case. The brief made reference to the *Maxwell* case and the arguments made there. But the racial issues were barely touched upon, presumably because the states involved (California and Ohio) were not southern and did not have a notable history of state-sanctioned discriminatory practices. Instead the Fund focused on the way juries arbitrarily chose life imprisonment for some defendants and death for others, even though the circumstances of the crimes were the same or similar. Jury sentencing was attacked for not being subject to legal rules, for its "lawlessness." Life and death decisions seemed to be based on chance, or on the whim of the moment. If evenhanded, objective standards or rules were given juries to assist them in their deliberations, then the sentences they arrived at would be more consistent.

Anthony Amsterdam asked to speak at oral argument, but ominously the court refused his request by a vote of six to three. The justices' law clerks were abuzz over the implications of the majority's slap at Amsterdam. They thought it was a "clear telegram" of things to come.[50] And they were right.

Decision Rendered

As the Fund lawyers feared, the court rejected both standards and split-verdict arguments in a six-three decision, with Justices Harlan, Burger, Stewart, White, Blackmun, and Black in the majority. The dissenters were Marshall, Brennan, and Douglas.

Harlan wrote the majority opinion. He wholeheartedly approved of the right of juries to use their "untrammeled discretion" in pronouncing life or death. "States are entitled to assume that jurors . . . will act with due regard for the consequences of their decision and will consider a variety of factors, many of which will have been suggested by the evidence or by the arguments of defense counsel."[51] He found it impossible to "catalog the appropriate factors in this elusive area [which] could inhibit rather than expand the scope of consideration."[52] Harlan also found no need for a separate trial on the appropriate punishment after the defendant was found guilty of the capital crime: "It does no violence to the privilege [against self-incrimination] that a person's choice to testify in his own behalf may open the door to otherwise inadmissible evidence which is damaging to his case."[53] Though the choice may be hard, it is a matter of judgment that had routinely been left to the discretion of the defendant and his counsel. There was no case precedent to indicate the Constitution was offended by a defendant assuming that risk.[54]

Brennan, Douglas, and Marshall met privately and decided that Brennan would write a dissent stressing the need for jury-sentencing standards. Douglas would write the dissent on the bifurcated trial issue. They each would then join in the two dissents. When Brennan received a draft copy of the majority opinion towards the end of February 1971, he let Harlan know he would need additional time to write and circulate his response. Fearing Brennan's persuasive talents, Harlan quickly summoned approval of his own draft from Justices White, Blackmun, Stewart, and Burger. Although Hugo Black was in agreement with the majority, he told Harlan he wanted to write a separate concurring opinion in which he would take special aim at the abolitionists.[55]

By April 20 Brennan had finished his opinion. Douglas saw him examining a copy of it while on the bench. Without even asking to read it, Douglas said he was ready to join. Bemused, Brennan retorted, "So this is the way we get the benefit of your thirty years' experience?" Douglas sheepishly took Brennan's copy, promised to read it, and later sent back a note inscribed with the word "Magnificent!"[56]

Brennan's Dissent

In his dissent, Brennan adopted wholesale the arguments of the Fund on the standards issue. He remained convinced that the southern death statutes had become impregnated with racial animus. "Due Process Clause," he wrote, ". . . commands us . . . to make certain that no State takes one man's life for reasons that it would not apply to another."[57] When statutes are left vague by the legislatures that created them, they can be applied in different ways to different individuals so as to deny equal protection of the laws.[58] He cited authorities holding that due process of law required protection against "arbitrary and discriminatory" punishment.[59] Sentencing should be alike for all who are similarly situated.[60]

Speaking for all three dissenters, Brennan pointed towards setting standards for imposing death as a way to insure due process. He wrote, "I see no reason to believe that juries are not capable of explaining . . . what facts they have found and what reasons they have considered sufficient to take a human life."[61] He differed with the majority's view that standards for death sentencing were too hard to establish.

Justice Black concurred with the majority and added something that none of the parties or any other justice had addressed. He wrote that the Eighth Amendment forbidding cruel and unusual punishment "cannot be read to outlaw capital punishment because that penalty was in common use . . . at the time the Amendment was adopted."[62] But instead of continuing with a lengthy historical look at the death penalty, his writing turned pithy and explosive. "It is inconceivable to me," he said, "that the framers intended to end capital punishment by the [Eighth] Amendment. Although some people have urged that this Court should amend the Constitution by interpretation to keep it abreast of modern ideas, I have never believed that lifetime judges in our system have any such legislative power."[63]

Was Black signaling a warning not to try an Eighth Amendment attack? What was certain was that any efforts to vitiate the death penalty laws in the South and elsewhere had been dealt, to all appearances, a mortal blow in *McGautha*. The court's broad acclamation of jurors' "untrammeled discretion" manifested a willingness to look the other way from any signs of racism creeping into death sentencing.

Other Cases Loom

Just as the reform efforts had seemed to falter, other cases were percolating from below, preparing to surface eventually and carrying with them a common message: the issue of discriminatory death sentencing in the South was not going away. Already the justices were on notice of the law students' 1965 rape surveys discussed in the earlier published cases of *Sims v. Abrams,*[64] *Moorer v. South Carolina,*[65] and *Maxwell v. Bishop.*[66] There were also state appellate court decisions that were dismissive of Wolfgang's conclusions. When *Swain v. State* and *Butler v. State* reached the U.S. Supreme Court in the early 1970s,[67] the petitions filed in each served again to remind the justices of the law students' work. Both cases discussed at length Wolfgang's statistical analyses and the data the students had extracted of racially influenced death sentencing in the South. Both petitions sought the same relief: to reverse the Alabama Supreme Court's decisions that had rubber-stamped the white jury verdicts.

At about the same time that the *Swain* and *Butler* cases were surfacing, Wolfgang's findings were being used in other cases, referenced and cross-referenced in countless petitions for review, briefs, and other pleadings. Much like the irrepressible drips that come from a leaky tap, these findings made their way into the subconscious of the justices, serving to remind the jurists of the basic justice of the death-sentenced defendants' cause. Like the rows of a phalanx, these court documents marched through the state and federal appellate systems, pounding away at the same points, until finally reaching the Supreme Court's doorstep.

Anthony Amsterdam later explained the rationale for this strategy. He felt that all the discrimination arguments were "important not only because of their potential legal force, but because they permit us to raise doubts in the minds of judges . . . and the general public about the fairness of the administration of the death penalty and its conformity to the supposed penological goals of capital punishment."[68]

Despite *McGautha,* the many cases raising discrimination issues that were still moving through the lower courts and the visibility of such issues produced by the Fund's aggressive abolition campaign meant that no consideration of a potential execution could ignore the racial dimension of death penalty sentencing. The public record symbolized by the moratorium and the costs of ending it would weigh on the consciences of some members of the court and help set the stage for the next and most dramatic inning of play.

Chapter 8

The High Court Acts

Whether or not Justice Hugo Black believed in the efficacy of the death penalty, he was sure that neither the Constitution's promise of equal protection of the laws nor the Eighth Amendment's ban on cruel and unusual punishments abolished it. To Black, arguments against capital punishment boiled down to claims of unfairness, and his entire career had been set against giving judges the discretion to define constitutional protections on this basis. Following the court's *McGautha* decision,[1] Black believed that a Supreme Court holding that death sentencing was not cruel and unusual would leave its fate forever "in the hands of the [state] legislatures," where he thought it belonged.[2]

Chief Justice Warren Burger, a death penalty proponent, liked the idea, and with Black's encouragement suggested that "four clean cases" be picked for review. He and Black probably had in mind four cases where the hideous facts of the murders and rapes demanded the ultimate penalty. Black's encouragement was well timed. Since 1967 stays and postponements of execution for most of the inmates on Death Row had been granted while the death penalty's fate was awaiting constitutional resolution. By 1971 the backlog of executions had grown so large that some feared a "bloodbath" once the moratorium was lifted. The Supreme Court was under intense public pressure to do something and with a court shifting to a more conservative bent, Black was confident of victory.

If Black was confident, Justice William Brennan was worried. He feared the effects of a public outcry over the rising crime rate and civil unrest. After a decade of decline, the popularity of capital punishment had recently surged,[3] probably because changing the death penalty from an almost invisible issue to a center-stage political controversy stoked anxiety that the criminal law had become too permissive. Brennan thought *McGautha* a dangerous precedent: without standards to guide predominantly white juries in the South, the defendant's race would continue to determine who would live and who would die.

But Brennan had one advantage. He was a master tactician, and he went to work. With Justice Potter Stewart's assent, he suggested that he and Stewart be assigned to find the "four clean cases." Burger agreed,[4] probably assured that Potter Stewart would keep Brennan in check. Burger, of course, was aware of Brennan's close ties to the former chief justice, Earl Warren, and of his dissenting opinion in *McGautha*. What Burger may have undervalued was the extent of Brennan's wiles and convincing ways. He had been on the court since 1956. To those who knew him, he was the "great conciliator" and "coalition builder."[5] Thurgood Marshall once opined that no other justice could "persuade the way Brennan can persuade."[6] Brennan also put his law clerks to work, encouraging them to befriend "the other clerks to find out what their Justices are thinking."

Once he knew the thoughts and leanings of his brethren, he went about trying to dissuade or persuade, not by buttonholing but by the sheer force of his logic. Brennan had the ability, according to Marshall, to "sit down with you and talk to you and show you where you're wrong." Warren had recognized Brennan for his intellectual firepower, resolve, and industry.[7] No one worked harder on the court.

Brennan's personal qualities aided his persuasiveness. Small in stature ("leprechaun-like"),[8] he took a delight in all those he met, and spoke warmly of his adversaries. Brennan, of course, downplayed his abilities. He did not claim victory or credit. Frequently he would write letters to his fellow justices attempting to explain his views on pending cases. He avoided confrontations and preferred to carefully craft his suggested changes in writing.[9] According to Warren, Brennan had a particularly strong influence on Potter Stewart and credited him with holding Stewart's vote for the majority in the great redistricting case of *Baker v. Carr*.[10] That strong influence would become critical once again in forming a new majority on the death penalty issue.

Brennan, with Stewart's acquiescence, culled through the numerous Death Row petitions and found a package of four cases he thought Burger and Black would agree to review. All involved black defendants[11] and white victims. Three cases came from the South. In two of those three, black defendants had been convicted of raping white women.

The Fund was counsel of record in two of the four cases (*Furman* and *Jackson*). The racial undertones of the crimes and the convictions would be before the court even if nothing about the cases immediately evoked any great sympathies for the defendants, and at least one of the cases presented a truly violent man whose culpability seemed clear.

The Facts

Furman v. Georgia

William Henry Furman was twenty-six years old with a sixth-grade education. He had been moving about his home state of Georgia, constantly looking for new employment. As his financial fortunes waned, he grew more depressed and hungry, and embarked on a life of petty thievery. On August 11, 1967, Furman broke into a home belonging to William Joseph Micke Jr., a twenty-nine-year-old, white, Coast Guard petty officer. When Micke heard sounds coming from the kitchen, he left his bed and rushed downstairs to pursue the intruder. Furman fled from the kitchen, ran out the back door, and tripped over a washing machine cord. When he fell and landed on the hardwood floor of the porch, the gun he was carrying discharged. A bullet passed through the solid back door that had closed behind him and struck Micke in the chest, killing him almost instantly.

Before his trial began, Furman had entered an insanity plea and had been examined by the staff of the Georgia Central State Hospital. The staff members had diagnosed Furman with "Mental Deficiency, Mild to Moderate with Psychotic Episode associated with Convulsive Disorder," and concluded he was in need of further psychiatric hospitalization and treatment. But the superintendent found Furman not to be psychotic at the time of the offense and concluded he could distinguish between right and wrong. At his trial the jury took only one hour and thirty-five minutes to return a verdict of guilty and a sentence of death. Furman's court-appointed attorney, Clarence Mayfield, received $150 for his services.[12]

Jackson v. Georgia

Lucius Jackson Jr., a twenty-one-year-old black man, was convicted of raping a white woman in 1968 in Chatham County, Georgia. He had escaped from a prison work gang and broke into the woman's home. The crying of her four-month-old infant at about 7:45 a.m. awakened Mary Rose. She heard a loud noise from the dining room or living room area of the house. She turned toward the baby's closet and saw "a young colored male." The intruder, Jackson, crossed the room and placed a half-pair of scissors against her neck. They went to the bedroom where Jackson spied a five-dollar bill and some change on the dresser. He put the half-scissors down to seize the money. Mrs. Rose seized the scissors and tried to stab him. They fell together on the bed, each struggling for the scissors. He finally grabbed them and while on top of her, he released her left hand, pulled her gown open, unzipped his pants, and had sexual intercourse with her. Finally the maid arrived and shouted Mrs. Rose's name from the front door. Jackson soon left through a window.[13]

Branch v. Texas

Elmer Branch was twenty years old when he crept into the home of his victim, Mrs. Grady Stowe. The victim was a white, sixty-five-year-old widow. Branch entered her bedroom as she slept, jerked off the bedcovers, grabbed her arm, pinned her against a wall as she lay on the bed, told her not to yell, and pinned his right arm on her throat when she tried to call for help. Then he took off her pajama bottoms and sexually assaulted her. Following that, Stowe retrieved her glasses and hearing aid and then sat in a chair. They engaged in a conversation for forty-five minutes.

"Why did you come out here and molest a woman my age?" she asked. "I am sixty-five years old, when there are plenty of nice, pretty girls in town."

Branch replied, "I wanted to see how you felt about colored people."

She then gave a detailed account of times she and her late husband had helped "Negroes." Mrs. Stowe asked to go to the bathroom to get a drink of water. Branch agreed. Branch told her to tell no one what happened, or he would return the next day to kill her. Branch had no weapon, and there were no apparent physical injuries to Mrs. Stowe requiring medical treatment. Branch was purported to have an IQ of only 67.[14]

Aikens v. California

Earnest James Aikens Jr. had been convicted in California of the murder of an elderly white woman, Mary Winifred Eaton, and sentenced to death. He had earlier raped and savagely stabbed Kathleen Dodd, who was alone with her two small children. Aikens's only mitigating circumstance was his age. He was under eighteen when he killed Mrs. Dodd and barely over that age when he murdered Mrs. Eaton. His case, along with the *Furman, Branch,* and *Jackson* cases, were orally argued before the before the Supreme Court on January 17, 1972.[15] (The following month the California Supreme Court rendered its decision in *People v. Anderson*,[16] declaring capital punishment in violation of California's state constitution. Aikens's punishment was modified to life in prison. Because of the *Anderson* ruling by the state court, there was no further reason for Anderson's sentence to be reviewed by the U.S. Supreme Court. His petition was ultimately dismissed,[17] leaving only the *Branch, Jackson,* and *Furman* cases for consideration.)

The Coalition Develops

Justice Brennan made clear his stance on the death penalty at the outset. At a conference of the justices before they recessed for the summer in 1971, he announced his decision to find capital punishment unconstitutional on Eighth Amendment grounds because it was cruel and unusual. None of the other justices would make such a commitment. But by the time summer was over, Brennan learned there might be more to join him.[18]

Douglas and White were heard to say they were undecided.[19] Douglas had been searching for a way to apply the ban on cruel and unusual punishment to the unequal treatment of blacks and whites convicted of capital crimes. Marshall already had directed his clerks to research the "cruel and unusual" arguments against the death penalty.[20] From his private conferences with Potter Stewart, Brennan was sure of another vote.[21] Beyond that, his notes reveal little of his efforts between the fall of 1971 and January 17, 1972, when oral argument was scheduled.

But in September 1971, before the argument of the cases, eighty-five-year-old Hugo Black and seventy-two-year-old John Harlan resigned due to ill health.[22] Both passed away within a few months thereafter. Black's leaving the court was, of course, not a loss to the Fund's efforts to invalidate the death penalty, but Harlan was harder to figure. He often opposed the Warren Court's majority views, but he nevertheless had endorsed a broad interpretation of the Fourteenth Amendment's Due Process Clause. In their places, Nixon nominated Lewis F. Powell Jr. and William H. Rehnquist.[23] Powell was sixty-four years old, a business attorney and former president of the American Bar Association, and had published articles critical of the Warren Court for its civil liberties stance. He wrote that the court had given defendants too many rights that were now "abused and misused by criminals." Rehnquist was an assistant attorney general in the Office of Legal Counsel from 1969 to 1971.

In this capacity he became the chief lawyer to Attorney General John Mitchell. He took a restrictive view of the Fourteenth Amendment, finding that it "does not prohibit even foolish or unauthorized information gathering by the government." After his appointment he was considered the most conservative of the justices, almost always favoring the prosecution in criminal cases.

Though the new justices had hardly replaced votes for abolition, the Burger Court now had a conservative look that made it difficult to imagine an Eighth Amendment victory for Fund lawyers.

On the morning that arguments were to be delivered, Marshall handed Brennan a typed draft of his opinion that capital punishment serves "no valid purpose and is repugnant to contemporary standards of decency."[24] Marshall also reported to Brennan that he had given Stewart a copy of it, an indication that Stewart was also on board. Despite having at most four committed votes, Brennan proudly wrote in his notes, "From being the lone dissenter, there was now at least a chance that WJB [Brennan] would be in the majority."[25]

Oral Argument

Next came the oral arguments. None of the counsel, of course, had any idea of the nature of any backroom discussions that had taken place. The first case called was *Aikens v. California*. Anthony Amsterdam was the Fund's counsel representing Aikens, and Ronald George, the deputy attorney general, represented the state of California. Stewart, Douglas, and Marshall peppered each attorney with questions, first Amsterdam by Stewart, then George. Stewart asked Amsterdam if there were any mandatory death statutes remaining. Douglas asked George whether he had any statistics showing the kinds of people executed. Stewart questioned George on the deterrent effect of capital punishment. Marshall questioned the evolving meaning of "cruel and unusual." The second case called was *Furman v. Georgia*. Again Amsterdam was closely questioned—this time by Burger, who asked how other countries had abolished capital punishment. Amsterdam admitted that courts elsewhere usually do not have the power to abolish what has been statutorily authorized.[26] Amsterdam argued again that previous statistical studies had shown how capital punishment was reserved for minorities and the poor.[27]

Rehnquist asked whether those statistics included judge-imposed death sentences. Amsterdam replied they did. Dorothy Beasley of the

State Attorney General's Office spoke for the State of Georgia. Douglas asked her if a state could discriminate as to which persons were put to death. She replied that such action would violate the Fourteenth Amendment. *Jackson v. Georgia* was the third case called. Jack Greenberg spoke for Jackson, and Beasley again represented the state. White asked her if a rare execution for rape would make the punishment unusual. Beasley replied that "unusual" under the Constitution meant the sentence was exotic but not infrequent.

The fourth case was *Branch v. Texas*. Marvin Carson Bruder was counsel for Branch, and prominent law professor Charles Alan Wright spoke for the state. White asked Wright what he thought about infrequency of executions for rapists. Wright replied that infrequency had much to do with due process and equal protection issues but not with whether the sentence was cruel and unusual under the Eighth Amendment.[28]

The Conference Vote

Four days later, on January 21, 1972, the justices convened in the conference chamber adjoining the courtroom to discuss the cases.[29] As was and still is the custom, no one else was allowed inside—no clerks, attorneys, secretaries, or pages.[30] This was the justices' opportunity to speak privately and frankly with one another[31] about the death penalty issues they had so tried to avoid in earlier cases. Unquestionably, the solemnity of the room added to the suspense over how the voting would go. The oak-paneled walls were lined with books on one side reaching from the floor to the ceiling.[32] Over the mantel was the only adornment, a portrait of John Marshall, the longest-serving chief justice, who repeatedly confirmed the supremacy of federal over state law. In the middle of the room stood a rectangular table around which the justices were seated. Custom required the justices upon entering to shake each other's hands to symbolize the harmony of their aims if not of their views.[33]

Chief Justice Burger, who sat on the south side,[34] began the discussion by upholding the death penalty, finding that the rarity of executions did not make them cruel and unusual. He said he had no trouble applying the death penalty to rapists, though he might with respect to lesser crimes.[35] The chief's pronouncements probably had little impact on his colleagues. His intellectual abilities and leadership skills were not well regarded. Brennan harbored particular contempt for one of Burger's opinions, which he described as "among the most ludicrous of his many ludicrous circulations of the year."[36] Burger was depicted as being aloof, plodding, and pompous.[37] He rewarded "his friends with choice assignments," and punished "his foes with dreary ones."[38] Brennan felt Burger had gone "berserk" in his efforts to keep secret the justices' deliberations on the *Furman* case.[39]

The senior associate justice was Douglas, who sat at the north end. Also predictably, Douglas came out against capital punishment, but he found its fault lay in unequal application of death sentences on African Americans, primarily in the South. He said death was being applied without standards and that the "lack of standards makes the system discriminatory." And being "discriminatory in practice, it's unusual under the Eighth Amendment."[40] He considered the *McGautha* case a "wild card" and felt that reversal was "compelled." He believed that statistics had shown the death penalty was being imposed primarily on minority groups.[41] His reference to statistics was a clear indication that Wolfgang's analyses, presented earlier in the *Maxwell* case, were much on his mind.

Blackmun, perhaps in response to Douglas's statistical references, countered that the court should not intrude on the authority of the state legislatures to match the punishment to the crime. Blackmun also acknowledged in the conference that reconciling death penalties for rape with the Constitution was "much harder."[42] Blackmun knew his brethren were fully familiar with the Fund's *Maxwell* brief, which contained the results of the law students' work and the evidence they had gathered in 1965 of discriminatory death sentencing in the South. To his credit, his decision to open this festering wound at the conference by mentioning the *Maxwell* case showed his willingness to directly confront this specter. Three of the dissenters—Burger, Powell, and Blackmun—later discussed *Maxwell* in their written opinions filed in the *Furman* case.

The discussions and votes continued in the order of seniority of the justices' appointment to the Supreme Court.[43] Brennan agreed with Douglas and voted to reverse the death sentences. Then came Stewart. He had rejected the need for standards in the *McGautha* case, joining with Harlan in the majority opinion. But now he found the arbitrary application of capital punishment to be objectionable and also voted to reverse.[44] The four Nixon appointees were in dismay! They did not know then but would learn five months later the reason for Stewart's change of heart. He wrote in his concurring opinion that while racial discrimination in death sentencing had not been proven, "my concurring brothers have shown that if there is any basis for the few to die, it is the unconstitutionally impermissible basis of race."

By "concurring brothers" he most likely meant Brennan, Marshall, and Douglas, who four years earlier had been persuaded by Wolfgang's statistical analyses and had voted to strike down the Arkansas death penalty statute. If so, then the capital punishment survey conducted in 1965 had had an impact far greater than previously believed.

Two more votes to go, and White was next. No friend to the criminal defense bar, he had dissented in *Miranda v. Arizona*[45] to the majority opinion requiring police to advise suspects of their right to remain silent and to speak with an attorney. He also voted with the majority in *McGautha v. California*.[46] But surprisingly this time he too switched his vote. He explained to the other justices: "The nub of the case is that only a small proportion are put to death."[47] He was concerned with arbitrary death-sentencing practices of juries and disapproved of one jury deciding on death while another jury decided on life though faced with the same or similar facts. Because capital punishment was being arbitrarily applied, he felt it was cruel and unusual. Additionally, he believed that the death penalty had been rejected in practice since it was seldom applied.[48]

The last vote for the majority was an easy one. Marshall predictably voted to reverse the Furman cases, leaving only Powell, Blackmun, and Rehnquist to speak. Powell claimed that the Framers never thought of the death penalty as cruel and unusual and that he had found eight cases that supported the penalty's constitutionality.[49] He voted to affirm, as did Rehnquist.[50] Blackmun was conflicted. He agreed the decision to void capital punishment should best be left with the legislatures even though he was personally opposed to the death penalty. Finally, he voted to abstain.[51]

The last justice had spoken, and the voting tally was now complete. Five justices favored reversal, finding that capital punishment violated the Constitution's ban on cruel and unusual punishment. Three had agreed to affirm the death sentences, and one had voted to abstain. The votes were tentative, and the justices were still free to switch positions. But they were all left stunned. The court appeared to be on the verge of changing two hundred years of accepted jurisprudence.

Holding onto White's Vote

Soon after the conference in January, 1972, Brennan received bad news. White had advised his colleagues that he was withdrawing his tentative vote to ban capital punishment. He was uncertain whether he would affirm the death sentences or abstain from voting. Brennan knew White's vote at the conference had been a weak one. White had been clear about his ambivalence. Brennan immediately huddled with Douglas and Marshall to plan how they would respond. They agreed that each would write a separate opinion covering different points and then circulate them with the hope that one or more of their points would have some appeal to White or possibly Powell. They were only one vote shy of a majority.

Douglas proposed arguing that the *McGautha* decision, permitting standard-less death sentencing, allowed juries to racially discriminate as to which defendant would face execution. Marshall indicated that he would cover the history of capital punishment and its limited deterrent effect. And Brennan would make a different point, that because death was "rarely and arbitrarily imposed," it was unusual. Once printed, the drafts could be sent to White and Stewart and maybe others to see whether a sympathetic response might be evoked.[52]

The final versions Marshall and Douglas wrote went much further. Both of them discussed the damage arbitrary death sentencing had wreaked on the entire criminal justice system. They argued that because death was being selectively applied, it fed upon jurors' prejudices against the poor and unpopular minorities. And they referenced an extensive number of articles written by recognized criminologists and sociologists supporting their views. Included were works by noted scholar Hugo Bedau as well as Rupert C. Koeninger's study of capital punishment in Texas from 1924 to 1968. Marshall specifically referenced Wolfgang and Cohen's publication, "Crime and Race, Conceptions and Misconceptions," which discussed the capital punishment survey conducted by the law students in 1965 in Arkansas and elsewhere in the South.[53] Marshall and Douglas also used the National Prisoner Statistics to back up their claims about the disproportionate number of African Americans historically executed.

Then, on February 18, 1972, the justices received word of the California Supreme Court's decision in *People v. Anderson* to find capital punishment unconstitutional under California's Constitution. The *Anderson* decision resolved the *Aikens* case then pending before the court because Aikens's death sentence was rendered in California and could be invalidated by that state's supreme court.[54] There had been a feeling among the justices that the California court was attempting to "beat this Court to the punch." According to Brennan, after a few days had passed the *Anderson* decision was never mentioned again, and it had virtually no impact on the justices' thinking with one exception.

On April 24, Burger distributed a draft of his opinion, which gave a restrictive interpretation of the Eighth Amendment. According to Burger, only "cruel" punishments were prohibited, and capital punishment was not necessarily cruel.[55] On May 12 Brennan received a draft of Lewis Powell's opinion calling for judicial restraint. By then Brennan realized Powell was a lost cause, and all attention turned to White.

Focus on White

Brennan took six weeks before his rough draft was ready. He sent a private copy to Stewart and White. Stewart lavished high praise on Brennan's work and said he would join it. White remained silent. By May, Douglas and Marshall had written their first and second drafts and had circulated and recirculated them. But still no word from White. Brennan learned from one of the clerks that White had isolated himself in his chambers and remained nonconversant and lost in his thoughts. Brennan searched desperately for a way to break through. White's written opinions were often written in the passive voice and relied heavily on the court's case law, not constitutional history. His reasoning was meticulously drawn, and he shunned rhetorical quotations. He admired English appellate opinions, which were written without much fanfare and relied heavily on precedent. During oral argument he frequently questioned whether the Supreme Court should first defer to the state court on the issues at hand. He favored deciding a case on the most limited basis. He was as unpretentious in his personal demeanor as he was in his written opinions.[56]

White had been a deputy attorney general under President Kennedy and was reluctant to accept a Supreme Court appointment when it was offered. He was a modest man with a towering intellect. While in college, he earned a Phi Beta Kappa key. He was awarded a Rhodes scholarship to study at Oxford. He was known affectionately as "Whizzer White" for his fabled football skills. While he was a law student, he played for the Pittsburgh Steelers and later the Detroit Lions. He led the National Football League in rushing while studying law at Yale, where he ranked first in his class. Potter Stewart was a classmate of his. Stewart recalled many times seeing White with his steel-rimmed glasses seated behind a desk in the Yale Law Library, absorbed in his studies. A few days later

Stewart would read about him on the sports pages.[57] White was thought to be the kind of man who usually listened to no counsel but his own.[58]

Perhaps it was Stewart's past association with White at Yale that prompted Brennan to discuss the possibility that Stewart might be able to forge a link with his elusive colleague. One of White's clerks indicated that nothing "we [presumably Brennan, Marshall, and Douglas] could write would make any difference to BRW [White]." Other rumors were circulating about, including one that another of White's clerks tried to foster—that White had decided to approve the death penalty. On June 7 Stewart told Brennan that he was shortly going to meet with White about the *Furman* cases and would report back what he learned.

Powell's Efforts

Meanwhile, Powell was at work trying to form his own majority. He suspected that Stewart and White were unsure of how they would vote and was convinced that he only needed to find sufficient Supreme Court case precedent to box them in. In the *McGautha* case they had already dispensed with the need for standards or a bifurcated trial on the issues of guilt and the penalty. Powell, a light sleeper, worked feverishly in the early morning hours and even gave up time for church to complete his research. He had a string of cases validating the death penalty that would become the focal point for his opinion, but he knew he needed first to counter the principal arguments Brennan, Douglas, and Marshall had raised.[59] He wrote that even if their statistical analyses pointed to the racially discriminatory application of death sentences, that was a matter of only past concern. The segregation of American society, "which contributed substantially to the severity of punishment for intra-racial crimes, is now no longer prevalent in this country." Blacks now sat on juries.[60] He commented on the rape survey performed by the law students in 1965, which was reviewed by the Eighth Circuit Appellate Court in *Maxwell v. Bishop*.[61] "In that case," he wrote, "substantial statistical evidence was introduced tending to show a pronounced disproportion in the number of Negroes receiving death sentences for rape in parts of Arkansas and elsewhere in the South. That evidence was not excluded but was found to be insufficient to show discrimination in sentencing in Maxwell's trial."[62]

And he quoted from Blackmun's earlier opinion that "we are not ready to . . . upset the result reached in every case of a Negro rape defendant . . . on the basis of broad theories of social and statistical injustice." In attacking Wolfgang's work, Powell did not deal with several recent Supreme Court decisions overturning southern convictions where blacks were systematically excluded from grand and petit juries.[63] His argument that racial segregation was "no longer prevalent" in the South only a few years after federal civil rights legislation had been enacted was at best naive and at worst disingenuous. Nevertheless, as one of the newer members of the court, he needed encouragement, and Stewart and White gave him that. They praised the draft of his written opinion for its "thoroughness" and "depth of research."[64] Powell might have been unfamiliar with the long-standing practice in the Supreme Court of paying verbal compliments to one's fellow jurists before smashing apart their written arguments. He took White's and Stewart's comments at face value and bragged to his clerks that he had won the needed majority.[65] Burger also referenced the *Maxwell* case and the irrelevancy of statistics demonstrating racially inspired death sentencing from "the distant past." He wrote: "While no statistical survey could be expected to bring forth absolute and irrefutable proof of a discriminatory pattern of imposition, a strong showing would have to be made, taking all relevant factors into account."[66]

Blackmun likewise could not resist quoting from his Eighth Circuit *Maxwell* opinion about his "distress and concern" over the ultimate sanction.[67] It was as though the dissenters sensed a chilly wind blowing, not only from the liberal wing of the court (Marshall, Douglas and Brennan) but also from the centrists (Stewart and White) that reflected a concern over the abusive use of capital punishment in the South for too long a time. That concern had been seeded by Wolfgang's statistical findings introduced in the *Maxwell* case and reinforced with the statistics in Koeninger's Texas studies, as well as those from the National Prisoner Statistics of racially induced jury sentencing. Burger, Powell, Blackmun, and Rehnquist instinctively knew they had to take on that evidence by reminding their other brethren of the Eighth Circuit's *Maxwell* decision, which rejected "statistical injustice."

The June 9 Conference

June 9 was a big day. The justices all met in conference. Stewart said nothing to Brennan about his discussions with White. Brennan wondered if they had even met. Brennan described the conference as "explosive," following a motion to continue the abortion cases for a year for re-argument. Blackmun said he did not want the country to hear on the same day that the court had struck down both the death penalty statutes and the statutes banning abortion. He feared the near-violent outcry that would follow. Then Douglas countered that it was unlikely capital punishment would be held unconstitutional. He had counted five votes in favor of affirming the death verdicts, specifically those of Burger, White, Blackmun, Powell, and Rehnquist. Blackmun responded that at the January conference White had voted against the death statutes. The justices continued to argue among themselves over which side had the upper hand, and all the while White watched but said not a word.

Stewart's and White's Intentions Revealed

Later in the day, following the conference, Brennan learned from one of Stewart's clerks that Stewart and White had been closeted together. Both were working on the death cases, along with all their clerks. On June 10 and 11, Brennan learned from the clerks that the two justices were writing their respective opinions together. Other than that, they could say nothing more. The mystery intensified when, on June 12, Powell mentioned to Brennan his belief that both White and Stewart were going to join his opinion to affirm the death judgments. Later that afternoon, Stewart's clerk called Brennan to say that a surprise would soon be arriving. And it did, at 4 p.m. Both White's and Stewart's opinions arrived together. With hands palsied with anticipation, Brennan first unfolded White's and read it aloud before his clerks. Then he read Stewart's. Other than some minor differences, both justices had agreed to strike down the death penalty![68]

Powell was crushed. He was incredulous about White's and Stewart's opinions. In *McGautha* they had approved of unguided jury discretion. In *Furman* they attacked that discretion because it yielded arbitrary, random results. Yet they were unwilling to admit they had reversed course. Powell was distressed at having almost won that majority he had tried so hard to form and disgusted with what he considered the specious reasoning of his two fellow jurists.[69]

Stewart later shed some light on the machinations of the past few days. He told Brennan that a deal had to be struck or White would be lost to the Nixon appointees. White had told Stewart he would join Powell and affirm death sentencing in this country unless a sufficiently narrow ground could be found to have the death statutes in their present form declared unconstitutional while leaving open the possibility of their later resurrection. At White's suggestion they agreed to include language that would allow the state legislatures to enact mandatory death sentences for specified crimes. While this language found its way into the final draft of Stewart's opinion, it was absent in White's. Stewart reported he labored for two weeks with White before agreeing to back down from his own positions.[70]

Muzzling Douglas

With victory at hand, Brennan received another jolt. This time his compatriot, Douglas, declared that he was furious with White and Stewart for taking positions inconsistent with what they wrote in the *McGautha* case. Douglas fumed about how they could both oppose the death statutes in the *Furman* cases yet had reached a contrary opinion a year earlier. In keeping with his nickname "Wild Bill," Douglas vowed he would get back at them by giving them a good lashing in his written opinion. Brennan feared that once White and Stewart received a whiff of Douglas's wrath, they would overreact and change their votes. So a friendship of sorts was quietly cultivated between Brennan and the clerk whom Douglas had assigned to do the rewriting. The clerk promised he would show Brennan the new version before it was sent to Douglas for approval. When Brennan received it, his worst fears were confirmed. Brennan described Douglas's rebuke of White and Stewart as "violent." Reluctantly, the clerk agreed at Brennan's insistence to "tone it down." The "attack" was rewritten so as to appear as a mere "tension" between the *Furman* and *McGautha* decisions, and the criticism was buried in a footnote. Apparently Douglas was never told of this change or of Brennan's handiwork. To this day it remains in its final version as "Footnote 11."[71]

After all the written opinions were completed and published, five of the justices (Brennan, Douglas, Marshall, Stewart, and White) had decided to reverse the judgments with directions to vacate the death sentences. The majority could not produce a controlling opinion, so they each wrote separately. The remaining four justices (Burger, Powell, Blackmun, and Rehnquist) dissented, each also writing a separate opinion.

Chapter 9

What the Law Students Set in Motion

For days the news agencies laid siege to the Supreme Court building in Washington, D.C. Reporters camped outside, waiting for any announcements. Finally, Thursday, June 29, 1972, arrived, the last day that the court would convene for its 1971–72 term.[1] Attorneys, litigants, the press, and members of the public packed the gallery,[2] awaiting with anticipation the arrival of the justices. Finally, at about 10 a.m., the marshal announced, "Oyez! Oyez!" and the nine robed men stepped from behind the curtains to take their seats.

Chief Justice Burger, in his deep-toned, sonorous voice, read the names of each case on the docket and a brief recitation of the court's holding. It was only a matter of moments before he arrived at the *Furman-Branch-Jackson* matters. After reciting the nature of the convictions and the sentence of death given by the juries, he tersely pronounced:

> Certiorari was granted limited to the following question: Does the imposition and carrying out of the death penalty . . . constitute cruel and unusual punishment in violation of the Eighth and Fourteenth Amendments? The Court holds that the imposition and carrying out of the death penalty in these cases constitutes cruel and unusual punishment in violation of the Eighth and Fourteenth Amendments. The judgment in each case is therefore reversed insofar as it leaves the death sentence imposed, and the cases are remanded for further proceedings.[3]

Audible gasps could be heard from beyond the bench. Shock waves of disbelief rippled through those in the audience who knew of the cases and what they meant. As quickly and surreptitiously as possible, lawyers and the press corps slipped out of the courtroom to report what they just heard and to read the *per curium* decision. But instead of one opinion with a dissent or two, they discovered nine separate opinions—a highly unusual occurrence. None could agree on identical bases for their decisions. The nine opinions, including those of the four dissenters, were spread over 243 pages or about 50,000 words. The sheer volume of the opinions made the Furman decision the longest ever issued to that time.[4]

Differing Reasons

The wire services broadcast the story within minutes.[5] One day later, on June 30, 1972, the *New York Times* published an article carrying differing public reactions. Lucius Jackson, one of the rape defendants, said, "I've been thinking of death for a long time. Now I can think about life."[6] Governor Ronald Reagan of California predicted passage of a November initiative to restore capital punishment for "cold-blooded, premeditated, planned murder."[7] President Nixon stated his hope that the death penalty would still be reserved for kidnappers and hijackers. Governor Jimmy Carter muted his criticism. He opined that someone convicted of premeditated murder should serve more than a term of years and that "this decision clears the way for us to re-examine all our laws in Georgia."[8]

Some were elated. Jack Greenberg, director of the Fund, predicted "there will no longer be any more capital punishment in America."[9] Governor Dan Evans of Washington said, "States that have the death penalty have not had less crime than those states that have not had it."[10] Earnest Lee Herron, on Death Row in Tennessee, said the decision would help "the poor and the black man."[11] Tony Amsterdam was driving along a freeway near San Francisco when he heard the terse radio announcement. Instantly he was in shock and had to pull to the side of the road, overcome by waves of emotion. He later reported: "I felt free for the first time in years. I thought, 'That job is done. Those guys live.'"[12] Michael Meltsner, by then a Columbia Law School professor, was editing a brief at the kitchen table of a vacation house on Cape Ann, Massachusetts, when he heard the news on the radio. His nine-year-old daughter, Jessie, was lying on a couch across the room deep in a book when she spied her father in tears.

The Dissecting Begins

What had happened? Lawyers from across the country pored over the printed words trying to see whether there was a common thread of logic binding the majority vote together, whether the death penalty was banned for all crimes, and whether it could be revived by future legislation or initiatives tailored to the court's dictates.[13] Reading the dissenters' opinions was important as well to understand the majority's findings and rulings and the fallacies that might lay therein. But what was most stupefying was how this so-called "Nixon Court," in just three years' time, could render a decision more radical from a civil libertarian's viewpoint than anything conjured up by the Warren Court in the preceding sixteen years. Of course, Nixon had appointed none of the justices in the majority.

A sampling of the opinions revealed a range of perspectives and significant conflict.

Justice Brennan spoke of "the dignity of human beings" that the Eighth Amendment was designed to protect. By killing a human being, the state violated that amendment. Nothing could so degrade a person than the taking of his or her life.[14] To this, Justice Rehnquist responded that judicial officers not elected by the people's will, but merely appointed to their positions, should not impose their own values of "truth and justice" on others.[15]

Brennan also argued that a country that rarely imposed the death penalty on those it convicted must have not been doing so either regularly or fairly. Those who suffered the ultimate penalty, he contended, were drawn at random and without a reason that distinguished them from the many other defendants convicted of the same or similar crimes.[16] Stewart joined in this argument, writing, "These death sentences are cruel and unusual in the same way that being struck by lightning" is cruel and unusual. Those on Death Row were chosen by capricious, freakish, and wanton means.[17] Justice White likewise wrote that "the death penalty is exacted with great infrequency . . . that there is no meaningful basis for distinguishing the few cases in which it is imposed from the many cases in which it is not."[18] Douglas also agreed. He quoted an article coauthored by former Supreme Court justice Arthur Goldberg: "[T]he extreme rarity with which applicable death penalty provisions are put to use raises a strong inference of arbitrariness."[19] Burger responded. To say that the rate of imposition is "freakishly rare," he wrote, is "unwarranted hyperbole," declaring, "[I]t is thought that

15% to 20% of those convicted of murder are sentenced to death in States where it is authorized."[20]

Brennan next contended that capital punishment ran against community values. By its rare application, "it has proved progressively more troublesome to the national conscience."[21] Marshall agreed with Brennan's assessment, stating that the American people would be opposed to capital punishment if they were fully apprised of how it was administered in practice, that the costs of executing a defendant most often exceeded the cost of life imprisonment, that no effort was being made in the sentencing process to ferret out likely recidivists, and that the death penalty was not an effective deterrent.[22] Again, Burger gave the unified response of the dissenters: "There are no obvious indications that capital punishment offends the conscience of society to such a degree that our traditional deference to the legislative judgment must be abandoned. It is not a punishment such as burning at the stake that everyone would ineffably find to be repugnant to all civilized standards."[23]

Burger then referenced a 1969 poll showing that 51 percent of the American people in favor of capital punishment, with only 40 percent opposed and 9 percent having no opinion.[24] Powell pointed to repeated efforts by abolitionists to repeal death penalty laws, which regularly were defeated either at the polls or within the state legislative bodies. The resistance to those efforts, he said, manifested a strong desire on the American people's part to maintain death among the arsenal of punishments to be meted out to particularly brutal offenders. And it was speculative to assert that Americans would be so revolted by death as a punishment if they knew more about it. Murder trials that became highly publicized had not shown a lessening of the public's appetite for death.[25]

Next Brennan contended that the threat of death had "no greater deterrent effect than the threat of imprisonment." Someone who planned a murder or rape was not likely to ponder over the likelihood of "a speedy death," particularly where the "risk of death is remote" and the risk of "long term imprisonment is near and great."[26]

Marshall agreed with that assessment, to which Burger replied that a reading of the available empirical evidence showed a stalemate as to whether or not capital punishment provided a deterrent effect. He retorted that the states should not bear the burden of proof on this issue and that it was not for the courts but for the legislatures to decide the appropriate punishment for serious crimes.[27]

White thought that because capital punishment was so rarely imposed, it served no purpose: "[T]he threat of execution is too attenuated to be of substantial service to criminal justice."[28] But Powell disputed White's claim that executions were rare, contending instead that juries returned death verdicts with sufficient regularity.

Douglas claimed that capital punishment was cruel and unusual when applied "selectively to minorities whose numbers are few, who are outcasts of society, and who are unpopular, but whom society is willing to see suffer though it would not countenance general application of the same penalty across the board."[29]

He pointed to statistics from Texas and those quoted in several national publications showing that "the Negro convicted of rape is far more likely to get the death penalty than a term sentence, whereas whites and Latins are far more likely to get a term sentence than the death penalty."[30] Douglas concluded by calling for the striking of capital punishment because of its discriminatory application against minorities and those of "lower castes."[31] Any law applied in such manner, he said, ran afoul of the Equal Protection Clause of the Fourteenth Amendment. Marshall, the only African American on the court, could not agree more. He wrote:

> Indeed a look at the bare statistics regarding executions is enough to betray much of the discrimination. A total of 3,859 persons have been executed since 1930 of whom 1,751 were white and 2,066 were Negro. Of the executions, 3,334 were for murder; 1,664 of the executed murderers were white and 1,630 were Negro; 455 persons, including 48 whites and 405 Negroes were executed for rape. It is immediately apparent that Negroes were executed far more often than whites in proportion to their percentage of the population.[32]

Burger replied that those statistics were meaningless. "It is not enough to show how the death penalty was applied in the distant past."[33] Also, those statistics "cover periods when Negroes were systematically excluded from jury service and when racial segregation was the official policy in many States. Data of more recent vintage are essential."[34]

Marshall narrated a lengthy history of capital punishment in this country. He described how the death penalty was transported from Europe to the United States and then became "tempered considerably." He postulated whether capital punishment's abolition should depend not on "grass roots movements"[35] but on the mandates of the Eighth

Amendment. Powell fumed at this utter disregard for the many death statutes enacted by state legislatures. The majority's approach, he said, ignored history and legal precedent. He believed that the continued existence of the penalty should be determined by the state legislatures who were more in touch with the popular will.

The View Today

The *Furman* opinions are viewed today as an enigma.[36] So many reasons were given for rejecting the death penalty, but no one seemed to loom above the rest. Why the de facto reversal of the *McGautha* holding rendered just a year earlier—that standards were not needed in jury death-sentencing? Why nine separate opinions? And why would the court, so roundly criticized for its activism, take on the ire of the public and the new administration by so quickly tossing out a penalty deeply rooted in American criminal jurisprudence?

Though Jack Greenberg was elated with the result, he acknowledged his confusion over the dizzying display of arguments and counterarguments. He was also puzzled over why the court had so quickly changed course from its ruling in the *McGautha* case one year earlier. *McGautha* had rejected the notion that a jury needed standards to guide it in determining death or life for a convicted felon. By contrast, in *Furman,* Douglas and Brennan both complained of the lack of standards and that juries had uncontrolled discretion that allowed the exercise of whim to decide a man's fate.[37] Stewart and White voiced similar complaints of the wanton and freakish infliction of the penalty,[38] carrying with it no distinction between when death should or should not be imposed. Greenberg could only hypothesize that "superior advocacy" and a couple of state court decisions invalidating capital punishment were the moving forces behind court's abrupt turnabout.[39]

A Slow Evolution

To understand *Furman* requires much more than looking at the four corners of the justices' concurring and dissenting opinions. The 1972 decision wasn't an epiphany for the Supreme Court. There was no one moment of inspiration when a majority of the bench suddenly resolved to abandon the death penalty in this country. The justices had been struggling with the issue since at least 1966, a year before the moratorium on executions began. And from that struggle had emerged a slow evolution of thought.

As the death case appeals kept mounting between 1967 and 1972, the justices became increasingly sensitized to the same issues being advanced. Most noteworthy were the repeated claims of disparate treatment presented in the petitioners' pleadings and briefs—that southern juries had been systematically selecting blacks for death in rape cases. Indications of the justices' increasing awareness of this phenomenon did not appear at once and even today are not altogether visible. Rather, they emerged over the years following a justice's retirement or death, when private notes were laid bare revealing long-ago machinations. The revelations also have come from later opinions written in other cases, when yesterday's battles could be spoken about more freely. These fragments of information can now be pieced together to unwind the *Furman* riddle.

The journey begins with the more recent writings of several of the justices. Brennan, who voted with the *Furman* majority, offered a dissent written sixteen years later in *McCleskey v. Kemp*[40] in which he revealed the "specter of race discrimination" as the determinative factor that propelled the court to strike down Georgia's death penalty statute in the *Furman* case.[41] He said that "the Court regarded the opportunity for the operation of racial prejudice a particularly troublesome aspect of the unbounded discretion afforded by the Georgia sentencing scheme."[42]

In his *McCleskey* dissent, Brennan referred to what five other justices had written in the Furman case that manifested their concern with the discriminatory application of the death penalty. Douglas had pointed to studies indicating that juries were handing out death sentences based on a defendant's race and that "standard-less statutes were pregnant with discrimination."[43] Marshall wrote that "Negroes [have been] executed far more often than whites in proportion to their percentage of the population."[44]

Stewart stated that "my concurring Brothers have demonstrated that, if any basis can be discerned for the selection of these few to be sentenced to die, it is the constitutionally impermissible basis of race."[45]

Burger, one of the dissenters, admitted that the statistics suggested that "Negroes pointedly have been sentenced to death with greater frequency than whites in several States, particularly for the crime of interracial rape."[46]

Powell disagreed with the majority's conclusion that the Eighth Amendment's ban on cruel and unusual punishment forbade death sentences. But he suggested that the Equal Protection Clause in the Fourteenth Amendment might be available for an African American "who could demonstrate that members of his race were being singled out for more severe punishment than others charged with the same offense."[47]

Not to be forgotten are Brennan's own words that the jury in the *Furman* case knew only about the defendant's age and where he worked, both presumably insignificant factors in their decision-making, and "*that he was black.*"[48] Apparently the latter fragmentary fact was all the jury needed to decide Furman must die. Marshall twice referenced articles Wolfgang had authored, one of which concerned the 1965 rape survey.[49] One of the dissenters in *Furman,* Harry Blackmun, acknowledged in a much later case (*Callins v. Collins,* 1994), that "*Furman* aspired to eliminate the vestiges of racism and the effects of poverty in capital sentencing."[50]

His view was joined by two more recent arrivals to the court. In *Graham v. Collins,*[51] Justice Clarence Thomas wrote a concurring opinion that echoed Brennan's comments about the specter of racial discrimination in death sentencing, especially in the South, and the statistics that bore out that conclusion. In particular, Thomas blamed that specter on "the [*Furman*] Court's condemnation of unguided discretion" and the "capricious and irrational" way the death penalty was being applied.[52] In the same case, Justice John Paul Stevens repeated Thomas's contention that "racial discrimination played a significant role in the development of our modern capital sentencing jurisprudence."[53]

Before capital punishment was outlawed in 1972, Stevens wrote, there was reason to believe that "racial discrimination infected the administration of the death penalty, particularly in the southern states and particularly in rape cases."[54]

The *Maxwell* case was much on the minds of the dissenters. Burger used it to support his claim that statistical surveys that evaluate past patterns of discriminatory sentencing are out of date.[55] Powell acknowledged that in *Maxwell* there was "substantial statistical evidence" showing disproportionate death verdicts given blacks "in Arkansas and elsewhere in the South."[56] And Blackmun said he expressed his "distress and concern" over the use of death as a type of punishment in the *Maxwell* case.[57] Some twenty-one years later, in *Callins v. Collins,* he revealed why: "Race . . . continues to play a major role in determining who shall live and who shall die."[58] Just as the majority struggled with this issue of differential capital sentencing, so did the dissenters.

Other Issues

What then of some of the other issues and arguments raised in the *Furman* case—that capital punishment affronted the dignity of the condemned man, that it was administered arbitrarily, that it was not effective as a deterrent to those contemplating criminal behavior, that it offended contemporary standards of decency, and that its usefulness was nil because of its infrequent application? If what Brennan, Blackmun, Thomas, Stevens, Burger, and Powell have said is accurate, then the guiding force behind the *Furman* decision was the concern that racial discrimination pervaded death sentencing. All the remaining issues and arguments that the majority addressed in *Furman,* familiar though they were, seem little more than window dressing. If not necessarily without merit themselves, they did cover what the court could not say explicitly—that capital punishment was being applied in this country according to a defendant's race. In short, reliance on arbitrariness was a surrogate for finding racial selection of the condemned. Not until 1987 did Powell explain why he and other justices on the high court could not admit to the apparent racism that infected southern death verdicts. Doing so, he wrote, would throw "into serious question the principles that underlie our entire criminal justice system. . . . [I]f we accepted . . . that racial bias has impermissibly tainted the capital sentencing decision, we could soon be faced with similar claims as to other types of penalties."[59]

A Clearer Perspective

All of these later writings provide a clearer perspective of not only the *Furman* decision but also what led up to it. First came Wolfgang's statistical evaluations of the data derived from the 1965 fieldwork of the law students. His conclusions became the catapult for the launching of attacks on death penalty verdicts across the South. Then came the arduous process of educating key members of the Supreme Court about the racial disparities in death sentencing, particularly for the crime of rape.

Wolfgang's analyses were played and replayed to the high court, most prominently in *Maxwell v. Bishop.*[60] Brennan, Marshall, Warren, and most particularly Douglas in early 1969 became so incensed at the excessive use of the electric chair on black defendants convicted of raping white women that they united in their efforts to seek standards for capital sentencing by juries. They believed that standards would guide white jurors away from their raw racial prejudices and allow them to focus instead on the severity of the crime and other objective factors. After Warren departed the court, the remaining three (Douglas, Brennan, and Marshall) held steadfast to those views despite the remaking of the "Warren Court" by Nixon and the later remand of the *Maxwell* case[61] on grounds unrelated to the issue of standards.

Because Brennan, Marshall, and Douglas were a minority, they had to win over two other justices to their viewpoint if the death statutes, particularly those in the South, were ever to be nullified. So they shifted their emphasis from asserting racism in death sentencing to the very random manner in which capital punishment was being administered (much like being "struck by lightning," according to Stewart).[62] Because that viewpoint created less controversy, it was woven into the opinions of three of the five justices constituting the *Furman* majority. Nevertheless, the specter of race discrimination was what principally goaded Marshall, Brennan, and Douglas and to a lesser extent Stewart and possibly White[63] to change the way the death business in America was done—for to leave it untouched would have countenanced the very evils our system of justice was designed to prevent.

The States Respond

In the wake of *Furman,* some 631 men and 2 women in thirty-two states had their death sentences converted to a term of years in prison.[64] In the days following the court's decision, legislators across the country huddled over the opinions trying to envision a way capital punishment could be constitutionally revived.[65] Justice Burger pointed the way. In his dissent he wrote: "[L]egislative bodies may seek to bring their laws into compliance with the court's ruling by providing *standards for juries and judges to follow in determining the sentence in capital cases* or by more narrowly defining the crimes for which the penalty is to be imposed [emphasis added]."[66]

Legislation was soon introduced to restore capital punishment but with provisions for standards to be given juries. Governor Rubin Askew demanded that all members of Florida's legislature return from their recess immediately after the Thanksgiving holiday. Within days they passed capital punishment legislation devised to address the problems raised in *Furman.*[67] The statute set forth factors a jury must consider before imposing death. Among those were the prior criminal record of the defendant and the manner in which the murder was conducted. Notably, the punishment for rape of an adult person was missing. Death was only reserved for an adult who raped a child. Mississippi and Tennessee soon followed with similar legislation.[68] In California an initiative was passed in November 1972 that amended the state constitution by reintroducing the death penalty.[69] Within four years of issuance of the *Furman* opinions, thirty-five states had restored capital punishment with an eye to addressing the concerns raised in *Furman*.[70]

Among those states, two principal types of death statutes emerged. First were the "guided discretion" laws that incorporated some or all of the American Law Institute's Model Penal Code list of aggravating and mitigating factors. Some state legislatures enacted new standards of their own. Florida's death penalty legislation was of this type. Then there were the "mandatory death penalty" laws that required automatic death for the commission of certain crimes. For instance, North Carolina required death for anyone convicted of first-degree murder, aggravated rape, or aggravated kidnapping. This approach removed any possibility that racism would factor into the decision-making since juries would have no discretion when it came to sentencing.[71]

Changing of the Guard

In response to the legislation sprouting across the country, numerous petitions were filed with the Supreme Court seeking to invalidate the new death statutes. Then came another changing of the guard at the court. Douglas, while on vacation, suffered a stroke on December 21, 1974. Initially he insisted on remaining despite his infirmities. Finally, former justice Fortas prevailed upon him to retire.[72] Douglas left on November 12, 1975, and was quickly replaced by John Paul Stevens, nominated by President Gerald Ford. Not until January 1976 did the justices decide on their next step. At an emergency Saturday conference, they considered some fifty death penalty petitions before granting review of five murder cases selected from five different states. Each of those states—Georgia, Texas, Florida, Louisiana, and North Carolina—had enacted new capital punishment laws, all designed to conform to the dictates of the *Furman* decision.[73] The lead case was *Gregg v. Georgia*.[74]

Justice Powell thought for sure the court would invalidate all the statutes on Eighth Amendment grounds. He believed Stevens or Blackmun would join the remaining four justices who had sided with the majority in *Furman*.[75] But Brennan knew better, probably thanks to what law clerks told him about was happening on other chambers.[76] He was also aware that White and Stewart had taken offense at Anthony

Amsterdam's stance during oral argument. Amsterdam asked for a total ban on capital punishment, claiming that the penalty was constitutionally "different" and that if the justices could not accept that view, then the petitioner's case was lost.[77]

The justices met in conference on April 2, 1976. The votes taken showed a seven-vote majority supporting the Georgia and Florida statutes. The validity of the other three statutes was in doubt. Stewart and Stevens both disliked the mandatory death statutes of North Carolina and Louisiana because jurors did not have to consider the character or record of the offender and the circumstances of the offense. Stevens thought that to be a "lawless use of the legal system." Also, no standards were given the jurors to guide them on whether death should be imposed. After the conference, the two justices (Stevens and Stewart) convinced Powell to side with them. The three formed an alliance with Brennan and Marshall, who were opposed to all the statutes. The resulting majority of five voted to strike down only the mandatory death laws passed by North Carolina and Louisiana.[78] The Georgia, Texas, and Florida statutes were upheld and the death sentences affirmed.[79]

Friday, July 2, 1976, was the day planned for the public announcements of the decisions for all five cases. In the robing room, the mood was somber. Considerable resentment had been building between the men. White had refused to share his research with Powell, Stewart, and Stevens. Burger had directed White to write the opinions for all five cases affirming the trial court judgments, leaving Stevens astounded at the chief's presumption that a majority would vote to uphold the Louisiana and North Carolina judgments. Stevens's description of the North Carolina statute as a "monster" probably did not appeal to Burger. Stewart was selected to read the majority opinions. He did so hesitantly, his voice straining at every other enunciation. Marshall delivered a passionate dissent, trying in vain to stifle his anger. Hugely disappointed, he returned home that evening and suffered a heart attack.[80]

Checks Restored

But while capital punishment had been restored in America, its implementation had been dramatically changed. No longer could a properly behaving jury indulge in its "unfettered discretion" and allow racial bias to influence a death verdict. Instead, it would supposedly have to weigh and be guided by objective factors—the aggravating and mitigating circumstances of a crime as defined by state law. The jurors' deliberative process had become more structured and disciplined. And no longer could a defendant be coerced to remain silent both during the guilt and penalty phases of a trial. With bifurcated proceedings, he or she could wait until the penalty phase before testifying. The *Gregg* decision and the accompanying cases also approved special procedures for state appellate review of the defendant's death sentence to insure it was imposed based on the facts of the case and by comparison with penalties imposed in similar cases.[81]

Today, these rules generally apply in any state with death laws, though the high court has tinkered with them over time. For instance, since the *Gregg* decision, the court has required that a jury hear all relevant mitigating evidence that might avoid a death sentence for the defendant.[82] And it has struck down statutes providing for excessively broad or vague aggravating factors such as "especially heinous, atrocious or cruel."[83] But the states have generally expanded their lists of aggravating circumstances qualifying a defendant for execution. In California, for instance, the penal code provides for seventeen "special circumstances," including the intentional killing of a victim because of his or her race, color, religion, nationality, or country of origin.[84] In Florida, the application of aggravating and mitigating factors was removed from the jury and given solely to the judge. Presumably, an experienced trial judge would be less influenced by extraneous factors such as race and more likely to apply the standards consistently. However, in 2002 the court held in *Ring v. Arizona*[85] that the right to a jury trial guaranteed under the Sixth Amendment requires a jury to make factual determinations on which a sentencing increase is based. Therefore, capital sentencing schemes allowing only judges to find if aggravating factors are present to warrant death are unconstitutional. Only juries can make those determinations.

Standards Spread

The use of standards has also spread to sentencing in non-capital cases. Marvin Frankel, a U.S. district court judge, largely instigated this expansion. In 1973 he published his book, *Criminal Sentences: Law Without Order*.[86] Frankel's book became a sensation within the country's legal community and influenced the lay public as well. The book was short, and Frankel's ideas were delivered pungently and with a persuasive style. He showed the public how criminal sentencing was done from an insider's vantage point. It was a book by a judge who knew what was wrong with judging.

Frankel complained of the patchwork of sentences that had cropped up across the country for crimes committed by similar defendants under similar circumstances. Frankel called federal criminal sentencing "lawless" because it lacked consistency and predictability.[87] He wedded his anger at the state of affairs with eloquent writing, arguing that federal judges were influenced by the same irrelevant factors such as race and class prejudice that had plagued jurors in capital cases. "There are powerful indications," he wrote," that . . . black people have drawn harsher sentences than whites for essentially similar crimes in essentially comparable circumstances."[88] He then examined the "bare statistics regarding executions [which] is enough to betray much of the discrimination."[89] He bewailed the longer periods of imprisonment given blacks and other minorities and urged the adoption of standards that would limit a judge's discretion so as to insure greater uniformity in sentencing.

The Fund, in its briefs filed in the *Maxwell, McGautha,* and *Furman* trilogy of cases, had argued that death sentencing was "arbitrary," "wanton," "capricious," and "freakish." Those same words appeared to have found their way into Justices White's and Stewart's concurring opinions in the *Furman* case and again into Frankel's book. But as emphasized by Justices Brennan, Douglas, and Marshall (and suggested by Stewart), behind this morbid lottery system of capital punishment lay the specter of racial discrimination, sometimes well camouflaged but ever present.

Frankel agreed with this assessment and made specific references to the *Furman* decision. He quoted Marshall's comparison of the number of blacks and whites executed since 1930. He concluded that because federal judges had no guideposts by which to sentence those convicted of non-capital crimes, it was widely suspected that "racial or religious prejudices"[90] and other forms of hidden biases played significant roles. Frankel urged the formation of a sentencing commission that would formulate a checklist of factors that would be coupled with a numerical or objective grading of offenses. He called for a narrowing of judicial discretion in non-capital sentencing to avoid influences of racial and class prejudices in much the same way that the Fund had urged the narrowing of jurors' discretion in death sentencing.

Frankel's Background

Frankel's concern for the "little guy" is understandable, considering the hardscrabble circumstances of his early life. He was raised in Newark, New Jersey. His father, who had only advanced to the third grade, thought little of education and believed his son had no need of it either. As a young boy, Frankel witnessed his mother's physical abuse and was a victim of his father's wrath as well. When he was around ten years old, his mother left the home, taking Marvin with her. Frankel escaped his family troubles by spending hours at his school's library. Soon after he graduated from high school, he left home following yet another vicious argument with his father. Virtually penniless, he entered Queens College, which then offered affordable prospects for New Yorkers to gain a higher education. He received his B.A. degree in 1943. He was so smart and articulate that he had no difficulty sailing through Columbia Law School with high grades and honors. He became editor-in-chief of the *Columbia Law Review*.[91]

After graduation in 1948, he went to Washington, D.C., to work for the Justice Department in the Supreme Court Section of the Claims Division. A series of career moves began in 1951. He was hired by the National Labor Relations Board, then by the Solicitor General's Office, and finally went into private practice in New York. He taught at Columbia Law School for three years while maintaining close ties with the Legal Defense Fund. He was a law school classmate of Jack Greenberg, the Fund's director, and became an important advisor. Frankel, upon Greenberg's request, helped assemble a faculty to teach Fund-cooperating attorneys about recent developments in civil rights law.[92] He was a frequent visitor to the Fund's New York offices. He was only a subway ride away from Columbia Law School, where he taught. Frankel invited the Fund's attorneys, such as Frank Heffron, to speak to his classes at the Law School.[93]

Frankel was also a member of the board of advisors of the Law Students Civil Rights Research Council (LSCRRC) in the mid-1960s.[94] LSCRRC was established with Greenberg's help, giving the organization a "start-up contribution" of $5,000.[95] As a board advisor, Frankel presumably would have known of the Fund's plans to conduct a rape–capital punishment survey in the South in 1965 and the reasons for it. In that same year, Frankel was appointed by President Johnson to a district court judgeship.[96] He quickly established himself as a thoughtful jurist, though he set very high standards for the lawyers who appeared before him, and his law clerks would describe him as a "notoriously difficult boss."[97]

Following his book's publication in 1973, Frankel became a regular contributor to a Yale workshop that brought together the nation's criminal justice policy makers once a month to formulate legislative reforms for sentencing. The workshop's report, titled "Toward a Just and Effective Sentencing System: Agenda for Legislative Reform," was published in 1977.[98] Soon Frankel had the ear of Senator Ted Kennedy, who agreed to base his proposed legislation in 1975 for federal sentencing reforms on an early draft of the workshop's report that had adopted many of Frankel's ideas.[99]

New Legislation

Kennedy became aware of a growing consensus of the country's criminal justice experts that rehabilitation of inmates was not working in the prisons. Rehabilitation was the foundation on which "indeterminate sentencing" had been built. Indeterminate sentencing called for maximum periods of imprisonment established by state and federal statutes with the sentencing decisions in particular cases being left to each judge's notions of justice. Discretion was also granted to the parole boards to release a defendant sooner than his maximum term because of good behavior or his efforts at rehabilitation, but high rates of recidivism reflected the limited resources made available to make rehabilitation a realistic goal.[100] Kennedy's two Senate bills introduced in the 1970s parroted Frankel's call for establishing a sentencing commission that would develop objective standards to guide federal judges to more consistent results. Thus began the birth of the "determinate sentencing" laws, which now are common in the federal courts and in the courts of a number of states.

Determinate sentencing prescribes confinement for a fixed or minimum period that is specified by statute. Courts are required to apply rules governing aggravating and mitigating circumstances to determine the length of confinement. Judicial discretion is restricted to a consideration of a prescribed set of factors.

Kennedy's proposed legislation initially went nowhere in Congress. Then, in the early 1980s, he teamed up with an unlikely pair of bedfellows, Senators Strom Thurmond of South Carolina and Orrin Hatch of Utah, both politically conservative Republicans. They viewed federal judges as being too lenient in sentencing criminals and wanted harsher terms for convicted defendants. A compromise was reached. In 1984, with the help of the Senate Republicans, Kennedy reintroduced his earlier proposals in new form, and the Sentencing Reform Act was born.[101]

Kennedy laid much of the credit for its passage on Marvin Frankel, dubbing him the "Father of sentencing reform."[102] The Act called for establishing a sentencing commission that would draft guidelines for federal judges, the same proposal outlined in Frankel's earlier book. The guidelines would be neutral as to race, sex, national origin, and socioeconomic status of the offender. Rehabilitation was abandoned as a goal. Instead, the purpose of incarceration was to deter criminals from committing further crimes, to incapacitate and educate them, and to acknowledge society's need to seek retribution for the harms inflicted. All sentences would be determinate and based on a complicated formula that reflected the seriousness and characteristics of the offense and the criminal history of the offender. The offender's sentence would be calculated on the grid, from which a judge could vary only within a narrow range and only after giving justifying reasons.[103]

The Sentencing Reform Act began to be used in the federal courts in 1987. At the state level, thirty-four jurisdictions followed suit. They created similar sentencing commissions, and as many as eighteen states, at different points, adopted sentencing guidelines.[104] In 2005 the Supreme Court in *United States v. Booker*[105] held that any enhancement of sentences by judges deprives a defendant of the right to have the facts affecting his sentencing determined by a jury of his peers. As a result of that decision, guidelines are now viewed as being advisory.[106] Nevertheless, the guidelines today remain influential in sentencing,[107] are largely still followed, and continue to influence reform efforts here and abroad.

The Dominos Topple

From my perspective, the events leading to the now widespread use of "guided discretion" statutes in capital and non-capital cases all had their origins in that boiling, violent summer of 1965, when twenty-eight law students roamed through eleven southern and border states. Each episode in this unfolding chapter of American jurisprudence triggered the next one, much like a string of dominos toppling one upon another. The data extracted by the students; Professor Wolfgang's statistical analysis and conclusions; the *Maxwell* decision; the minority alliance formed by Brennan, Marshall, and Douglas; the majority decision in the *Furman* case; the new legislation passed by the state legislatures; the Supreme Court's approval of the guided-discretion statutes; Judge Frankel's book; and the federal sentencing standards enacted in 1984—each event played a role leading to the next until finally criminal sentencing, including the death penalty, had been transformed from an arbitrary, discriminatory exercise of judicial power and brutal tool of race control, to a more measured and objectively applied system of punishment.

Chapter 10

To Save a Mockingbird

Yet another domino—a last piece of unfinished business from the law students' 1965 survey of southern rape cases—needed to fall. Of the sixteen states that had authorized death for the crime of rape in 1971, only three states, Georgia, North Carolina and Louisiana, included rape among capital felonies after the *Furman* decision in 1972.[1] Discriminatory death sentences for black males convicted of raping white women were off-limits. So most state legislatures had gotten that message.

In 1976 the Supreme Court struck down the death statutes of North Carolina and Louisiana because the death penalty was made mandatory for certain crimes.[2] The court reasoned that automatic death penalties violated the ban on cruel and unusual punishment because no consideration was given to the character and record of the offender, among other matters.

Georgia was then left as the only state authorizing death for rape. Still unresolved was whether the high court would allow Georgia's death statute to stand. Would it also be stricken because historically it had been discriminatorily and arbitrarily applied? A statute not administered evenhandedly was tainted with unconstitutionality and could not be enforced even where both the victim and the defendant were white.[3] The discrimination issue had been raised at the state appellate level and summarily dispensed with by the Georgia Supreme Court.[4]

Or, would the high court find an alternative reason to declare the statute's unconstitutionality so as to avoid the prickly thicket of Georgia's racist sentencing practices? In 1977 the answer came. The crime Wolfgang and the law students had studied a decade earlier would be scrutinized in *Coker v. Georgia*.[5]

It all began on the evening of September 2, 1974, when several inmates escaped from the Ware County Correctional Institution in Georgia. While attending an Alcoholics Anonymous meeting at the prison chapel, one of them held up a six-pound steel bar and warned the corrections counselor, George Silver, "Be still . . . this is an escape." Silver asked those not involved to stand behind him. Several inmates complied. Three inmates did not, among them Ehrlich Anthony Coker. Those three used the steel bar to rip through the plywood ceiling. They then lifted themselves through the hole and escaped by dashing across the chapel roof to another building not enclosed by the prison fence. From there they jumped to the ground and fled into the nearby woods.

The Crime

Three hours later, Coker, a white man still dressed in prison clothes, broke open the back door of a young couple's home. The husband, Allen Carver, only sixteen years old, was helping his wife in the kitchen while their three-week-old son slept in a back bedroom. Coker directed Carver's young wife to tie her husband's hands and feet. Coker then pulled off Carver's belt and used it to tie him to the bathroom shower rod. With Carver now disabled, Coker grabbed some clothes, money, and a four-inch steak knife from the kitchen. He then gagged Carver with one of his wife's underpants.

Next, he turned his attention to Mrs. Carver. She had only recently left the hospital following childbirth and was still weak. Using the knife he found, he forced the terrified young woman to submit. After he had finished his rape, he directed her into the couple's car while warning her husband not to call the police or "your wife is gong to be dead." A few hours later Coker was arrested, and Mrs. Carver was released.

After a trial, Coker was found guilty of several offenses, including rape, for which he was sentenced to death.[6] The jury had had enough of him after learning of his past crimes, which included two rapes and the murder of one of his rape victims. The Georgia Supreme Court affirmed the death verdict, and Coker took his case to the U.S. Supreme Court. There the justices split, with White, Stewart, Blackmun, and Stevens concluding that the sentence of death for the crime of rape was grossly disproportionate, excessive, and therefore forbidden by the Eighth Amendment because no human life had been taken. Justices Brennan and Marshall found the death penalty to be cruel and unusual and, therefore, should be held unconstitutional on that ground.

Justice Lewis Powell gave a clue as to his leanings in an interchange he had with David Kendall, Coker's attorney, during oral argument. "What would be an appropriate punishment for a convicted rapist serving life who escapes and commits another rape?" Powell asked Kendall. "Incarceration," replied Kendall. Powell, looking at his colleagues, wryly noted, "The same punishment he had before." Powell would later write that because the woman had not been brutally raped and suffered no permanent injuries, death for Coker was too severe. But Powell did not rule out capital punishment where the circumstances were more egregious.[7] Chief Justice Burger and Justice Rehnquist dissented and agreed with the State of Georgia that the sentence fit the crime. The majority also observed that Georgia was the sole jurisdiction left in the country that still executed defendants convicted of rape of an adult. Absent from the majority's discussion was whether Georgia had been applying the statute in a discriminatory manner. Amazingly, Georgia's past use of the electric chair on black males convicted of raping white women was never mentioned.

Racism as a Factor

But did race play its silent role in the decision, as it had in *Furman*? Had the majority opted to ban the death penalty for rape on one basis—that the penalty was excessive and disproportionate to the crime—when it really had in mind another reason? And was that disguised reason the belief that predominantly southern white jurors must never again be allowed to use death in punishing black males for interracial transgressions? Justice Brennan thought so, and he would have known because he sat on the *Coker* case and was privy to the justices' private discussions. In one of his later dissenting opinions,[8] he mentioned Wolfgang's statistical evidence presented in *Maxwell* that pointed to discriminatory death-sentencing practices.[9] In the very next paragraph he wrote,

> Although the [Coker] court did not explicitly mention race, the decision had to be informed by the specific observations on rape both by the Chief Justice and Justice Powell in *Furman*. Furthermore, evidence submitted to the court indicated that black men who committed rape, particularly of white women, were considerably more likely to be sentenced to death than white rapists.[10]

Brennan's statements reveal the long-lasting impact the statistical studies had on the justices, beginning with the *Maxwell* case in the late 1960s, continuing to *Furman* in 1972, and then to the *Coker* case in 1977.

In addition to the lingering effects of the earlier evidence presented in *Maxwell,* the justices hearing the *Coker* case were likely moved by the racism issue for another reason. The racial issue was openly and unabashedly presented in the briefing preceding oral argument. Fund lawyer David Kendall, Coker's attorney, provided statistics showing that in southern states, execution for rape had been typically based on race. Before the Civil War in Georgia, a white man who raped a black woman would usually pay a fine. Perhaps he might receive a short time in jail. A slave or even a "free person of color" who dared attempt to rape a white woman, would be hanged—or worse. That was the southern way, and it had never really changed, even well into the twentieth century. Most significantly, the petitioner's brief addressed Wolfgang's examinations of sentencing patterns from Georgia and across the country[11] and used them to show that "charges of racially discriminatory application of capital punishment were 'most often justified when the penalty was inflicted for rape.'"[12]

And there is no likelihood the *Coker* justices would have forgotten about Wolfgang's rape studies. A year earlier in *Gregg v. Georgia,* his conclusions were cited in the appendix to the brief filed by the U.S. government as *amicus curiae,*[13] and by the time of the *Coker* ruling, many eminent academicians had described Wolfgang's studies as "one of the 'most definitive pieces of research ever done on capital punishment.'"[14]

The court would later apply the same proportionality test used in the *Coker* case in other contexts. For example, in 1986 the justices held that the criminally insane could likewise not be executed.[15] In 2002 the court recognized that executing those suffering from mental retardation offended society's evolving standards of decency and forbade the practice.[16] In 2005 it banned death for defendants who committed their crimes prior to their eighteenth birthdays.[17] And in 2008 the court held that a death sentence for one who raped but did not kill a child, and who did not intend to assist another in killing the child, was unconstitutional under the Eighth and Fourteenth Amendments.[18] In each of those cases, the court found the death penalty to be cruel and unusual either because it was disproportionate to the crime for which the defendant was convicted or disproportionate to the type of offender convicted.

A Final Effect

The racial statistics first presented in *Maxwell* in the late 1960s had one final, if modest, effect. They had sensitized the justices to racism's insidious reach into the jury room and thereby prodded the court into keeping a watchful eye on death verdicts. In *Zant v. Stephens,*[19] the Supreme Court specifically held that race was not an appropriate factor to consider when deciding on death. In *Turner v. Murray,*[20] Justice White, speaking for the plurality, found that there was some risk of racial prejudice influencing a jury whenever a crime that is charged involves interracial violence. That prejudice becomes especially serious when it affects capital sentencing "in light of the complete finality of the death sentence." In that case a black defendant was convicted of murdering a white shopkeeper. Could it be that White's penchant for banning arbitrary death sentences in *Furman* was also founded on concerns over racism? Clearly that was so in the *Turner* decision that White wrote fourteen years later. In *Turner,* the court vacated the death sentence because the trial judge had failed to question the jurors about racial prejudice. In Justice Stevens's dissent in *Graham v. Collins,* he expressed this concern:

> An aggravating factor that invites a judgment as to whether a murder committed by a member of another race is especially "heinous" or "inhuman" may increase, rather than decrease, the chance of arbitrary decision making, by *creating room for the influence of personal prejudices.* In my view, it is just such aggravating factors, which fail to cabin sentencer discretion in the determination of death eligibility. [Emphasis added.][21]

Stevens also expressed concern about racism when a statute overly restricts what the jury can consider as mitigating factors. Under those circumstances, "there is more, not less, reason to believe that the sentencer will be left to rely on irrational considerations like racial animus." And in *Callins v. Collins,*[22] Justice Blackmun wrote that "arbitrariness inherent in the sentencer's discretion to afford mercy is exacerbated by the problem of race. . . . [R]ace continues to play a major role in determining who shall live and who shall die. . . . [A]s long as the sentencer has discretion, he can discriminate."[23]

The Baldus Study

In *McCleskey v. Kemp,*[24] the black defendant was convicted on two counts of armed robbery and one count of murder. At the penalty hearing, the jury imposed the death penalty because he did not provide any mitigating circumstances. The Georgia Supreme Court affirmed the trial court's decision and denied a petition for writ of certiorari. The defendant then filed a petition for a writ of habeas corpus in federal court in which he alleged the state's capital-sentencing process was administered in a racially discriminatory manner in violation of the Fourteenth Amendment. The defendant based his claim on a study indicating a risk that racial consideration entered into capital-sentencing determinations.

In support of this position, the Fund proffered a statistical study performed by Professors David C. Baldus, Charles Pulaski, and George Woodworth that showed a disparity in the imposition of the death sentence in Georgia based on the race of the murder victim and, to a lesser extent, the race of the defendant. The Baldus study actually comprised two sophisticated statistical studies that examined over two thousand murder cases occurring in Georgia during the 1970s. The raw numbers collected by Professor Baldus—a worthy successor to Marvin Wolfgang, who died in 2011—indicated that defendants charged with killing white persons received the death penalty in 11 percent of the cases, but defendants charged with killing blacks received the death penalty in only 1 percent of the cases. The raw numbers also indicated a reverse racial disparity according to the race of the defendant: 4 percent of the black defendants received the death penalty, as opposed to 7 percent of the white defendants.

Baldus also divided the cases according to the combination of the race of the defendant and the race of the victim. The study found that the death penalty was assessed in 22 percent of the cases involving black defendants and white victims, 8 percent of the cases involving white defendants and white victims, 1 percent of the cases involving black defendants and black victims, and 3 percent of the cases involving white defendants and black victims. Similarly, Baldus found that prosecutors sought the death penalty in 70 percent of the cases involving black defendants and white victims, 32 percent of the cases involving white defendants and white victims, 15 percent of the cases involving black defendants and black victims, and 19 percent of the cases involving white defendants and black victims.

Baldus subjected his data to an extensive and demanding analysis, taking account of 230 variables that could have explained the disparities on nonracial grounds. One of his models concludes that even after taking account of thirty-nine nonracial variables, defendants charged with killing white victims were 4.3 times as likely to receive a death sentence as defendants charged with killing blacks. Thus, the Baldus study indicated that black defendants, such as McCleskey, who killed white victims, had the greatest likelihood of receiving the death penalty.

The Supreme Court held that the statistical study did not present substantial evidence that would require a reversal of petitioner's conviction. For a defendant to meet his burden of proof of racially discriminatory practices, he or she must provide "exceptionally clear proof" that in his or her particular case, discrimination had influenced the outcome. Then, with either resignation or indifference, the court concluded that "apparent disparities in sentencings are an inevitable part of our criminal system."

Because McCleskey's sentence was imposed under Georgia sentencing procedures that focus discretion "on the particularized nature of the crime and the particularized characteristics of the individual defendant," the court found that McCleskey's death sentence was not "wantonly and freakishly" imposed and not disproportionate within any recognized meaning under the Eighth Amendment. But for Justice Lewis Powell, writing for the majority, there must have been something greater at stake than merely reaffirming the rules and principles previously announced in *Gregg*. If McKleskey's claims were given credence, they would jeopardize

> the principles that underlie our entire criminal justice system. The Eighth Amendment is not limited in application to capital punishment, but applies to all penalties. . . . Thus, if we accepted McCleskey's claim that racial bias has impermissibly tainted the capital sentencing decision, we could soon be faced with similar claims as to other types of penalty. Moreover, the claim that his sentence rests on the irrelevant factor of race easily could be extended to apply to claims based on unexplained discrepancies that correlate to membership in other minority groups, and even to gender.[25]

Yale law professor Robert A. Burt suggested another, more sinister reason for the court's decision to disregard the statistics. He wrote that to acknowledge them would impeach "society's commitment" to "the rule of law":

> The ideal is impeached because this law enforcement regime devalues blacks as such. The practical achievement of the rule of law . . . is also undermined because insofar as blacks perceive their systemic devaluation by the dominant whites, they are provoked toward overt acts of racial hostility. . . . Thus comes a spiraling self-fulfilling impetus toward civil warfare: the destruction of our mutual confidence, even the bare tolerance, on which the civic order depends.[26]

Even worse, according to Professor Dennis Dorin of the University of North Carolina, would be the acknowledgment that "hundred of blacks in rape cases went to their deaths as victims of racially discriminatory sentencing. It would have suggested that perhaps thousands more had suffered the same fate through murder sentences."[27]

Professor Baldus's efforts to follow in Wolfgang's tracks had failed. Baldus did not have the advantage of several years to allow his statistical studies to percolate in appellate cases through the state and federal court system, thereby acclimatizing the justices to the data.

By contrast, Wolfgang's studies appeared initially in a scattering of lower court decisions, then in a few federal appellate cases before finally arriving before the Supreme Court in *Maxwell.* Much like artillery fired from naval vessels before an amphibious landing, the Wolfgang studies peppered the Supreme Court's shoreline, preparing the battlefield until the justices were ready to tackle serious reforms in the *Furman* case.

Baldus had another disadvantage: his statistics were generated long after the civil rights movement of the early 1960s, when fewer protections against racism were in place. By 1987, when *McCleskey* was decided, the concern over racism had subsided after a plethora of civil rights legislation and court decisions had produced at least surface protections against jury mischief. Finally, by 1987 three Republican presidential administrations had planted a conservative majority on the Supreme Court that holds sway to this day.

The *McCleskey* case did demonstrate, through the dissenting opinions, the court's continuing concern with the effects of racial decision-making, especially by jurors. Justices Marshall, Blackmun, Brennan, and Stevens were all troubled that Georgia's guided-discretion statute had not fully worked as planned. Indeed, the 1980s saw a more conservative court water down protections against unregulated discretionary decision-making put in place to address the evil identified in *Furman* and to restrict arbitrary death sentencing. *McCleskey* confronted the justices with powerful proof, the result of methods even more elaborate than those employed in 1965, that the race of a homicide victim significantly affected death sentencing but it also collided with the now entrenched unwillingness of court majorities to admit that their previous efforts to ease the problem had failed. And when confronted with a choice between allowing racial selection to continue or to abolish (or just to adopt more stringent procedural protections), Justice Powell in *McCleskey* decided discretion had to be maintained. When Powell compared racial discrimination in capital cases to how differences in personal appearance might bring about differential results, it was clear that the court had accepted the notion that while weighing race on the scales of justice was inevitable, greater efforts to ameliorate the practice were not going to be considered. Of course, Congress and the states were still free to pass legislation aimed at authorizing a defendant to prove racial discrimination by statistics. Bills in Congress seemed likely to pass in the nineties but ultimately failed; however, in 2009 a North Carolina statute specifically allowed statistics to support such claims. Its fate in the courts is still undecided.

Literary Parallel?

In 1960 Harper Lee of Alabama published *To Kill a Mockingbird*. Her hugely successful novel takes place in the fictional town of Maycomb, Alabama. A black man, Tom Robinson, stands accused of raping a young white female, Mayella Ewell. Yet the evidence of his innocence is compelling. During the trial, Tom's white attorney, Atticus Finch, notices that Tom's left hand is withered and realizes that Tom could not have hit Mayella's face on the right side. Atticus suggests that her father, who repeatedly abused her, may have inflicted Mayella's injuries.

Then Tom testifies as to what really happened. Mayella made advances on him; her father saw them, became enraged, and beat her. Atticus appeals to the jurors to put aside their racial prejudices and return an acquittal. Nevertheless, the all-white jury takes only two hours to convict Tom of rape and sentences him to death. Tom is later shot and killed while trying to escape from jail. The mockingbird in the title of the book symbolizes that which is innocent and inoffensive, such as Tom.

It is comforting to believe that no such trial would take place today with the many post- *Furman* safeguards now in place. But legal institutions are checkered with flaws. In 1984 a black marine, William Henry Hance, was arrested for the murder of several women, both white and black, around Columbus, Georgia. He had an IQ of 75 to 79 points, placing him close to being mentally retarded. He was prosecuted in both the military and Georgia state criminal courts. His military convictions were vacated in 1980. He was found guilty in the civilian court for the murder of Gail Jackson, a black prostitute. In his second sentencing trial (the first one was reversed), all the jurors were white except for one twenty-six-year-old black woman, Gayle Lewis Daniels. After initially leaning toward life imprisonment, all the jurors except Daniels switched course and opted for death. According to Daniels, she held out for life because she "did not believe (Hance) knew what he was doing at the time of his crimes."[28] One white juror, Patricia Lemay, reported, "There was a good deal of racial tension in the jury room, and the other jurors made repeated comments between themselves about the race of the defendant and the one black woman holding out. I specifically remember one white woman, back in the hotel room, stating, 'the nigger admitted he did it; he should fry.'"[29] Lemay went on:

> The pressure was particularly strong because of Mother's Day, which was that Sunday. I finally gave in and went along with a death sentence because someone said if the jury was hung, there would have to be another trial. If I had known a hung jury meant the judge would impose a life sentence, I would definitely have held out for life. Gayle continued to hold out. She refused to take part in the vote for death.[30]

The story worsens. Lemay said she heard one white woman say that if Hance got death there would be "one less nigger to breed." She also heard descriptions of Hance as a "typical nigger" and that he would be "just one more sorry nigger that no one would miss."[31]

The other jurors then told Daniels that if she refused to join them, she could be convicted of perjury because she had previously told the court she could vote for the death penalty. Daniels still held firm. Finally, the white jurors decided to bypass her by reporting to the judge that they were unanimous on a verdict. When all the jurors were polled, Daniels said that she was too intimidated to say how she felt and decided to go along with the death verdict.

Hance exhausted his state court appeals. As his execution date came closer, he filed a petition for a writ of certiorari with the Supreme Court requesting a stay of his death sentence. In *Hance v. Zant,* the court denied both requests. Justice Harry Blackmun wrote a dissent, finding "substantial evidence" that Hance was "mentally retarded as well as mentally ill. There is reason to believe that his trial and sentencing proceedings were infected with racial prejudice."[32]

On March 31, 1994, at 10:10 p.m., he was executed by electrocution.[33] Hance was guilty of his crime, having been convicted of the murder. But if the facts were true as reported, then like the mockingbird Hance should not have been judged to die because of the accident of his birth—his race. Of that, at least, he was "innocent."

The Hance case underlines the continuing risk that prejudice can pose to decision-making, no matter how hard the efforts to prevent it. Just before the *McCleskey v. Kemp* decision was announced in 1987, Justice Antonin Scalia wrote this pessimistic memorandum to his colleagues: "The unconscious operation of irrational sympathies and antipathies, *including racial,* upon jury decisions is real, acknowledged in the decisions of this court, and *ineradicable* [emphasis added]."[34]

Justice Harry Blackmun agreed but could not accept this inevitability. In his dissent, he found Baldus's statistical evidence convincing and showed a "constitutionally intolerable level of racially based discrimination leading to the imposition of his [the defendant's] death sentence."[35] And by 1994, in another dissent, he wrote, "From this day forward I shall no longer tinker with the machinery of death," concluding that capital punishment was irremediably infected with racism. What a turnaround! In 1968 he could not accept Wolfgang's statistical conclusions in the *Maxwell* case. Almost twenty years later, similar evidence convinced him Wolfgang had been right. And by 1994 he declared himself a vote for abolition. And then the final irony: Justice Lewis Powell Jr., who wrote the majority opinion in *McCleskey v. Georgia,* came to a similar conclusion. In the summer of 1991, he confessed to his biographer that if there were one vote he could change, it would be his vote in *McCleskey.* To which he added, "I would vote the other way in any capital case."[36]

Reform Changes

In light of recent studies, however, it appears to me that Scalia's and Blackmun's pessimistic assessments may have been premature. Recent indications suggest that the post-*Furman* reforms have been working. In California the Rand Corporation was commissioned by the Attorney General's Office to study the death penalty in that state. The Rand study found no effect based either on the race of the victim or the defendant.[37] Nebraska commissioned a study headed by Baldus and his colleague George Woodworth. They reached the same conclusion.[38] In New Jersey, that state's supreme court appointed several "special masters" to examine the effects of bias on capital punishment there. Retired Judge David Baime found no effect, whether based on the race of the victim or of the defendant.[39] Although the defendants in white-victim cases were more likely to advance to the death penalty phases of their trials, this was due to differing prosecutorial practices in different counties. Prosecutors in urban centers with a greater number of black-victim crimes sought fewer death penalties than in less populated areas where white-victim crimes predominated.[40]

Other researchers have also concluded that most jurors will try to exclude racial considerations when evaluating the defendant. However, where a great majority of the jurors are white, they will not be as likely to identify with black victims by seeing them as family or friends. And they are more likely to be horrified by the murder of a white than a black. However, the impetus for this reaction comes not from racial hostility but from "the natural product of patterns of interracial relations in our society. It is simply an emotional fact."[41]

A Better Place

Clearly, our judicial system is in a better place than it was before the *Furman* decision in 1972. And this would not have happened but for the pioneering efforts of Anthony Amsterdam, Marvin Wolfgang, Marvin Frankel, Michael Meltsner, Frank Heffron, Norman Amaker, and all the other Legal Defense Fund attorneys, including Jack Greenberg, the Fund director who planned the southern invasion in 1965. What is remarkable about this whirlwind journey through a half-century of sentencing law is where it all began. The seeds were planted in the fertile soil of the discriminatory practices of southern white juries who sent many a black man to the chair for the rape (imagined or otherwise) of a white woman. The Fund was long involved in defending blacks sentenced to death in questionable interracial rape cases. Then came Justice Arthur Goldberg's dissenting opinion in 1963, questioning whether the death penalty should ever be given for the crime of rape. His opinion prompted the Fund's attorneys to expand their efforts to challenge capital punishment as it was applied in the South. The claim would be based on Fourteenth Amendment violations, specifically that black males were being sent to their deaths disproportionately because they had breached the southern social order by having sexual intercourse with a white woman.

The law students played the essential role of gathering the data at a time when most of the South was aflame with racist violence and hate. They confronted dangerous circumstances and with stealth avoided a southern citizenry seething at the second invasion of northern meddlers. The students' success in extracting the data and Wolfgang's expertise in making sense of it began the launch of a "Seven Years' War" through the state and federal courts waged by Amsterdam and the Fund's lawyers. The lawyers emphasized Wolfgang's statistics to the Supreme Court justices in the *Maxwell* case, initially convincing four of them of the need for standards to prevent race from affecting death sentencing. The minority became a bare majority in the *Furman* case that followed. With *Furman,* the pillars came tumbling down. All capital punishment laws throughout this country were declared unconstitutional and void. From the ashes of the old capital punishment laws sprang new ones that included nonracial standards to guide juries, bifurcated (or separate) trials on the issues of guilt and punishment, and regular state appellate review in the hope that it would ensure the constitutional rules were followed. Also from those same ashes emerged standardized sentencing laws for non-capital crimes to prevent judges from committing the same sins as those previously perpetrated by southern white juries.

The success of these developments in removing the scourge of racial sentencing is controversial.[42] Racism does not disappear just because laws and legal procedures are changed. Capital punishment, though less popular, less widespread, and less cited as a cure for crime, is still with us. And with the exoneration of many innocent prisoners, its flaws are now even more obvious than before.

But my experience in 1965 and the events that followed convince me that while much remains to be done, much was accomplished. Mockingbirds have been saved.

"Alone we can do so little; together we can do so much," said Helen Keller. And in this great play, all the characters that swept across the stage of American jurisprudence played vital roles that were interdependent. But the play could not have begun without the first act performed by the twenty-eight young law students who, propelled by their zeal and idealism, scattered across the battlefields of eleven southern states in the summer of 1965, extracting the evidence that would eventually end racism's stranglehold on our sentencing laws.

Epilogue

Where Are They Now?

After the tumultuous summer of 1965, the twenty-eight law students, most toughened and touched by the experience, returned to law school to complete their educations and launch careers in the law. In the intervening decades, they took on all manner of roles. Some gravitated to family law, others to corporate law, while others became legal advocates for the poor. They were a talented lot with several winning honors and awards, and one even having a building named after him.

This epilogue includes a brief look at the later lives of some of those law student researchers, as well as those of the legal advocates who directed the project and the criminologist who made sense of the data recovered. They generously contributed to the author's memories of the research project, though, of course, this book's interpretation of what sprang from those efforts is his alone.

The Law Students

Thomas C. "Tim" Brayton

Brayton completed his studies at the UCLA School of Law, graduating in 1967 and earning admission to the California State Bar the following year. He became a research attorney with the appellate department of the Superior Court of Los Angeles County where he worked for a couple of years before moving on to private practice specializing in family law. He became—and still remains—a partner in the law firm of Jones and Brayton in Claremont, California, and is certified as a family law specialist by the state bar's Board of Legal Specialization.

Philip Brown

Brown also graduated in 1967 from UCLA Law School, where he founded the UCLA chapter of the Law Students Civil Rights Research Council. After law school, Brown began law practice as an associate at a law firm but opened his own practice in Los Angeles in 1969. He is now a partner in Egerman & Brown, LLP, with his brother-in-law Mark Egerman, and specializes in civil litigation, both trial and appellate. He has handled a wide range of matters ranging from securities fraud, general contract/business tort litigation, and institutional lender litigation to will contests, health insurance law matters, financial elder abuse, medical and legal malpractice, and products liability.

Brown served for seven years as a judge pro tem for the Los Angeles Municipal Court, for eight years as an arbitrator for the American Arbitration Association, for ten years as an arbitrator for attorney/client disputes for the Beverly Hills Bar Association, for nine years as a probation monitor for the State Bar Court, and for five years as a director of the Beverly Hills Education Foundation. He and his wife, Terry, have run the New York Marathon four times. They have two adult daughters, one of whom is also a lawyer.

Bennett Brummer

Brummer graduated from the University of Miami Law School in 1965 and has spent much of his career as a public defender, winning election as Dade County public defender for eight consecutive terms.

His service career began early, as he spent two years with the Peace Corps in Venezuela, where he became fluent in Spanish. Later, a fellowship brought him to the Legal Services of Greater Miami, where he attended to the legal needs of low-income, multiracial, and multiethnic persons in Dade and Monroe counties. In 1971 he joined the Dade County Public Defender's Office as an assistant public defender and by 1976 was elected to head the agency, which includes two hundred attorneys who handle about 100,000 cases per year.

In 2002 the American Civil Liberties Union Foundation of Florida and the Florida Bar's Criminal Justice Section bestowed their highest awards upon him. Most recently, Brummer was awarded a Lifetime Achievement Award from the Association for Retarded Citizens of South Florida. And from Florida's Children First! he was honored with an award for being one of Miami–Dade County's outstanding child advocates.

The *Miami Herald* described him as an "intelligent, cultivated and thoughtful public servant," who "stick[s] up for those who can't stick up for themselves." He was recently honored with the dedication of the six-story Bennett H. Brummer Building by Miami-Dade County. Brummer now serves as senior advisor to his successor, Carlos Martinez, and as a consultant on public defender and court management.

Richard Burns

One of the law students who researched Florida's rape cases, Burns worked under the direction of Tobias Simon, a well-known civil rights attorney in the Miami area and an inspirational mentor who influenced the future direction of his law practice. Following law school graduation, Burns developed a clientele of mostly Hispanic Americans and Cuban exiles. Still practicing in Miami, he is presently the general counsel for the Dade County Federal Credit Union.

Karen Davis

After graduating from Stanford Law School, Davis was appointed by the American Civil Liberties Union as its Tennessee director. Later she moved to Portland, Oregon, where she worked for the Legal Aid Society for several years. She practiced law in Oregon before becoming a justice of the peace. Karen Davis focused on public interest law for much of her legal career before her untimely death in the late 1980s.

Henning Eikenberg

A German citizen, Eikenberg completed his studies at the Yale University School of Law in 1966 with the assistance of a DAAD (German Academic Exchange Service) scholarship and Fulbright travel scholarship. He earned his master of laws degree from Yale in 1965 and stayed there for another year to work on his doctoral thesis, which was later accepted by the Saarland University.

From 1970 to 2004, he worked for the German Ministry for Education and Research, where he was engaged in the planning and promotion of research and technology. He represented the ministry before the European Space Agency (ESA), a Paris-based intergovernmental organization dedicated to the exploration of space. He also represented the ministry before the European Southern Observatory (ESO), an intergovernmental research organization for astronomy that is composed of fourteen European countries and has built some of the most advanced telescopes in the world.

From 1973 to 1976 and again from 1990 to 1996, Eikenberg joined the "Permanent Representation"—similar to a diplomatic mission—of Germany to the European Union (EU), the economic and political partnership governing the relations of almost 500 million people living within twenty-seven member states. He became the German representative to the International Association for the Promotion of Cooperation with Scientists from the New Independent States of the former Soviet Union (INTAS); later he served as the science and environment counselor of the German embassy in Tel Aviv, Israel. After returning to Germany, he became a director in his ministry in charge of scientific cooperation with Western European, Middle Eastern, Mediterranean, and African countries.

Eikenberg worked as the representative of Hebrew University of Jerusalem, and since 2004 he has been a board member of the German Technion Society (GTS), which provides support to the Technion-Israel Institute of Technology. Eikenberg has written and published articles about European law, science in Israel, and scientific cooperation between Israel and Germany. He is married with four adult children and resides in Koenigswinter, Germany, in the Rhine Valley.

Charles "Chuck" Farnsworth

Graduating from Stanford Law School in 1966, he soon married Susan Fink, another Stanford student, who was pursuing a master's degree in history. He traveled to Peru with his wife on a Ford Foundation grant to study tax policy with an economic development organization.

The couple lived in a grimy bungalow near the cliffs of Miraflores, where they were almost daily enshrouded with fog. On returning to the United States a couple of years later, Farnsworth eventually became a staff attorney with the California Rural Legal Assistance Office in El Centro, California. He represented individual farm workers primarily in employment, school, and consumer law cases. He recalls the birth of his daughter there during a heat wave in October 1968, when the temperature was 118 degrees.

A year later he went to work for the United Farm Workers union (UFW) in Delano. From 1969 to 1971, he drove all over California representing the UFW during its heyday of striking and picketing the many farming conglomerates that dominated the state's agricultural market. In one case he secured reversal of a court order banning the waving of

UFW's red-and-black flag on picket lines. The trial judge had ruled that the flag incited violence.

In 1972 the Farnsworths moved to the Bay Area, where he started a law firm in Oakland, emphasizing employment law, including race and gender class actions, wrongful termination, and industrial accidents. From 1990 to the present, he has served as an arbitrator and mediator specializing in employment cases.

His wife, Susan, is a television journalist and has been a reporter for *The News Hour with Jim Lehrer* on PBS. She most recently completed a documentary film on the prosecution of General Pinochet in Chile titled *The Judge and the General*. Chuck and Susan have two adult children.

John C. "Chip" Gray

Returning to Harvard Law School following the 1965 southern trip, Gray served as editor-in-chief of the *Harvard Civil Rights–Civil Liberties Law Review*. He graduated cum laude from Harvard Law School in 1967 and then was a graduate fellow in the Arthur Garfield Hays Liberties Law Program while studying for his master of laws degree at the New York University School of Law.

In 1968 he became a staff attorney for the Community Action for Legal Services (now Legal Services for New York City), where he specialized in welfare and education law. Later, Gray became the project director of South Brooklyn Legal Services, Inc., and continues to serve in that capacity. As director, he oversees all aspects of a successful antipoverty program that provides legal services to low-income people in Brooklyn on issues pertaining to housing, pension benefits, consumer law, child care employment, family law, domestic violence, government benefits, special education, and a host of other matters.

Gray also served as an adjunct professor at the New York University School of Law from 1985 to 1988, teaching welfare law. His many articles on poverty law have been published in the law reviews of the University of Pennsylvania, New York University, and the University of Michigan. Since 1997, he has served as a board member of the HOPE Program, which provides job training for low-income people. He was chair of the Committee on Public Interest Law of the New York Bar Association from 1995 to 1997.

Douglas Hedin

Hedin graduated from the University of Pennsylvania Law School in 1967. After a two-year army stint, he clerked in 1971 for the late federal judge Earl R. Larson of the district court in Minnesota. From 1971 to 2006, he practiced law, representing litigants in civil rights and employment cases.

He also served as a qualified mediator and arbitrator in Minnesota from 1992 to 2006. He is the founder and editor of the Minnesota Legal History Project, which seeks to add to the knowledge of the state's legal history by making available previously published articles and by publishing new or original studies.

Hedin also founded the Minnesota chapter of the National Employment Lawyers Association (NELA) and received the First Distinguished Service Award and the Karla R. Wahl Advocacy Award from the Minnesota Chapter of NELA. He also served as president of the League of Minnesota Human Rights Commissions and was a member of the Minneapolis Civil Rights Commission. Hedin retired in 2006 to write articles on the legal history of Minnesota.

Layton Olson

Olson graduated from Boalt Hall (the University of California law school at Berkeley) in 1967 and gained admission to the California and Illinois state bars. After a stint with the Vista Project in Chicago in 1968, he became a community activist managing initiatives to improve the economically distressed areas of northeast Illinois and northwest Indiana.

Among his legislative accomplishments are helping to foster legislative and regulatory initiatives in education, health care, transportation, and community technologies in Washington, D.C., Springfield, and Chicago. For instance, he drafted the Integrated Telecom and Digital Literacy Act, which was passed by both houses of the Illinois General Assembly in February 2006. He also drafted the Eliminate the Digital Divide Act that was introduced in the Illinois General Assembly and adopted in 2000. He drafted and secured adoption by the U.S. Congress of two sets of higher education financial aid and student access amendments to the Education Amendments of 1972 and 1976.

He is also a recognized leader of those assisting the start-up and regulation of nonprofit institutions in Illinois. From 1980 to 2008, Olson served as an attorney and business consultant for nonprofit organizations and businesses working with nonprofits. He has been of counsel since 1995 with the law firm Howe and Hutton, Ltd., in Chicago, which specializes in representation of nonprofit organizations, including trade and professional organizations, charities and related foundations, and firms that work with them.

He is married to Annette Robinson, a probate and trust attorney and since 1980 has lived in the Lincoln Park community area of Chicago, where he is active in community affairs.

The Advocates

Norman Amaker

Hired by Thurgood Marshall to work for the NAACP Legal Defense and Education Fund, Amaker was a lawyer in numerous civil rights cases. Well known for tenacity and personal courage, he defended Martin Luther King Jr. in Birmingham and Selma, Alabama, demonstration cases. In fact, he was the courier who brought out to the world Dr. King's famous essay "Letter from a Birmingham Jail."

In addition to teaching law at Rutgers and Loyola University Chicago, he was executive director of the Neighborhood Legal Services Program in Washington, D.C., and general counsel for the National Committee against Discrimination in Housing. He died in 2000 at age sixty-five.[1]

Anthony Amsterdam

Once a clerk for U.S. Supreme Court Justice Felix Frankfurter, Amsterdam became one of the nation's leading legal scholars and advocates. He left the University of Pennsylvania for Stanford in 1969 and later moved on to New York University, where he was credited with ground-breaking changes to the law school curriculum.

Over the years, he has served a variety of civil rights bodies, legal aid organizations, and public defender groups. He has litigated cases involving the death penalty; claims of access to the courts for detainees at Guantanamo Bay, Cuba; and numerous free speech, free press, and equal opportunity lawsuits.

Amsterdam has been much praised for his legal acumen and his concern about racism in sentencing, such a dominant theme of his legal life in the 1960s and '70s. He continues to teach at the New York University School of Law.[2]

Jack Greenberg

As a young lawyer, Greenburg was one of the attorneys who argued *Brown v. Board of Education* before the Supreme Court. In 1961 Greenberg succeeded Thurgood Marshall and served as director of the Legal Defense Fund until 1984. Since then, he has been on the faculty of Columbia University Law School and lectured widely, as well as remaining active in civil rights and human rights causes.[3] With Greenberg's leadership, the Fund's anti–capital punishment campaign transcended a focus on a few extreme cases and instead took on the death penalty as a comprehensive state-supported system of injustice.

In 2001 he was awarded the Presidential Citizens Medal and cited by President Clinton as "a crusader for freedom and equality for more than half a century." A movie (*The Crusaders*) based on his life, and starring Tobey Maguire as the young, idealistic Greenberg, then the only white attorney for the Fund, is in development.[4]

Frank Heffron

After graduating from Columbia Law School in 1962, Heffron was hired as one of only nine lawyers on the staff of the NAACP Legal Defense Fund, then in the forefront of the nation's civil rights movement. He traveled throughout the South, assisting local lawyers in cases involving Freedom Riders, student sit-ins, and desegregation of public facilities.

He left the Fund in 1965 and practiced corporate and banking law in Boston before opening his own general practice office. When his wife, Margery, became an associate vice president at State University of New York (SUNY), Binghamton, he embarked on the final phase of his career, practicing municipal law with the Broome County (New York) Attorney's Office from 1989 to 1999. Heffron retired in 2000.

In 2005 he became active in the local Amnesty International group and coordinated its efforts in advocating for Murat Kurnaz, a Turkish resident of Germany who was one of the first persons to be detained at Guantanamo Naval Base in 2002. (Kurnaz was finally released in 2006, thanks to a personal appeal by the recently elected German chancellor Angela Merkel to President George W. Bush.)

Michael Meltsner

Joining Greenberg in 1961, Meltsner became the second white lawyer on the Fund's staff. An Oberlin College and Yale Law graduate, he filed hundreds of lawsuits to integrate major southern institutions and argued dozens of them before the U.S Supreme Court and lower federal courts. He brought the case that integrated hundreds of southern medical facilities and also represented Muhammad Ali in a case that allowed the boxer's return to the ring after refusing induction into the Army.

As a Columbia Law School professor, Meltsner cofounded the school's first poverty-law clinic. He later became dean of the Northeastern Law School in Boston and has been a visiting professor at Harvard Law

School.[5] His book about death case litigation, *Cruel and Unusual: The Supreme Court and Capital Punishment,* was reissued by Quid Pro Books in 2011.

The Expert

Marvin Wolfgang

A pioneering criminologist, Professor Wolfgang wrote more than thirty books, but his most famous work came in 1972 with *Delinquency in a Birth Cohort,* which marked the beginning of large-scale longitudinal studies of crime and delinquency. He went on to win numerous awards in the United States and abroad and in his later years continued to speak out against the death penalty. However, because the rape statistical study is barely mentioned in most books on the history of capital punishment, Wolfgang is little recognized for his contribution to changing American jurisprudence. Nonetheless, he was named by a British journal as "the most influential criminologist in the English-speaking world."

Wolfgang succumbed to cancer in 1998 at age seventy-three.[6]

Notes

1 A Showdown Looms

1. This incident was described briefly by Barrett Foerster in "Law Students Sent to South," *UCLA Summer Bruin,* Sept. 9, 1965, 1, 4. It was mentioned again by Philip Brown, one of the law students participating in the project, in a telephone interview with the author on April 21, 2008.

2. Law Students Civil Rights Research Council (LSCRRC), letter re: acceptance into program, n.d., p. 1, box 21, folder: Capital Punishment Rape Survey, Seeley G. Mudd Manuscript Library, Princeton University. Subsequent references to this archived file are abbreviated CPRS.

3. Nadya Labi, "A Man Against the Machine," *New York University Law School Magazine,* 2007, http://blogs.law.nyu.edu/magazine/2007/a-man-against-the-machine/. See also "Prodigious Professor," *Time,* Dec. 10, 1965, http://www.time.com/time/magazine/article/0,9171,898415,00.html.

4. LSCRRC, "Preliminary Survey of Capital Rape Cases in Southern States," Mar. 15, 1965, p. 1, CPRS.

5. Michael Kaufman, "Obituary: Marvin E. Wolfgang, 73, Dies; Leading Figure in Criminology," *New York Times,* Apr. 18, 1998, http://www.nytimes.com/1998/04/18/us/marvin-e-wolfgang-73-dies-leading-figure-in-criminology.html?pagewanted=1. See also Robert A. Silverman, "Biographical Memoirs: Marvin Eugene Wolfgang," *Proceedings of the American Philosophical Society* 148, no. 4 (Dec. 2004): 547–54.

6. *Capital Punishment Survey* booklet, copy in author's file.

7. LSCRRC, instructions document, n.d., p. 2, CPRS.

8. Marvin E. Wolfgang, "The Social Scientist in Court," *Journal of Criminal Law and Criminology* 65, no. 2 (1974): 241.

9. Ibid., 1, 6, 7.

10. Philip Dray, "Civil Rights Workers: Death in Mississippi," in *Free At Last: The U.S. Civil Rights Movement* (Washington, DC: Bureau of International Programs, U.S. Dept. of State, 2008), 48–49, http://www.america.gov/media/pdf/books/free-at-last.pdf.

11. LSCRRC, "Statewide Analysis—Louisiana," n.d., p. 1, CPRS.
12. Ibid.
13. Ibid., 3.
14. LSCRRC, "Additional Comments on Parish Research, Louisiana," n.d., p. 2, CPRS.
15. Amy Ruth Tobol, "Badge of Honor: The Law Students Civil Rights Research Council" (PhD diss., University of New York at Buffalo, 1999), 149, 151. These instructions given by the LSCRRC to the law students working on the rape–capital punishment survey were similar to those given the law student interns assigned to southern law firms.
16. Ibid., 224.
17. Ibid., 223.
18. Ibid., 224.
19. See, for example, LSCRRC, Preliminary Survey of Capital Rape Cases in Southern States, Additional Comments on Parish Research, Louisiana, Types of Rape Punishable by Death (marked as "File Copy"), n.d.; Statewide Survey–Georgia by Howard Moore, n.d., CPRS.
20. Richard Burns, telephone interview with author, June 2, 2008; Bennett Brummer, telephone interview with author, June 3, 2008.
21. LSCRRC, paper: "Rape: Selective Electrocution Based on Race," submitted by Tobias Simon, n.d., 19 pp., CPRS; Burns and Brummer interviews.
22. Petitioner's brief filed with Clerk of the U.S. Supreme Court, Jan. 21, 1969, in *William L. Maxwell, Petitioner v. O. E. Bishop, Superintendent of Arkansas State Penitentiary, Respondent,* on writ of certiorari to U.S. Court of Appeals, 8th Circuit, 14–15.
23. See, for example, *Florida v. Thomas,* 253 F. 2d 507 (5th Cir. 1958), wherein the defendant produced statistics showing that over a twenty-year period, twenty-four blacks and no whites had been executed for rape in Florida. The court did not find the statute unconstitutional in its application in light of the inviolability of jury deliberations and the uncontrolled character of their deliberations.
24. Tobol, "Badge of Honor," 52–53.
25. *Brown v. Board of Education,* 347 U.S. 483 (1954).
26. Tobol, "Badge of Honor," 45–46.
27. Ibid., 47.
28. James R. Acker, *Scottsboro and Its Legacy: The Cases That Challenged American Legal and Social Justice* (Westport, CT: Praeger Publishers, 2007), 53–104; also "Scottsboro Boys," Encyclopedia Article, available at www.absoluteastronomy.com/topics/Scottsboro_Boys
29. Eric Rise, *The Martinsville Seven: Race, Rape, and Capital Punishment* (Charlottesville: University Press of Virginia, 1995), 2–47.
30. Ibid., 88–92.
31. Hugo Adam Bedau, "The Case Against the Death Penalty," n.d., *Ethics Updates* website, http://ethics.sandiego.edu/applied/deathpenalty/bedeau.

html. See also the dissenting opinion of Justice William Brennan in *Glass v. Louisiana,* 471 U.S. 1080 (1985); and Mark D. Harris (United Press International), "Witness to an Execution," May 4, 1983, http://en.wikisource.org/wiki/Execution_of_John_Louis_Evans_May_4,_1983:_First_Person_Account.

32. David Krajicek, "He Cheated the Chair," *New York Daily News,* Apr. 28, 2008, http://origin.nydailynews.com/news/crime/2008/04/27/2008-04-27_he_cheated_the_chair.html.

33. *Louisiana ex rel. Francis v. Resweber,* 329 U.S. 459 (1947).

34. Gilbert King, *The Execution of Willie Francis: Race, Murder and the Search for Justice in the American South* (Boulder, CO: Perseus Publishing, 2008).

35. *Rudolph v. Alabama,* 375 U.S. 889.

36. Ibid., 890–91.

37. See Dennis D. Dorin, "Two Different Worlds: Criminologists, Justices and Racial Discrimination in the Imposition of Capital Punishment in Rape Cases," *Journal of Criminal Law and Criminology* 72, no. 4 (1981): 1667, 1681. According to Dorin, Justice Goldberg had recognized in an earlier draft of his *Rudolph* opinion the "well-recognized disparity in the imposition of the death penalty for sexual crimes committed by whites and nonwhites." This reference was subsequently removed from the final written opinion.

38. Robert A. Burt, "Disorder in the Court: the Death Penalty and the Constitution," *Michigan Law Review* 85 (Aug. 1987): 1741, 1744.

39. The term "white collar guerrilla bands" is used in Michael Meltsner, *Cruel and Unusual Punishment: The Supreme Court and Capital Punishment* (New York: William Morrow, 1974), 87.

2 Into the Southern Cauldron

1. Jack Greenberg, *Crusaders in the Courts: How a Dedicated Band of Lawyers Fought for the Civil Rights Revolution* (New York: Basic Books, 1994), 441.

2. Margalit Fox, "Obituary: Jim Clark, Sheriff Who Enforced Segregation, Dies at 84," *New York Times,* June 7, 2007, http://www.nytimes.com/2007/06/07/us/07clark.html.

3. Diary of John Gray, p. 2, in author's file.

4. Wolfgang, "The Social Scientist in Court," 240.

5. Charles Farnsworth, telephone interview with author, Feb. 6, 2010.

6. Gray diary, 1.

7. Ibid., 9. Montgomery was the political capital of the Confederacy only temporarily. It was soon moved to Richmond, Virginia.

8. Ibid.

9. Diary of Henning Eikenberg, p. 11, in author's file.

10. Ibid., 1, 3.

11. Associated Press, "Negro Rape Executions Challenged," undated newspaper clipping from *Los Angeles Times* in author's possession.

12. Foerster, "Law Students Sent to South," 1, 4.

13. Ibid.
14. Ibid.
15. Gray diary, 6.
16. Ibid., 10–11.
17. Foerster, "Law Students Sent to South," 1, 4.
18. Gray diary, 8.
19. *Miranda v. Arizona*, 384 U.S. 436 (1966).
20. Gray diary, 10.
21. "Preliminary Survey-Iberville Parish-Louisiana" prepared by the Law Students' Civil Rights Research Council which is in the author's possession.
22. Gray diary, 2.
23. Ibid., 4.
24. Ibid.
25. Ibid., 5–6.
26. Ibid., 7.
27. Ibid., 11.
28. Eikenberg diary, 4.
29. Gray diary, 6.
30. Ibid., 5; Eikenberg diary, 6.
31. Eikenberg diary, 4.

3 Meeting the Klan

1. J. C. Lester and D. L. Wilson, *Ku Klux Klan: Its Origins, Growth and Disbandment* (New York: Neale Publishing Co., 1905), 51.
2. James W. Clarke, "Without Fear or Shame: Lynching, Capital Punishment, and the Subculture of Violence in the American South," *British Journal of Political Science* 28, no. 2 (1998): 269–89.
3. Ibid.
4. Ibid., 271n5, which references the *Joint Select Committee to Inquire into the Condition of Affairs in the Late Insurrectionary States, House Reports,* U.S. House of Representatives, 42nd Congress, 2nd sess. (Washington, 1872), 13 vols (hereinafter cited as U.S. Congress, KKK Investigation, 1872).
5. Clarke, "Without Fear or Shame," 276n23, which references W. J. Cash, *The Mind of the South* (New York: Alfred A. Knopf, 1941); Joel Williamson, *The Crucible of Race: Black-White Relations in the American South since Emancipation* (New York: Oxford University Press, 1984); George C. Wright, *Racial Violence in Kentucky: Lynchings, Mob Rule, and "Legal Lynchings"* (Baton Rouge: Louisiana State University Press, 1990); and W. Fitzhugh Brundage, *Lynching in the New South: Georgia and Virginia, 1880–1930* (Urbana: University of Illinois Press, 1993). Also see 277n25, which references U.S. Congress, KKK Investigation, 1872; Allen W. Trelease, *White Terror: The Ku Klux Klan and Southern Reconstruction* (New York: Harper & Row, 1971); and Richard

Maxwell Brown, *Strain of Violence: Historical Studies of American Violence and Vigilantism* (New York: Oxford University Press, 1975).

6. Clarke, "Without Fear or Shame," 271n3, which references the files of the Department of Records and Research, Tuskegee Institute, Tuskegee, AL; and Harry A. Ploski and James D. Williams, eds., *The Negro Almanac: A Reference Work on the Afro-American* (New York: Wiley, 1983), 347.

7. Clarke, "Without Fear or Shame," 283n42, which references George B. Tindall, *The Emergence of the New South, 1913–1945* (Baton Rouge: Louisiana State University Press, 1967), 175–83; and Harvard Sitkoff, *A New Deal for Blacks: The Emergence of Civil Rights as a National Issue* (New York: Oxford University Press, 1978), 274–75. See also 283n43, which references Neil Fligstein, *Going North: Migration of Blacks and Whites from the South, 1900–1915* (New York: Academic Press, 1981), 120–36; and 284n44, which references Will W. Alexander, "Better Race Relations," *Southern Workman* 51 (Jan. 1922): 362–64; Tindall, *The Emergence of the New South,* 179–83; George M. Frederickson, *The Black Image in the White Mind: The Debate on Afro-American Character and Destiny, 1817–1914* (New York: Harper & Row, 1971), 272–75; and Brundage, *Lynching in the New South,* 208–44.

8. Clarke, "Without Fear or Shame," 251n51, which references Neil R. McMillen, *Dark Journey: Black Mississippians in the Age of Jim Crow* (Urbana: University of Illinois Press, 1989). See also 285n52, which references Tindall, *Emergence of the New South,* 173–80; Williamson, *Crucible of Race,* 335; and Wright, *Racial Violence in Kentucky,* 12–13.

9. Clarke, "Without Fear or Shame," 286n55, which references William J. Bowers, *Executions in America* (Lexington, Mass.: D. C. Heath, 1974), 55–57, 191–93; and Hugo Adam Bedau, ed., *The Death Penalty in America: An Anthology,* 3rd. ed. (New York: Oxford University Press, 1982), 32.

10. Clarke, "Without Fear or Shame," 286n55.

11. Mark Robert Schneider, *We Return Fighting: The Civil Rights Movement in the Jazz Age* (Boston: Northeastern University Press, 2002), 369–70.

12. "Ku Klux Klan," *The Free Dictionary,* http://legaldictionary.thefreedictionary.com/Ku+Klux+Klan.

13. Ibid.

14. Ibid.

15. James C. Cobb, "The Real Story of the White Citizens' Council," *HNN: George Mason University's History News Network,* http://hnn.us/articles/134814.html.

16. See Crystal N. Feimster, *Southern Horrors: Women and the Politics of Rape and Lynching* (Cambridge, MA: Harvard University Press, 2009).

17. Duncan Howlett, *No Greater Love: The James Reeb Story* (Boston: Skinner House Books), 209–24; Eikenberg diary, 3.

18. Eikenberg diary, 3.

19. Associated Press, "Sheriff Jim Clark, segregationist icon, dies at 84," June 6, 2007, MSNBC website, http://www.msnbc.msn.com/id/19075327/.

20 Eikenberg diary, 3.

21. Ted Robert Gurr, ed., *Violence in America,* vol. 2, *Protest, Rebellion, Reform* (Newbury Park, CA: Sage Publications, 1989), 243.

22. Eikenberg diary, 11; "Alabama: The Trial," *Time,* May 14, 1965, http://www.time.com/time/magazine/article/0,9171,898795,00.html.

23. "Alabama: The Trial."

24. Gary May, *The Informant: The FBI, the Ku Klux Klan, and the Murder of Viola Liuzzo* (New Haven, CT: Yale University Press, 2005), 150–65, 243–70.

25. Thomas C. Smith, "Collie Leroy Wilkins Trial," in *Great American Trials,* vol. 2, ed. Edward W. Knappman (Detroit, MI: Visible Ink Press/Gale Research, 1994), 533–36.

26. Front cover, *Life,* May 21, 1965.

27. Eikenberg diary, 12. Matthew Murphy Jr. was killed in a vehicular accident later that year. See "The Press: Fifty-Fifty in the South," *Time,* Oct. 15, 1965, http://www.time.com/time/magazine/article/0,9171,834527,00.html.

28. Associated Press, "Reputed Klansman found guilty in 1964 deaths," June 14, 2007, MSNBC website, http://www.msnbc.com/id/19234202.

29. Stanley Nelson, "Why Frank? A New Probe of the 1964 Murder of Ferriday Shoe Shop Owner Frank Norris," *Concordia (LA) Sentinel,* Jan. 10, 2008, http://www.concordiasentinel.com/news.php?id=1249.

30. Ibid.

31. Ibid.

32. Ibid.

33. Ibid.

34. Joseph Crespino, *In Search of Another Country: Mississippi and the Conservative Counterrevolution* (Princeton, NJ: Princeton University Press, 2007), 112–13.

35. Edward L. McDaniel led one of four Klan groups in the southwestern part of Mississippi during the 1960s. He joined the Original Knights of the Ku Klux Klan in 1961 and organized klaverns across Mississippi. After he was expelled from the Original Knights for alleged financial improprieties, he joined the White Knights of the Ku Klux Klan and was again expelled. Finally, Robert Shelton, the Imperial Wizard of the United Klans of America, appointed McDaniel Grand Dragon of Mississippi in 1964. McDaniel was credited with leading Klan members down a path of intimidation, threats, and burnings. See Jack E. Davis, *Race Against Time: Culture and Separation in Natchez since 1930* (Baton Rouge: Louisiana State University Press, 2004), 162–64.

36. Adam Fairclough, *Race and Democracy: The Civil Rights Struggle in Louisiana, 1915–1972* (Athens: University of Georgia Press, 1999), 349–55.

37. Ibid., 353.

38. Ibid., 356–57.
39. Ibid., 356.
40. Ibid., 358–59.
41. Ibid., 354.
42. Ibid., 356.
43. Ibid., 357–59.
44. Ibid., 360.
45. Ibid., 366.
46. Ibid.
47. Ibid., 355.
48. Ibid., 363, 354, 369.
49. Photograph, *New Orleans Times-Picayune,* July 18, 1965, sec. 1, p. 14.
50. George Lipsitz, *A Life in the Struggle: Ivory Perry and the Culture of Opposition* (Philadelphia: Temple University Press, 1988), 97–99.

4 The "Underground" Mobilizes

1. Albert C. "Buck" Persons, *Sex and Civil Rights: The True Selma Story* (Birmingham, AL: Esco Publishers, 1965), page facing 1, 4.
2. Frank Heffron, telephone interview with author, May 15, 2008; Frank Heffron, email correspondence with author, June 12, 2008, and Feb. 9, 2010.
3. W. Lewis Burke and Belinda F. Gergel, *Matthew J. Perry: The Man, His Times, and His Legacy* (Columbia: University of South Carolina Press, 2004), 189–92. See also *Gantt v. Clemson Agricultural College of South Carolina,* 220 F. 2d 611 (4th Cir. 1963).
4. Thomas Charles ("Tim") Brayton, telephone interview with author, Aug. 26, 2008.
5. "Oscar W. Adams, Jr.: Alabama's First African American Supreme Court Justice," *Alabama Moments in American History* website (Mont gomery: Alabama Dept. of Archives and History, 1999–2001), http://www.alabamamoments.state.al.us/sec65.html.
6. John Gray, telephone interview with author, Aug. 18, 2008.
7. "Oscar Adams: 1925–1997," Alabama State Bar website, http://www.alabar.org/members/hallfame/adams.cfm. See also Holcomb B. Noble, "Obituary: Oscar Adams, 72, a Pioneer as Alabama Top Court Justice," *New York Times,* Feb. 18, 1997, http://ww.nytimes.com/1997/02/18/us/oscar-adams-72-a-pioneer-as alabama-top-court-justice.html?pagewanted=1.
8. Gray telephone interview.
9. Gray diary, 15.
10. *United States v. Jefferson County Board of Education, et al.,* Docket No. 65–396, case summary available at the Civil Rights Litigation Clearinghouse, University of Michigan Law School website, http://www.clearinghouse.net/detail.php?id=1050.

11. *United States, et al., v. Jefferson County Board of education et al.,* 380 F. 2f 385 (5th Cir. 1967). See also *United States, et al., v. Jefferson County Board of education et al.,* 372 F. 2d 836 (5th Cir. 1966).
12. Gray diary, 16; Eikenberg diary, 9.
13. Lawrence Kestenbaum, Political Graveyard.com website, http://politicalgraveyard.com/bio/holten-hook.html.
14. Office of C. B. King to Frank Heffron, Apr. 7, 1965, box 21, CPRPS.
15. Tobol, "Badge of Honor," 210.
16. Ibid., 210–11.
17. "C.B. King (1923–1988)," *The New Georgia Encyclopedia: History and Archaeology,* http://www.georgiaencyclopedia.org/nge/Article.jsp?id=h-1100.
18. Tobol, "Badge of Honor," 193.
19. Ibid., 230.
20. Ibid.
21. "C. B. King (1923–1988)," *New Georgia Encyclopedia.*
22. Ibid.
23. Roy Reed, "Obituary: Sidney S. McMath, 91, Former Arkansas Governor," *New York Times,* Oct. 6, 2003, http://www.nytimes.com/2003/10/06/us/sidney-s-mcmath-91-former-arkansas-governor.html?pagewanted=1,
24. William Kopit (Lawyers Constitutional Defense Committee, Inc.) to Steven Antler, Apr. 13, 1965, CPRPS.
25. "Virginia Foster Durr," *Encyclopedia of Alabama,* http://www.encyclopediaofAlabama.org/face/Article.jsp?id=h-1574. See also Douglas Hedin, "That Summer in the South," June 2003, Civil Rights Movement Veterans website, http://www.crmvet.org/vet/hedin.htm.
26. Hedin, "That Summer in the South."
27. Gray diary, 3.
28. "Clifford Durr," *Encyclopedia of Alabama,* http://www.encyclopediaofalabama.org/face/Article.jsp?id=h-1254. See also Hedin, "That Summer in the South."
29. "Clifford Durr," *Encyclopedia of Alabama.*
30. Hedin, "That Summer in the South."
31. Gray diary, 3.
32. "Virginia Foster Durr," *Encyclopedia of Alabama.*
33. Gray diary, 8.
34. Gray diary, 3, 9.
35. Charles Farnsworth, telephone interview with author, May 1, 2008.
36. Gray diary, 8, and Gray telephone interview.
37. *Norris v. Alabama,* 294 U.S.587 (1935).
38. Farnsworth telephone interview, May 1, 2008.
39. "Thomas Seay Lawson," Alabama Academy of Honor website, http://www.archives.alabama.gov/famous/academy/t_lawson.html.
40. Farnsworth telephone interview, May 1, 2008.

41. Ibid.
42. Gray diary, 17.
43. Eikenberg diary, 10; Gray diary, 17.
44. Gray diary, 16; Eikenberg diary, 10.
45. Gray diary, 13.
46. Ibid., 9.
47. 42 U.S.C. 1973 et seq.
48. Associated Press, "Obituary: Richard Flowers, 88; Chief Alabama Lawyer was a moderate on race," *Los Angeles Times,* Aug. 11, 2007, http://articles.latimes.com/2007/aug/11/local/me-flowers11.
49. Eikenberg diary, 12.
50. Ibid.
51. Gray diary, 8.
52. For a general discussion on this subject, see Tobol, "Badge of Honor," 154–57.
53. Eikenberg diary, 12.
54. Ibid.
55. Ibid., 8–9.
56. Ibid., 3.
57. Ibid.
58. Ibid., 7.
59. Eikenberg diary, 6.
60. Thomas Charles "Tim" Brayton, telephone interview with author, Aug. 26, 2008.

5 Wolfgang Fuels the Assault

1. Meltsner, *Cruel and Unusual,* 31.
2. Ibid., 35.
3. Ibid., 87.
4. Wolfgang's evaluation of the schedules began in September 1965. See Meltsner, *Cruel and Unusual,* 87–88.
5. Deposition of Marvin Wolfgang, Jan. 13,1967, pursuant to Written Interrogatories propounded upon him by Defendant Robert Butler in *State of Alabama v. Robert Butler* in the Circuit Court of Etowah County, Alabama, Case No. 1160, p. 23. This deposition was later submitted to the U.S. Supreme Court in support of Robert Butler's Petition for Writ of Certiorari, which Petition was later dismissed in *Butler v. Alabama,* 406 U.S.939 (1972). Dr. Wolfgang explained that he received the capital punishment surveys from the Legal Defense Fund in late September 1965 by mail.
6. Wolfgang deposition, p. 88.
7. "Biographical Memoirs: Marvin Eugene Wolfgang," *Proceedings of the American Philosophical Society* 148, no. 4 (2004): 553.

8. The processing of the schedules was prioritized based upon which defendants faced critical court proceedings. See Meltsner, *Cruel and Unusual,* 88.

9. Ibid.

10. *Moorer v. State of South Carolina,* 368 F. 2d 458 (4th Cir. 1966).

11. Meltsner, *Cruel and Unusual,* 88.

12. Ibid., 89.

13. *Patterns in Criminal Homicide* was published in 1958 and *The Measurement of Delinquency* with Thorsten Sellin was published in 1964. See also "Biographical Memoirs: Marvin Eugene Wolfgang," 550.

14. "Biographical Memoirs: Marvin Eugene Wolfgang," 548.

15. Ibid., 548, 550.

16. Marvin E. Wolfgang and Franco Ferracuti, *The Subculture of Violence: Towards an Integrated Theory in Criminology* (London: Tavistock Publications, 1967), 104, 106–7, 140, 152–53. In this book he attributes the disproportionately high rates of crime committed by black males to what he termed their "subculture of violence." Relying on his 1958 study of 588 criminal homicides in Philadelphia, he described the high value placed on violence by the black subculture, which if deviated from would be punished by ostracism and similar sanctions. But he explained that the subculture shares major values in common with the general society of which it is a part.

17. "Biographical Memoirs: Marvin Eugene Wolfgang," 548.

18. Ibid.

19. Kaufman, "Obituary: Marvin E. Wolfgang."

20. "Biographical Memoirs: Marvin Eugene Wolfgang," 548.

21. Ibid., 553.

22. Ibid.

23. Wolfgang, "The Social Scientist in Court," 243.

24. Ibid., 240.

25. Ibid., 245.

26. Wolfgang and Ferracuti, *The Subculture of Violence,* 158, 314.

27. C. G. Ellison, "An Eye for an Eye? A Note on the Southern Subculture of Violence Thesis," *Social Forces* 69 (1991): 1224.

28. The seven states were Alabama, Arkansas, Florida, Georgia, Louisiana, South Carolina, and Tennessee. See Wolfgang, "The Social Scientist in Court," 242.

29. "Biographical Memoirs: Marvin Eugene Wolfgang," 548.

30. Marvin Wolfgang and Marc Riedel, "Race, Judicial Discretion, and the Death Penalty," *Annals of the American Academy of Political and Social Science* 407 (May 1973): 129.

31. Meltsner, *Cruel and Unusual,* 95–97.

32. Petitioner William Maxwell's Brief filed with the Clerk of the U.S. Supreme Court, Jan. 21, 1969, in Case No. 622, *Maxwell v. Bishop,* appendix A, 9a.

33. Ibid., 9b.
34. Wolfgang and Riedel, "Race, Judicial Discretion, and the Death Penalty," 130.
35. Ibid.
36. "The chi-square statistic is a summary measure of how well the observed frequencies of categorical data match the frequencies that would be expected under the null hypothesis that a particular multinomial probability model for the data is correct." Philip B. Stark, "Scout Report for Business and Economics," Dept. of Statistics, University of California, Berkeley, http://stat-www.berkeley.edu/~stark/SticiGui/Text/chiSquare.htm.
37. Wolfgang and Riedel, "Race, Judicial Discretion. and the Death Penalty," 130–31.
38. Marvin Wolfgang and Marc Riedel, "Rape, Racial Discrimination, and the Death Penalty," in *Capital Punishment in the United States,* ed. Hugo Adam Bedau and Chester M. Pierce (New York: AMS Press, 1975), 109.
39. Wolfgang and Riedel, "Race, Judicial Discretion, and the Death Penalty," 131.
40. Ibid., 131–32.
41. Ibid., 132.
42. Ibid.
43. Ibid., 133.
44. Wolfgang, "The Social Scientist in Court," 240.
45. Ibid., 242.
46. Marvin Wolfgang and Bernard Cohen, *Crime and Race: Conceptions and Misconceptions* (New York: Institute of Human Relations Press, 1970), 81.
47. Wolfgang, "The Social Scientist in Court," 242–43.
48. Ibid.
49. Meltsner, *Cruel and Unusual,* 98.
50. Wolfgang, "The Social Scientist in Court," 44.
51. Meltsner, *Cruel and Unusual,* 98.
52. Greenberg, *Crusaders in the Courts,* 444.
53. Meltsner, *Cruel and Unusual,* 91.
54. See *Calderon v. Coleman,* 525 U.S. 141(1998).
55. See *Fay v. Noia,* 372 U.S. 391 (1963).
56. Meltsner, *Cruel and Unusual,* 91–92.
57. *Sims v. Balkcom,* 220 Ga. 7, 12 (1964).
58. *Sims v. Georgia,* 389 U.S. 404, 406–8 (1967).
59. *Sims v. State,* 223 Ga. 465, 466 156 S.E. 2d 65 (1967).
60. *Sims v. State,* 221 Ga. 190 (1965).
61. *Sims v. Balkcom,* 220 Ga. 7 (1964).
62. *Sims v. Georgia,* 384 U.S. 998, 999 (1966). The evidence would have shown that nineteen times as many Negroes as whites had been executed for rape in Georgia.

63. Michael J. Henry (N.A.A.C.P. Legal defense and Educational Fund, Inc.) to Barrett J. Foerster, Aug. 17, 1966. Original letter is in the author's possession.

64. Fred P. Graham, "The Law: Rape, Race and Death in the South," *New York Times,* July 10, 1966, http://select.nytimes.com/gst/abstract.html?res=F10F16FF3559117B93C2A8178CD85F428685F9&scp=1&sq=Fred%20P.%20Graham%20Rape,%20Race%20and%20Death%20in%20the%20South&st=cse; Thomas A. Johnson, "Rape Penalties in the South Studied," *New York Times,* Apr. 24, 1966 http://select.nytimes.com/gst/abstract.html?res=FB0F1EFC355812718DDDAD0A94DC405B868AF1D3&scp=1&sq=Thomas%20A.%20Johnson,%20%E2%80%9CRape%20Penalties%20in%20the%20South%20Studied&st=cse; Henry to Foerster, Aug. 17, 1966.

65. *Sims v. Georgia,* 386 U.S. 538 (1967).

66. *Sims v. Georgia,* 223 Ga. 126 (1967).

67. "Old Sparky," *The New Georgia Encyclopedia,* http://www.georgiaencyclopedia.org/nge/Multimedia.jsp?id=m-704

68. See Wolfgang, "The Social Scientist in Court," 242. The four other states where, according to Wolfgang, depositions were taken were Alabama, South Carolina, Louisiana, and Florida.

69. In the Matter of Isaac Sims, Jr., 389 F. 2d 148 (5th Cir. 1967).

70. Petition for Writ of Certiorari filed in U.S. Supreme Court in *Robert Butler v. Alabama,* No. 5492, July 2, 1970, p. 6.

71. Deposition of Marvin Wolfgang taken in *Alabama v. Wheeler Billingsley, Jr., James Liddell and Robert Butler* (Case Nos. 1159, 1160 and 1161) and executed on Jan. 23, 1967, pp. 23–24, on file with Clerk of U.S. Supreme Court.

72. Ibid., 33–34.

73. Ibid., 59.

74. Meltsner, *Cruel and Unusual,* 89.

75. Wolfgang, "The Social Scientist in Court," 242.

76. Transcript of proceedings in *Alabama v. Wheeler Billingsley Jr. et al.,* filed on Aug. 22, 1969, with Clerk of Alabama Supreme Court appeal from Circuit Court of Etowah County, Circuit Court No. 1160, vo. II, 588–95.

77. See *Butler v. Alabama,* 406 U.S. 939 (1972). Butler's petition for writ of certiorari was dismissed due to his death, presumably not at the hands of the state.

78. *Swain v, State,* 275 Ala. 508 (1963).

79. *People v. Adamson,* 34 Cal. 2d 320, 326 (1949).

80. *Swain v. State,* 285 Ala. 292, 300; 231 So. 2d 737 (1970).

81. *Maxwell v. State,* 236 Ark. 694 (1963).

82. *Maxwell v. Stephens,* 229 F. Supp. 205 (1964).

83. *Maxwell v. Stephens,* 348 F. 2d 325 (1965).

84. *Maxwell v. Stephens,* 382 U.S. 944 (1965).

85. Meltsner, *Cruel and Unusual,* 95.
86. Petitioner's Brief, *Maxwell v. Bishop,* in support of Petition for Writ of Certiorari, Case No. 622, filed with U.S. Supreme Court, October Term, 1968, 7.
87. Ibid., 8.
88. *McGautha v. California,* 402 U.S. 183, 213–17 (1971).
89. Meltsner, *Cruel and Unusual,* 96.

6 *Maxwell* Climbs the Appellate Ladder

1. Meltsner, *Cruel and Unusual,* 78.
2. Ibid., 84.
3. Ibid., 79.
4. Ibid., 80–81
5. Labi, "A Man Against the Machine."
6. Ibid.
7. Meltsner, *Cruel and Unusual,* 79–80.
8. Ibid., 82.
9. Ibid., 86.
10. Ibid., 83.
11. Ibid., 82–83.
12. Ibid., 86.
13. Ibid., 76–78, 97.
14. *Moorer v. South Carolina,* 368 F. 2d 458 (4th Cir. 1966).
15. Meltsner, *Cruel and Unusual,* 99.
16. Jeffrey B. Morris, "Jesse Smith Henley (1917–1997)," *The Encyclopedia of Arkansas History and Culture,* http://www.encyclopediaofarkansas.net/encyclopedia/entry-detail.aspx?entryID=417.
17. Meltsner, *Cruel and Unusual,* 99.
18. *Maxwell v. Bishop,* 257 F. Supp. 710, 718–19 (E.D. Ark., Pine Bluff Div., 1966).
19. Wolfgang, "The Social Scientist in Court," 244.
20. Ibid.
21. Petitioner William Maxwell's Brief filed with Clerk of the U.S. Supreme Court, Jan. 21, 1969, in Case No. 622, *Maxwell v. Bishop,* appendix A, 8a.
22. *Maxwell v. Bishop,* 398 F.2d 138, 144 (8th Cir. 1968).
23. *Maxwell v. Bishop,* 257 F. Supp. 710, 719 (E.D. Ark., 1966).
24. Ibid., 719–20.
25. *Maxwell v. Bishop,* 398 F.2d 138, 144 (8th Cir. 1968).
26. *Maxwell v. Bishop,* 257 F. Supp. 710, 718–19 (E.D. Ark., 1966).
27. *Maxwell v. Bishop,* 398 F.2d 138, 141 (8th cir. 1968).
28. *Maxwell v. Bishop,* 257 F. Supp. 710, 719 (E.D. Ark., 1966).

29. Ibid., 718.
30. Ibid., 710, 718–19.
31. Ibid., 720.
32. Meltsner, *Cruel and Unusual,* 103.
33. Ibid.
34. Ibid. 103–4; *Maxwell v. Bishop,* 385 U.S. 650 (1967).
35. JOS, "The Death Penalty: Cruel and Unusual?" *Time,* Jan. 24,1972, http://www.time.com/time/magazine/article/0,9171,905684,00.html.
36. Ibid.
37. Bruce Solheim, *The Vietnam War Era: Personal Journey* (Westport, CT: Praeger Publishers, 2006), xxxii.
38. Walter Rucker and James Nathaniel Upton, *Encyclopedia of American Race Riots* (Westport, CT: Greenwood Press, 2007), lxii.
39. "United States Crime Rates 1960–2010," *The Disaster Center,* http://www.disastercenter.com/crime/uscrime.htm.
40. Jonathan J. Bean, "'Burn Baby Burn': Small Business in the Urban Riots of the 1960s," *Independent Review* 5 no. 2, (2000): 173–76.
41. James Richardson, *Willie Brown: A Biography* (Berkeley: University of California Press, 1996), 136.
42. *Trop v. Dulles,* 356 U.S. 86, 100 (1958).
43. See, for example, *Roper v. Simmons,* 543 U.S. 551, 560–61 (2005), where the court, in banning capital punishment for minors (under eighteen years of age), stated: "The prohibition against 'cruel and unusual punishments,' like other expansive language in the Constitution, must be interpreted according to its text, by considering history, tradition, and precedent, and with due regard for its purpose and function in the constitutional design. To implement this framework we have established the propriety and affirmed the necessity of referring to 'the evolving standards of decency that mark the progress of a maturing society' to determine which punishments are so disproportionate as to be cruel and unusual. *Trop v. Dulles,* 356 U.S. 86, 100–101 (1958) (plurality opinion)." See also *Weems* v. *United States,* 217 U.S. 349 (1910).
44. Meltsner, *Cruel and Unusual,* 106.
45. Ibid, 109.
46. Ibid., 106.
47. *Witherspoon v. Illinois,* 391 U.S. 510 (1968).
48. "If the State had excluded only those prospective jurors who stated in advance of trial that they would not even consider returning a verdict of death, it could argue that the resulting jury was simply 'neutral' with respect to penalty. But when it swept from the jury all who expressed conscientious or religious scruples against capital punishment and all who opposed it in principle, the State crossed the line of neutrality. In its quest for a jury capable of imposing the death penalty, the State produced a jury uncommonly willing to condemn a man to die." Ibid., 520–21.

49. *Whitus v. Georgia*, 385 U.S. 545 (1967).
50. Ibid., 107.
51. Ibid.
52. Meltsner, *Cruel and Unusual*, 111.
53. Ibid., 112–13.
54. Ibid., 112.
55. Greenberg, *Crusaders in the Courts*, 446.
56. Meltsner, *Cruel and Unusual*, 148.
57. "Colorado: No. 77," *Time*, June 9, 1967, http://www.time.com/time/magazine/article/0,9171,843865,00.html.
58. "The Law: Fatal Decision," *Time*, May 17, 1971, http://www.time.com/time/magazine/article/0,9171,944372,00.html.
59. Labi, "A Man Against the Machine," cover page.
60. *Maxwell v. Bishop*, 398 F. 2d 138, 146–47 (8th Cir. 1968).
61. Ibid., 148.
62. Ibid., 147–48.
63. Greenberg, *Crusaders in the Courts*, 445.
64. Eugene Grossman, Kenneth Geller, Stephen Shapiro, Timothy Bishop, and Edward Hartnett, *Supreme Court Practice*, 9th ed. (Arlington, VA: Bureau of National Affairs Books, 2007), 57.
65. Ibid., 262.
66. Ibid., 15.
67. *Maxwell v. Bishop*, 398 F. 2d 138, 138–39 (8th Cir. 1968).
68. *Maxwell v. Bishop*, 393 U.S. 997 (1968).
69. Brief for Petitioner, William L. Maxwell on Writ of Certiorari filed with U.S. Supreme Court, October Term, 1968, Case No. 622, 7.
70. Ibid., 8.
71. Ibid., 7.
72. The Petitioner's Brief filed in the *Maxwell v. Bishop* case mentioned that the survey covered 250 counties in eleven states of the South for the period from 1945 to 1965. In Arkansas nineteen counties were selected, representing 47 percent of the state's population. The field researchers investigated each case of a rape conviction and gathered information on predetermined "critical variables" that could have affected a jury's sentencing verdict. See pp. 16–18 of Petitioner's Brief.
73. Ibid., appendix A, 14a.
74. Ibid., 13–16.
75. Ibid.
76. *Gideon v. Wainwright*, 372 U.S. 335 (1963).
77. Joan Rapczynski, "The Legacy of the Warren Court" (New Haven, CT: Yale–New Haven Teachers Institute, 2010), http://www.yale.edu/ynhti/curriculum/units/2004/1/04.01.07.x.html.
78. *Kent v. United States*, 383 U.S. 541 (1966).

79. *Malloy v. Hogan,* 378 U.S. 1 (1964).

80. Bruce Allen Murphy, *Wild Bill: The Legend and Life of William O. Douglas* (New York: Random House, 2003), 235, 247.

81. Meltsner, *Cruel and Unusual,* 156.

82. *Daughterty v. Tennessee,* 384 U.S. 435, 505 (1966).

83. *Witherspoon v. Illinois,* 391 U.S. 510, 542 (1968).

84. See, for example, McGautha v. California, 402 U.S. 183, 306 (1971).

85. Meltsner, *Cruel and Unusual,* 158–62

86. Ibid., 159.

87. Ibid.

88. Ibid., 161.

89. Ibid., 160.

90. Ibid., 154.

91. Ibid., 163.

92. Ibid.

93. Ibid., 167.

94. Ibid.

7 Momentum Builds, Then Stalls

1. Stephen K. Shaw, William D. Pederson, and Frank J. Williams, eds., *Franklin D. Roosevelt and the Transformation of the Supreme Court* (Armonk, NY: M. E. Sharpe, 2003), 133–36.

2. David Garrow, "The Tragedy of William O. Douglas," *The Nation,* Apr. 14, 2003, http://www.thenation.com/doc/20030414/garrow.

3. Alden Whitman, "Vigorous Defender of Rights" (subsection, William O. Douglas obituary), *New York Times,* Jan. 20, 1980, http://query.nytimes.com/mem/archive/pdf?res=F10F10F93F59107788DDA90A94D9405B8084F1D3.

4. Ibid.

5. James F. Simon, *Independent Journey: The Life of William O. Douglas* (New York: Harper & Row, 1980), 253, 357–58.

6. Ibid., 436.

7. Ibid., 362.

8. Ibid., 363.

9. Ibid., 363–65.

10. A letter from "J.M.H." (Justice John Harlan) dated March 7, 1969, stated, "I am not at rest on my yesterday's vote to reverse this case." Thurgood Marshall's Case Histories, box 58, folder 3 ("Maxwell v. Bishop"), Manuscript Div., Library of Congress, Washington, DC. Subsequent references to this archive are abbreviated LOC.

11. Howard Ball and Phillip Cooper, "Fighting Justices: Hugo L. Black and William O. Douglas and Supreme Court Conflict," *American Journal of Legal History* 38, no. 1 (1994): 1.

12. William J. Brennan's Case Histories, box II: 6, folder 11., xii, LOC.
13. Marshall's Case Histories, box 58, folder 3 ("Maxwell v. Bishop"), LOC.
14. Draft opinion on *Maxwell v. Bishop,* No. 622, prepared by Justice William O. Douglas, p. 7, Brennan's Case Histories, box 196, LOC.
15. "Memorandum to the Conference," Apr. 4, 1969, from Justice William O. Douglas, Marshall's Case Histories, box 58, folder 3 ("Maxwell v. Bishop"), LOC.
16. Thomas Sowell, *The Vision of the Anointed* (New York: Basic Books, 1996), 206.
17. In his personal notes, Brennan reported that at the second conference Douglas, Warren, and he favored requiring the jury be provided standards before they decided on life imprisonment or execution. See William J. Brennan's Notes, box II: 6, folder 11, xii, LOC.
18. Hunter R. Clark, *Justice Brennan: The Great Conciliator* (Secaucus, NJ: Carol Publishing Group, 1995), 131.
19. Ibid.
20. Ibid., 132.
21. "The Law: Earl Warren's Way: Is it Fair?" *Time,* July 22, 1974, http://www.time.com/time/magazine/article/0,9171,942946,00.html.
22. Paul Craig Roberts and Lawrence M. Stratton, *The New Color Line: How Quotas and Privilege Destroy Democracy* (Washington, DC: Regnery Publishing, 1997). The pertinent chapter is available at http://www.lewrockwell.com/orig/brown.html. See also Greenberg, *Crusaders in the Courts,* 164, 174.
23. Clark, *Justice Brennan,* 242.
24. "Thurgood Marshall," *Encarta Encyclopedia,* 2008 ed.
25. Eric Rise, *The Martinsville Seven: Race, Rape and Capital Punishment* (Charlottesville: University Press of Virginia, 1995), 66.
26. Roger Goldman and David Gallen, *Thurgood Marshall: Justice for All* (New York: Carroll and Graf, 1992) 156.
27. Bob Woodward and Scott Armstrong, *The Brethren* (New York: Simon and Schuster, 1979), 205–6.
28. *McGautha v. California,* 402 U.S. 183 (1971).
29. Justice Abraham Fortas to Justice William O. Douglas, Apr. 7, 1969, Marshall's Case Histories, box 58, folder 3 ("*Maxwell v. Bishop*"), LOC.
30. Brennan's Case Histories, box II: 6, folder 11, xiii, LOC.
31. Brennan's Notes, box II: 6, xii–xiii, LOC.
32. Justice William O. Douglas, "Memorandum to the Conference," Apr. 22, 1969, Brennan's notes, LOC.
33. Woodward and Armstrong, *The Brethren,* 206.
34. Meltsner, *Cruel and Unusual,* 157.
35. Clark, *Justice Brennan,* 247.
36. Linda Greenhouse, "Obituary: Warren E. Burger is Dead at 87: Was Chief Justice for 17 Years," *New York Times,* June 26, 1995, http://www.nytimes.

com/1995/06/26/obituaries/warren-e-burger-is-dead-at-87-was-chief-justice-for-17-years.html?pagewanted=1. See also Warren E. Burger, "Paradoxes in the Administration of Justice," *Journal of Criminal Law, Criminology and Police Science* 58, no. 4 (1967): 428.

37. Greenhouse, "Obituary: Warren E. Burger."
38. Clark, *Justice Brennan,* 248.
39. David M. O'Brien, "Filling Justice William O. Douglas's Seat: President Gerald R. Ford's Appointment of Justice John Paul Stevens," in *The Supreme Court Historical Society 1989 Yearbook* (Washington, DC: Supreme Court Historical Society, 1989), http://www.supremecourthistory.org/docs/schs_publications-1989.pdf. Douglas was married four times; his last two wives were in their twenties.
40. Clark, *Justice Brennan,* 249.
41. Alexander Charns, *Cloak and Gavel: The F.B.I., Wiretaps, Bugs, Informers, and the Supreme Court* (Champaign: University of Illinois Press, 1992), 63.
42. Laura Kalman, *Abe Fortas: A Biography* (New Haven, CT: Yale University Press, 1990), 341.
43. Clark, *Justice Brennan,* 248.
44. Meltsner, *Cruel and Unusual,* 203–10.
45. *Witherspoon v. Illinois,* 391 U.S. 510 (1968).
46. *Maxwell v. Bishop,* 398 U.S. 262 (1970).
47. *Alexander v. Louisiana,* 405 U.S. 625 (1972).
48. *Sims v. Georgia,* 389 U.S. 404, 407 (1967).
49. *Maxwell v. Bishop,* 398 U.S. 262, 267, fn. 4 (1970).
50. Brennan's Notes, box II: 6, folder 3, lxxv, LOC.
51. *McGautha v. California,* 402 U.S. 183, 208 (1971).
52. Ibid.
53. Ibid., 213.
54. Ibid., 214–16.
55. Brennan's Notes, box II: 6, folder 3, lxxvi, LOC.
56. Ibid.
57. *McGautha v. California,* 402 U.S. 183, 306 (1971).
58. Ibid., 259.
59. Ibid., 265.
60. Ibid., 298.
61. Ibid., 311.
62. Ibid., 226.
63. Ibid.
64. *Sims v. Abrams,* 389 F. 2d 148 (5th Cir. 1967).
65. *Moorer v. South Carolina,* 368 F. 2d 458 (4th Cir. 1966).
66. *Maxwell v. Bishop,* 257 F. Supp. 710 (E.D. of Ark. 1966); 398 F. 2d 138 (8th Cir. 1968).
67. See Petition for Writ of Certiorari filed in *Robert Butler v. Alabama* in the U.S. Supreme Court on July 2, 1970 during the October Term of 1970, Case

No. 5492; that petition is on file with the Clerk of the United States Supreme Court, Washington, D.C. See also *Swain v. State,* 285 Ala. 292, 231 So. 2d 737 (1970); subsequent petition for writ of certiorari filed with the U.S. Supreme Court was granted on June 29, 1972, in *Swain v. Alabama,* 408 U.S. 936 (1972).

68. Dorin, "Two Different Worlds," 1693n91, which cites the quote from NAACP Legal Defense Fund and Center for Studies in Criminology and Law, "Death Penalty Conference" (1977), 47n34.

8 The High Court Acts

1. *McGautha v. California,* 402 U.S. 183 (1971).
2. Brennan's Case Histories, box II: 6, folder 5, LOC.
3. Hazel Erskine, "The Polls: Capital Punishment," *Public Opinion Quarterly* 34, no. 2 (1970): 290. In 1966, 42 percent of those polled favored capital punishment and 47 percent were opposed. In 1969, 51 percent were in favor and 40 percent were opposed.
4. Ibid.
5. Clark, *Justice Brennan,* 5.
6. Ibid., 7.
7. Ibid., 117.
8. Ibid., 116.
9. Ibid., 7.
10. In *Baker v. Carr,* 369 U.S. 186 (1962), the State of Tennessee had been challenged to reapportion its state legislators according to the population sizes of its counties.
11. *Lance-Star* (Fredericksburg, VA), Jan. 17, 1972, 4.
12. Brief for Petitioner, William Furman, filed with Clerk of the U.S. Supreme Court in Case No. 69–5003, 1–10.
13. Brief for Petitioner, Luscious Jackson, filed with the Clerk of the U.S. Supreme Court on Sept. 9, 1971, 2–10.
14. Brief for Petitioner, Elmer Branch, filed with Clerk of the U.S. Supreme Court on Sept. 13, 1971, in Case No. 69–5031, 3–6.
15. *People v. Aikens,* 70 Cal. 2d 369 (1969).
16. *People v. Anderson,* 6 Cal. 3d 628 (1972).
17. *Aikens v. California,* 406 U.S. 813 (1972).
18. Brennan's Case Histories, box II: 6, folder 5, cxxxv, LOC.
19. Ibid.
20. Woodward and Armstrong, *The Brethren,* 207.
21. Brennan's Case Histories, box II: 6, folder 5, cxxxviii, LOC.
22. Ibid., 248.
23. Ibid.
24. Ibid.
25. Ibid.
26. Meltsner, *Cruel and Unusual,* 269–73.

27. Woodward and Armstrong, *The Brethren,* 207.
28. Meltsner, *Cruel and Unusual,* 274–78.
29. Stuart Banner, *The Death Penalty: An American History* (Cambridge, MA: Harvard University Press, 2002), 260.
30. Stephen J. Friedman, ed., *William J. Brennan, Jr.: An Affair with Freedom* (New York: Atheneum Publishers, 1967), 335.
31. Grossman, Gelber, et al., *Supreme Court Practice,* 22.
32. Ibid.
33. Ibid., 335–36.
34. Stephen J. Friedman, ed., *William J. Brennan, Jr.: An Affair with Freedom,*
35. The chief justice sits at the south end of the rectangular conference table and the senior associate justice at the north end. See Justice Brennan's address given at Maxwell Air Force Base on Sept. 9, 1963, reported in ed. 35. Brennan's Case Histories, box II: 6, folder 5, LOC.
36. Brennan's Papers, box II, folder 3, LOC.
37. Joan Biskupic, *Sandra Day O'Connor: How the First Woman on the Supreme Court Became Its Most Influential Justice* (New York: HarperCollins, 2005), 111.
38. "Reagan's Mr. Right," *Time,* June 30, 1986.
39. Brennan's Case Histories, box II: 6, folder 5, LOC.
40. Banner, *The Death Penalty,* 260.
41. Brennan's Case Histories, box II: 6, folder 5, LOC.
42. Ibid., cxxxvii.
43. Ibid., 336.
44. Banner, *The Death Penalty,* 260–61.
45. *Miranda v. Arizona,* 384 U.S. 436 (1966).
46. *McGautha v. California,* 402 U.S. 183 (1971).
47. Ibid.
48. Brennan's Case Histories, box II: 6, folder 5, LOC.
49. Ibid., cxxxvi, cxxxvii.
50. Banner, *The Death Penalty,* 260–61.
51. Brennan's Case Histories, box II: 6, folder 5, cxxxvii, LOC.
52. Ibid., cxxxviii, cxxxix.
53. Wolfgang and Cohen, *Crime and Race,* 81.
54. Brennan's Case Histories, box II: 6, folder 5, cxxxix–cxliii, LOC; Greenberg, *Crusaders in the Courts,* 450.
55. Brennan's Case Histories, box II: 6, folder 5, cxxxvii –cxliii, LOC.
56. Dennis J. Hutchinson, *The Man Who Once Was Whizzer White: A Portrait of Justice Byron R. White* (New York: Free Press, 1998), 363–65.
57. Paul Tagliabue, "A Tribute to Byron White," *Yale Law Journal* 112 (2003): 999–1001.
58. Ibid., 1005.
59. Woodward and Armstrong, *The Brethren,* 213–14.

60. *Furman v. Georgia,* 408 U.S. 238, 449 (1972).
61. *Maxwell v. Bishop,* 398 F. 2d 138 (1968).
62. *Furman v. Georgia,* 408 U.S. 238, 449 (1972).
63. See, for example, *Peters v. Kiff,* 407 U.S. 493 (1972); *Alexander v. Louisiana,* 405 U.S. 625 (1972); *Whitus v. Georgia,* 385 U.S.545 (1967); *Sims v. Georgia,* 389 U.S. 404 (1967).
64. Woodward and Armstrong, *The Brethren,* 215.
65. Ibid.
66. *Furman v. Georgia,* 408 U.S. 238, 390.
67. Ibid., 406.
68. Brennan's Case Histories, box II: 6, folder 5, cxlvi-cxlix, LOC.
69. Woodward and Armstrong, *The Brethren,* 219.
70. Brennan's Case Histories, box II: 6, folder 5, cxlix, LOC.
71. Ibid., cl–cli.

9 What the Law Students Set in Motion

1. Meltsner, *Cruel and Unusual,* 289.
2. D. J. Herda, *Furman v. Georgia: The Death Penalty Case* (Hillsdale, NJ: Enslow Publishers, 1994), 66.
3. Ibid. See also Burt M. Henson and Ross Olney, *Furman v. Georgia: The Constitution and the Death Penalty* (New York: Franklin Watts,), 70.
4. Woodward and Armstrong, *The Brethren,* 220.
5. Meltsner, *Cruel and Unusual,* 290.
6. Bradley Steffens, *Furman v. Georgia: Fairness and the Death Penalty* (San Diego: Lucent Books, 2001), 80.
7. Ibid.
8. Ibid.
9. Ibid.
10. Meltsner, *Cruel and Unusual,* 290.
11. Steffens, *Furman v. Georgia: Fairness and the Death Penalty,* 80.
12. Labi, "A Man Against The Machine."
13. Meltsner, *Cruel and Unusual,* 293.
14. Ibid., 294.
15. Ibid., 299.
16. Ibid., 294.
17. Ibid., 296.
18. *Furman v. Georgia,* 408 U.S. 238, 313 (1972).
19. Ibid., 249.
20. Ibid., 385–86.
21. Ibid., 299.
22. Ibid., 354–64. See also Meltsner, *Cruel and Unusual,* 294–95.
23. *Furman v. Georgia,* 408 U.S. 385 (1972).
24. Ibid., 386.

25. Ibid., 298–99.
26. *Furman v. Georgia,* 408 U.S. 238, 302 (1972).
27. Meltsner, *Cruel and Unusual,* 297–98.
28. *Furman v. Georgia,* 408 U.S. 238, 313 (1972).
29. Ibid., 245.
30. Ibid., 251.
31. Ibid., 257.
32. Ibid., 364.
33. Ibid., 389.
34. Ibid.
35. Ibid., 341.
36. Greenberg, *Crusaders in the Courts,* 451.
37. *Furman v. Georgia,* 408 U.S. 238, 253, 295 (1972).
38. Ibid., 310.
39. Greenberg, *Crusaders in the Courts,* 451.
40. *McCleskey v. Kemp,* 481 U.S. 279 (1987).
41. *McCleskey v. Kemp,* supra, 331.
42. Ibid., 330.
43. *McCleskey v. Kemp,* supra, 330. See also *Furman v. Georgia,* supra, 257.
44. *McCleskey v. Kemp,* supra, 330. See also *Furman v. Georgia,* supra, 364.
45. *McCleskey v. Kemp,* supra, 330. See also *Furman v. Georgia,* supra, 310.
46. *McCleskey v. Kemp,* supra, 330. See also *Furman v. Georgia,* supra, 289n12.
47. *McCleskey v. Kemp,* supra, 303–4. See also *Furman v. Georgia,* 449.
48. *Furman v. Georgia,* supra, 295.
49. Ibid., 365 fn., 152, 154.
50. *Callins v. Collins,* 510 U.S. 1141, 1148 (1994).
51. *Graham v. Collins,* 506 U.S. 461 (1993).
52. Ibid., 461, 484 (1993).
53. Ibid., 501.
54. Ibid., 500.
55. *Furman v. Georgia,* 408 U.S.238, 389 (1972).
56. Ibid., 449.
57. Ibid., 406.
58. *Callins v. Collins,* 510 U.S. 1141, 1153 (1994).
59. *McCleskey v. Kemp,* 481 U.S. 279 (1987).
60. *Maxwell v. Bishop,* 398 U.S. 262 (1970).
61. Ibid.
62. *Furman v. Georgia,* 408 U.S. 238, 309 (1972).
63. In *Pulley v. Harris,* 465 U.S. 37, 54 (1984), Justice White noted that absence of perfection in state death penalty statutes was "a far cry from the major systemic defects identified in *Furman.*" Among those defects addressed was the discriminatory imposition of the death penalty on black males.

64. Michael Radelet, "Thirty Years after Gregg" (Amnesty International, 2005), http://www.docstoc.com/docs/52614599/Thirty-Years-After-Gregg-Michael-L-Radelet1.
65. Herda, *Furman v. Georgia: The Death Penalty Case,* 75.
66. *Furman v. Georgia,* 408 U.S. 238, 400 (1972). See also Douglas's and Brennan's remarks, pp. 247, 253, 295.
67. Meltsner, *Cruel and Unusual,* 307–8.
68. *Coker v. Georgia,* 433 U.S. 584, 595 (1977).
69. Scott G. Parker and David P. Hubbard, "The Evidence for Death," *California Law Review* 78 (July 1990): 973, 977. See also Herda, *Furman v. Georgia: The Death Penalty Case,* 76.
70. Woodward and Armstrong, *The Brethren,* 430.
71. Greenberg, *Crusaders in the Courts,* 452–53.
72. Woodward and Armstrong, *The Brethren,* 394, 399.
73. Ibid., 431–32.
74. *Gregg v. Georgia,* 482 U.S. 155 (1976).
75. Woodward and Armstrong, *The Brethren,* 432.
76. Ibid., 433.
77. Ibid., 434–35.
78. See *Woodson v. North Carolina,* 428 U.S. 280 (1976); and *Roberts v. Louisiana,* 428 U. S.325 (1976).
79. *Gregg v. Georgia,* 482 U.S. 155 (1976); *Proffitt v. Florida,* 428 U. S. 262 (1976).
80. Woodward and Armstrong, *The Brethren,* 435–31.
81. *Gregg v. Georgia,* 428 U.S. 153, 195,198 (1976); *Proffitt v. Florida,* 428 U.S. 242, 250–53 (1976).
82. *Lockett v. Ohio,* 438 U.S. 586 (1978); *Eddings v. Oklahoma,* 455 U.S. 104 (1982).
83. *Maynard v. Cartwright,* 486 U.S. 356 (1988).
84. California's Penal Code, Section 190.2, includes the following among the seventeen "special circumstances" that qualify a defendant for death: the defendant was previously convicted of first- or second-degree murder; the intentional murder was for financial gain; the victim was a peace officer or firefighter while engaged in his or her duties; or the victim was a judge, former judge, or prosecutor who was murdered so as to prevent any of them from performing his or her official duties. Additionally, a murder committed while the defendant is engaged in twelve specified felonies can also be death qualifying. First-degree murder is murder by the use of an explosive device or poison, or committed while lying in wait, or by other specified means. It can also include any other kind of willful, deliberate, and premeditated killing or a killing in the perpetration of a listed felony. See California Penal Code Sections 187 and 189. All other kinds of murder are in the second degree. California Penal Code, Section 189.

85. *Ring v. Arizona,* 536 U.S. 584 (2002).
86. Marvin Frankel, *Criminal Sentences: Law Without Order* (New York: Hill and Wang, 1973).
87. Ibid.; Gerard Lynch, "Marvin Frankel: A Reformer Reassessed," *Federal Sentencing Reporter* 21, no. 4 (Apr. 2009): 235–41.
88. Frankel, *Criminal Sentences,* 43.
89. Ibid.
90. Ibid., 42.
91. Arthur Murphy, "Marvin Frankel: A Lawyer Scholar," *Columbia Law Review* 102, no. 7, 1750–52 (Nov. 2002); Jack Greenberg, "What A Life," *Columbia Law Review* 102, no. 7 (Nov. 2002): 1743–47.
92. Greenberg, *Crusaders in the Courts,* 377–78.
93. Frank Heffron, email message to author, June 3, 2008.
94. "Report on the Internship Program, Summer, 1964," issued on behalf of the Executive Committee of the Law Students Civil Rights Research Council bearing the name of Marvin E. Frankel as a member of the Board of Advisors. Copy in author's possession.
95. Greenberg, *Crusaders in the Courts,* 377.
96. Kaufman: "Obituary: Marvin Frankel."
97. Nina Burleigh, "White Power," *New York Magazine,* July 9, 2001, http://nymag.com/nymetro/news/politics/national/features/4926/.
98. Michael O'Hear, "The Original Intent of Uniformity in Federal Sentencing," *University of Cincinnati Law Review* 74 (2006): 749–817.
99. Ibid.
100. Ibid.
101. Ibid.; "Sentencing Reform Act (1984)," Answers.com, http://www.answers.com/topic/sentencing-reform-act-1984.
102. Naomi Murakawa, "The Racial Antecedents to Federal Sentencing Guidelines: How Congress Judged the Judges from Brown to Booker," *Roger Williams University Law Review* 11, no. 2 (2006): 473, 478.
103. Ilene Nagel, "Sentencing Structuring Discretion: The New Federal Sentencing Guidelines," *Journal of Criminal Law and Criminology* 80 (1990): 883–943.
104. Rachel Barkow and Kathleen O'Neill, "Delegating Punitive Power: The Political Economy of Sentencing Commission and Guideline Formation," *New York University School of Law, Public Law and Legal Theory Working Papers* (2006), 5–6, http://lsr.nellco.org/cgi/viewcontent.cgi?article=1023&context=nyu_plltwp.
105. *United States v. Booker,* 543 U.S. 220, 232 (2005).
106. *United States v. Quirante,* 486 F. 3d 1273, 1276 (11th Cir. 2007).
107. Nancy Gertner, "What Yogi Berra Teaches about Post-Booker Sentencing," *Yale Law Journal,* Pocket 115, pt. 137 (2006), http://www.thepocketpart.org/2006/07/gertner.html.

10 To Save a Mockingbird

1. *Coker v. Georgia,* 433 U.S. 584, 594 (1977).

2. *Woodson v. North Carolina,* 428 U.S. 280 (1976); *Roberts v. Louisiana,* 428 U.S. 325 (1976).

3. This principle was applied in *Peters v. Kiff,* 407 U.S. 493 (1972), where a white defendant successfully challenged jury selection procedures that consistently excluded African Americans from serving as jurors. The court found the defendant had standing since his due process rights had been violated.

4. *Coker v. The State,* 234 Ga 555,216 SE 2d 782, 788 (1975).

5. *Coker v. Georgia,* 433 U.S. 584, 594 (1977).

6. *Coker v. The State,* 234 Ga. 555, 216 S.E.2d 782 (1975).

7. "The Law: Arguing About Death for Rape,' *Time,* Apr. 11, 1977, http://www.time.com/time/magazine/article/0,9171,918840,00.html.

8. *McCleskey v. Kemp,* 481 U.S. 279 (1987).

9. Ibid., 332.

10. Ibid., 333.

11. See Wolfgang and Riedel, "Rape, Racial Discrimination, and the Death Penalty," 99, 105–7, 109–14, 118–19.

12. Dorin, "Two Different Worlds," 1669–70

13. See *Graham v. Collins,* 506 U.S. 461, 481 (1993). There the government acknowledged that in eleven Southern states between 1945 and 1965 "the data revealed that among all those convicted of rape, blacks were selected disproportionately for the death sentence." App. to Brief for United States as Amicus Curiae in *Gregg v. Georgia,* O.T. 1975, No. 74–6257, p. 4a.

14. Dorin, "Two Different Worlds," 1669.

15. *Ford v. Wainwright,* 477 U.S. 399 (1986).

16. *Atkins v. Virginia,* 536 U.S. 304 (2002).

17. *Roper v. Simmons,* 543 U.S. 551 (2005).

18. *Kennedy v. Louisiana,* 554 U.S. 407 (2008).

19. *Zant v. Stephens,* 462 U.S. 862, 885 (1983).

20. *Turner v. Murray,* 476 U.S. 28, 36 (1986).

21. *Graham v. Collins,* 506 U.S. 461, 502–3 (1993).

22. *Callins v. Collins,* 510 U.S. 1141, 1153 (1994).

23. Ibid.

24. *McCleskey v. Kemp,* 481 U.S. 279 (1987).

25. Ibid., 279, 315.

26. Robert A. Burt, "Disorder in the Court: the Death Penalty and the Constitution," *Michigan Law Review* 85 (Aug. 1987): 1741, 1799.

27. Dorin, "Two Different Worlds," 1686.

28. Jill Smolowe and Lisa Towle-Raleigh, "Doubts on Death Row," *Time,* Apr. 11, 1994, http://www.time.com/time/magazine/article/0,9171,980479,00.html.

29. Bob Herbert, "Injustice in a Georgia Jury Room," *Gainesville Sun,* Mar. 31, 1994, http://news.google.com/newspapers?nid=1320&dat=19940330&id=MaYpAAAAIBAJ&sjid=bOoDAAAAIBAJ&pg=3032,8980856.

30. Ibid.

31. Bob Herbert, "In America; Judicial Coin Toss," *New York Times,* Apr. 3, 1994, http://www.nytimes.com/1994/04/03/opinion/in-america-judicial-coin-toss.html?pagewanted=1.

32. *Hance v. Zant,* 511 U.S. 1013 (1994).

33. Smolowe and Towle-Raleigh, "Doubts on Death Row."

34. Nat Hentoff, "Color-Coded Executions," *Jewish World Review,* June 5, 2003, http://www.jewishworldreview.co,/cols/hentoff060503.asp.

35. *McCleskey v. Kemp,* 481 U.S. 279, 345 (1987).

36. John C. Jeffries Jr., *Justice Lewis F. Powell Jr.* (New York: Charles Scribner's Sons, 1994), 451.

37. See Stephen P. Klein and John E. Rolph, "Relationship of Offender and Victim Race to Death Penalty Sentences in California," *Jurimetrics Journal* 32 (Fall 1991): 33, 44.

38. David C. Baldus, George Woodworth, Gary L. Young, and Aaron M. Christ, "Executive Summary," *The Disposition of Nebraska Capital and Non-Capital Homicide Cases (1973–1999): A Legal and Empirical Analysis* (Lincoln: Nebraska Commission on Law Enforcement and Criminal Justice, 2001) 14–22, http://www.ncc.state.ne.us/pdf/others/other_homicide/FinalReport2.pdf.

39. David S. Baime, "Report to the Supreme Court: Systemic Proportionality Review Project: 2001–2002, Term 54–55 (2002)," http://www.judiciary.state.nj.us/pressrel/baimereport.pdf.

40. Ibid., 62.

41. Samuel Gross and Robert Maura, *Death and Discrimination: Racial Disparities in Capital Sentencing* (Boston: Northeastern University Press, 1989), 112–15.

42. Carol Steiker, "Remembering Race, Rape and Capital Punishment," *Virginia Law Review* 83, no. 3 (1997): 693; Robert Weisburg, "Deregulating Death," *Supreme Court Review* 1983: 305, 311–13. Much of the work of legal scholar—and former Fund lawyer—Derrick Bell argues that the "traditional civil rights communities assumption that racism would be progressively eradicated has failed." George H. Taylor, "Derrick Bell's Narratives As Parables," *N.Y.U. Review of Law and Social Change* 31, no. 225 (2007): 264.

Epilogue: Where Are They Now?

1. "In Memoriam: Norman C. Amaker (1935–2000)," Loyola University Chicago–School of Law website, http://luc.edu/law/faculty/amaker.html.

2. "Anthony G. Amsterdam: Biography," New York University School of Law website, https://its.law.nyu.edu/facultyprofiles/profile.cfm?section=bio&personID=19743.

3. "Jack Greenberg (1926–): Biography," Howard University–School of Law website, http://brownat50.org/brownBios/BioJackGreenberg.html.

4. "The Crusaders," *Internet Movie Database,* http://www.imdb.com/title/tt0418277/. See also United Press International, "Maguire to Play Jack Greenberg," *UPI.com,* http://www.upi.com/Entertainment_News/2008/07/22/Maguire-to-play-Jack-Greenberg-in-film/UPI-79281216739214/.

5. Michael Meltsner, *The Making of a Civil Rights Lawyer* (Charlottesville: University of Virginia Press, 2006). See also Meltsner's website, http://michaelmeltsner.com/bio.html.

6. "The Tradition Continues: Marvin Wolfgang," Jerry Lee Center of Criminology website, University of Pennsylvania, http://www.sas.upenn.edu/jerrylee/history.htm; Kaufman, "Obituary: Marvin E. Wolfgang."

Index

Race, Rape, and Injustice was designed and typeset on a Macintosh OSX computer system using InDesign CS5 software. The body text is set in 10/13 Mercury text G2 and display type is set in Avant Garde Gothic STD. This book was designed and typeset by Barbara Karwhite and manufactured by Thomson-Shore, Inc.